TYPOGRAPHERS ON TYPE

TYPOGRAPHERS
ON TYPE

AN ILLUSTRATED ANTHOLOGY
FROM WILLIAM MORRIS TO
THE PRESENT DAY

Edited by
Ruari McLean

LUND HUMPHRIES PUBLISHERS
LONDON

First published in Great Britain in 1995 by
Lund Humphries Publishers Limited
Park House
1 Russell Gardens
London NW11 9NN

Texts by Ruari McLean © 1995 the author
Extracts © 1995 as listed
Typographers on Type © 1995 Lund Humphries Publishers

British Library Cataloguing in Publication Data
A catalogue record for this book is available from the British Library

ISBN 0 85331 657 0

Designed by Ruari McLean
Typeset in FF Quadraat by Typographic Assistance, Edinburgh
Output on Kodak film by Ikon Communications Limited, Manchester
Printed and bound in Great Britain by
Butler & Tanner Limited, Frome and London

for WALTER TRACY RDI

CONTENTS

ACKNOWLEDGEMENTS

The sources of the texts included in this anthology are acknowledged at the foot of each extract.

Apart from works in the public domain, every effort has been made to identify and locate the copyright holders in each case. I apologise for any inadvertent omissions, and would like to thank and acknowledge the following for permission to reproduce the pieces indicated:

BRUCE ROGERS Syndics of Cambridge University Press

WILLIAM ADDISON DWIGGINS Dorothy Abbe

BERNARD NEWDIGATE Tabard Press

FRANCIS MEYNELL Dame Alix Meynell

DANIEL BERKELEY UPDIKE Reprinted by permission of the publishers from *In the Day's Work* by Daniel Berkeley Updike, Cambridge, Mass.: Harvard University Press, Copyright © 1924 by the Harvard University Press

JAN TSCHICHOLD Jan Tschichold, *The new typography* Copyright © 1994. Reprinted with permission of the University of California Press

STANLEY MORISON The Literary Executors of Stanley Morison

HARRY CARTER Matthew Carter

ELMER ADLER Limited Editions Club, New York

CARL PURINGTON ROLLINS The Typophiles, New York

FREDERIC W. GOUDY Oxford University Press, New York

THOMAS MAITLAND CLELAND Reprinted with permission of R. R. Bowker, a Reed Reference Publishing Company, from *Heritage of the Graphic Arts* © 1972, by Reed Elsevier Inc.

FRED ANTHOENSEN The Anthoensen Press, Portland, Maine, USA

JOHN DREYFUS John Dreyfus

GEORGE BERNARD SHAW National Library of Scotland

P. J. CONKWRIGHT Reprinted by permission of the publishers from *Graphic Forms: The Arts as Related to the Book* by Ġyorgy Kepes et al, Cambridge, Mass.: Harvard University Press, Copyright © 1949 by the President and Fellows of Harvard College

JAN VAN KRIMPEN The Typophiles, New York

The texts are unaltered except for the standardisation of spelling in accordance with English usage, and the introduction, where applicable, of single quotes and the omission of a full point where the last letter of an abbreviated word is the actual last letter, eg. 'Mr'. Omitted matter is indicated by dots.

FOREWORD

My requirements in putting together this anthology were fairly obvious: no item should be boring, every contribution must say something useful and relevant to the main and related subjects of typography and calligraphy, and no article should – if possible – repeat too exactly what another contributor had written. A few well-known pieces had to be included (for what one generation knows too well may be unfamiliar to the next), but unfamiliarity was an advantage. The problems of copyright had also to be taken account of.

All contributions are in date order of first publication, as far as it can now be ascertained.

Some distinguished names will be seen to be missing – regrettable but inevitable. Not every excellent performer also writes well, nor has this editor read everything that he ought to have read.

I am extremely grateful to Walter Tracy RDI for having allowed me to ask constantly for his advice, and for his prompt flow of wisdom and corrections. Thank you also to Greer Allen at Yale for help with contacts in the USA, and to many other friends, especially Brooke Crutchley and Matthew Carter, for the trouble they took in answering questions. I am also very grateful to Neil Macmillan for his assistance in the production of this book, and for his setting of the text in FF Quadraat designed by Fred Smeijers of Ontwerpbureau Quadraat.

R. McL.

KELMSCOTT PRESS EDITION OF CHAUCER'S WORKS.

The above is now approaching completion, and Mr. Morris hopes to issue it to subscribers early in June. As already announced, the ordinary binding will be half holland, similar to that of the Golden Legend; but special bindings in oak boards & stamped white pigskin have been designed by Mr. Morris. The prices of these, executed under Mr. Cobden-Sanderson's direction at the Doves Bindery, and by Messrs. J. & J. Leighton, are as follows:

For full white tooled pigskin, executed under Mr. Cobden-Sanderson's direction at the Doves Bindery from Mr. Morris' design — 13 Pounds.

For half pigskin and oak boards ditto — 9 Pounds.

For full white pigskin, with tooling of a different pattern, executed by Messrs. J. & J. Leighton from Mr. Morris' design — 9 Pounds.

For half pigskin and oak boards ditto — 5 Guineas.

All orders should be sent to the Secretary of the Kelmscott Press, Upper Mall, Hammersmith, W., and will be executed in rotation, as the binding will necessarily take some time.

N.B. Owing to the strength and slow-drying qualities of the ink used, the Chaucer will not be fit for ordinary full binding, with the usual pressure, for at least a year from its issue.

Prospectus for the Kelmscott *Chaucer*, published in 1896. Actual size, printed in black on hand-made paper 205 x 142 mm, folded into envelope with embossed halfpenny stamp.

THIS ANTHOLOGY starts with William Morris because he, more than anyone else, inspired the changes, especially in book design, which introduced the twentieth century. He was born in England at a time when, as he grew up, he could see that quality – of nearly everything that was manufactured -- was being sacrificed to speed and cheapness.

Morris was a man of many parts – poet, painter, articled architect, manufacturer of textiles and furniture, and social reformer. His first two books, The Defence of Guinevere, 1858, and Life and Death of Jason, 1867, were printed and designed by the leading book printer of the day, Charles Whittingham, and to us look better than most English printing at that time; but Morris, typically, was not satisfied. He looked back to medieval manuscripts, collected them, and practised calligraphy himself. He did not decide to take up printing seriously until he heard Emery Walker's lecture on printing at the Arts & Crafts Exhibition in London on 15 November 1888. Emery Walker, himself a great printing technician, not a designer, was a friend and neighbour of Morris, and helped Morris to found the Kelmscott Press: he was asked to be a partner, but 'having some sense of proportion', as he said later, he declined the invitation.

There is no need here to describe the work of the Kelmscott Press. It is well known that Morris looked back in time for his inspiration – to find perfect craftsmanship – when other thinkers and designers were beginning to look forward, but it must be emphasised that the influence of Kelmscott was felt throughout the printing trade of England, Europe, and the United States. Again and again we find individuals who later became famous typographers getting their first inspiration when they saw, and handled, a Kelmscott Press book.

The standard biography is J. W. Mackail's Life, 1899. In an evergrowing literature, see especially William Morris and the Art of the Book, with essays by Paul Needham, Joseph Dunlap, and John Dreyfus, Pierpont Morgan Library, 1976; Susan Otis Thompson, American Book Design and William Morris, Bowker, New York, 1977; Duncan Robinson, William Morris, Edward Burne-Jones and the Kelmscott Chaucer, Gordon Fraser, London 1982; C. Harvey and J. Press, William Morris, design and enterprise in Victorian England, Manchester University Press, 1991; William S. Peterson, The Kelmscott Press, Clarendon Press, Oxford, 1991; and Fiona MacCarthy, William Morris: a Life for Our Time, Faber & Faber, 1994.

AIMS IN FOUNDING THE KELMSCOTT PRESS

I began printing books with the hope of producing some which would have a definite claim to beauty, while at the same time they should be easy to read and should not dazzle the eye, or trouble the intellect of the reader by eccentricity of form in the letters. I have always been a great admirer of the calligraphy of the Middle Ages, and of the earlier printing which took its place. As to the fifteenth-century books, I had noticed they were always beautiful by force of the mere typography, even without the added ornament, with which many of them are so lavishly supplied. And it was the essence of my undertaking to produce books which it would be a pleasure to look upon as pieces of printing and arrangement of type. Looking at my adventure from this point of view then, I found I had to consider chiefly the following things: the paper, the form of the type, the relative spacing of the letters, the words, and the lines, and lastly the position of the printed matter on the page.

It was a matter of course that I should consider it necessary that the paper should be hand-made, both for the sake of durability and appearance. It would be a very false economy to stint in the quality of paper as to price: so I had only to think about the kind of hand-made paper. On this head I came to two conclusions: 1st, that the paper must be wholly of linen (most hand-made papers are of cotton today), and must be quite 'hard', i.e. thoroughly well sized; and 2nd, that though it must be 'laid' and not 'wove' (i.e. made on a mould of obvious wires), the lines caused by the wires of the mould must not be too strong, so as to give a ribbed appearance. I found that on these points I was at one with the practice of the papermakers of the fifteenth century; so I took as my model a Bolognese paper of about 1473. My friend Mr Batchelor, of Little Chart, Kent, carried out my views very satisfactorily, and produced from the first the excellent paper which I still use.

Next as to type. By instinct rather than by conscious thinking it over, I began by getting myself a fount of Roman type. And here what I wanted was letter pure in form; severe, without needless excrescences; solid, without the thickening and thinning of the line, which is the essential fault of the ordinary modern type, and which makes it difficult to read; and not compressed laterally, as all later type has grown to be owing to commercial exigencies. There was only one source from which to take examples of this perfected Roman type, to wit, the works of the great Venetian printers of the fifteenth century, of whom Nicholas Jenson produced the completest and most Roman characters from 1470 to 1476. This type I studied with much care, getting it photographed to a big scale, and drawing it over many times before I began designing my own letter; so that though I think I mastered the essence of it, I did not copy it servilely; in fact, my Roman type, especially in the lower case, tends rather more to the Gothic than does Jenson's.

After a while I felt that I must have a Gothic as well as a Roman fount; and herein the task that I set myself was to redeem the Gothic character from the charge of unreadableness which is commonly brought against it. And I felt that this charge could not be reasonably brought against the types of the first two decades of printing: that Schoeffer at Mainz, Mentelin at Strasburg, and Gunther Zainer at Augsburg, avoided the spiky ends and undue compression which lay some of the later printers open to the above charge. Only the earlier printers (naturally following therein the practice of their predecessors the scribes) were very liberal of contractions, and used an excess of 'tied' letters, which, by the way, are very useful to the compositor. So I entirely eschewed contractions, except for the '&', and had very few tied letters, in fact none but the absolutely necessary ones. Keeping my end steadily in view, I designed a black-letter type which I think I may claim to be as readable as a Roman one, and to say the truth I prefer it to the Roman. This type is of the size called Great Primer (the Roman type is of 'English' size); but later on I was driven by the necessities of the Chaucer (a double-columned book) to get a smaller Gothic type of Pica size.

The punches for all these types, I may mention, were cut for me with great intelligence and skill by Mr E. P. Prince, and render my designs most satisfactorily.

Now as to the spacing: First, the 'face' of the letter should be as nearly conterminous with the 'body' as possible, so as to avoid undue whites between the letters. Next, the lateral spaces between the words should be (*a*) no more than is necessary to distinguish clearly the division into words, and (*b*) should be as nearly equal as possible. Modern printers, even the best, pay very little heed to these two essentials of seemly composition, and the inferior ones run riot in licentious spacing, thereby producing, *inter alia*, those ugly rivers of lines running about the page which are such a blemish to decent printing. Third, the whites between the lines should not be excessive; the modern practice of 'leading' should be used as little as possible, and never without some definite reason, such as marking some special piece of printing. The only leading I have allowed myself is in some cases a 'thin' lead between the lines of my Gothic pica type; in the Chaucer and the double-columned books I have used a 'hair' lead, and not even this in the 16mo books. Lastly, but by no means least, comes the position of the printed matter on the page. This should always leave the inner margin the narrowest, the top somewhat wider, the outside (fore-edge) wider still, and the bottom widest of all. This rule is never departed from in medieval books, written or printed. Modern printers systematically transgress against it; thus apparently contradicting the fact that the unit of a book is not one page, but a pair of pages. A friend, the librarian of one our most important private libraries, tells me that after careful testing he has come to the conclusion that the medieval rule was to make a difference of 20 per cent from margin to margin. Now these matters of spacing and position are of the greatest importance in the production of beautiful books; if they are properly considered they will make a book printed in quite ordinary type at least decent and pleasant to the eye. The disregard of them will spoil the effect of the best designed type.

It was only natural that I, a decorator by profession, should attempt to ornament my books suitably; about this matter I will only say that I have always tried to keep in mind the necessity for making my decoration a part of the page of type. I may add that in designing the magnificent and inimitable woodcuts which have adorned several of my books, and will above all adorn the Chaucer which is now drawing near to completion, my friend Sir Edward Burne-Jones has never lost sight of this important point, so that his work will not only give us a series of most beautiful and imaginative pictures, but form the most harmonious decoration possible to the printed book.

William Morris (1834 – 1896), *Aims in founding the Kelmscott Press*, Kelmscott House, Upper Mall, Hammersmith, 11 November 1895.

Wood engraving designed by William Morris, first used in *The History of Godefrey de Boloyne*, 1893.

THIS PIECE *forms the end of a monograph which appeared originally in the New York Evening Post of 12 January 1901. It gives an authoritative account of the problems and options facing printers at the end of the nineteenth century in America (where technical advances were being made faster than in Britain); it also shows with what acuteness the highly intelligent De Vinne evaluated the work of William Morris.*

De Vinne was a printer: he also wrote The Practice of Typography, 1899–1904, *four volumes which became a basic text for men like Updike, Bruce Rogers, and Stanley Morison.*

De Vinne's Title-pages as seen by a Printer, published by the Grolier Club of New York in 1901, was a limited edition from which the volume in The Practice of Typography *was developed. It is a beautiful, richly illustrated book, full of wisdom, often provocative, and still extremely worth reading.*

See also Theodore Low De Vinne *by C. P. Rollins, Typophile Chapbook 47 (2 vols), 1968.*

PRINTING IN THE NINETEENTH CENTURY

In 1870 a great change took place in the methods of book printing. To receive a good impression from types it had always been thought necessary that paper must be dampened and made pliable before printing. As an aid to this good impression an elastic woollen or india-rubber blanket was used for the impressing surface. When types only were printed, the dampened paper and elastic impression made strong and easily readable print, but this method that was good for types was bad for wood-cuts, in which shallow engraving was unavoidable. Elastic impression pressed surplus ink in the counters or depressions of the engravings and seriously damaged the contrasts of light and shade made by the engraver. Printers of cards and circulars on dry and smooth paper already had proved that it was possible to print sharp lines clearly without dampening the paper, and the printers of books, following this lead, began to use calendared paper and to print it dry, with better effect on wood-cuts. The new method of printing compelled much greater care in the adjustment of impression on the type and wood-cuts, but it saved the expense of wetting the paper and of smoothing the sheets in the hydraulic press after impression.

In 1880 the recently discovered art of photo-engraving had been developed to such an extent that it was supplanting wood-cuts as illustrations in pictorial magazines and books. The counters or depressed surfaces made by this process were so shallow that they could not be properly printed even on ordinary calendered paper. Papermakers removed this objection by covering a thin fabric of paper with a thick coat of whiting, which, after repeated calendering, left it with a surface as smooth as polished glass. On this coated paper it was possible for an expert pressman to bring out a delicacy from a relief plate almost equal to that made by photography or stipple engraving, and consequently coated paper has been the fabric most approved for the printing of fine illustrations. It was soon found that delicate lines and receding perspective were had at the expense of strength, for photo-engravings were first made weak and monotonous. The engraver on wood, whose art was threatened with extinction, had to be recalled to burnish and touch up the weak spots of feeble half-tone plates. So treated, photo-engraving made merchantable illustrations. The value of this relatively new art in the reproduction of pen drawings, facsimiles of old prints, and writings cannot be overestimated.

In 1884 the circulation of illustrated magazines had increased so largely that it was impracticable to print them properly and in time on any form of flat-bed cylinder press. A new form of web press was made by R. Hoe & Co., for the advertising forms and plain forms of the *Century Magazine*, which printed them from curved electrotype plates and performed the work of ten cylinder presses in an entirely satisfactory manner. The success of this machine led the same mechanicians to make for the same periodical the rotary art press. This machine also prints, from curved plates, sixty-four pages of the magazine at each revolution, quite as well as it had been done on the ordinary stop-cylinder. Although rotary machines have been found indispensable in newspaper offices that use one size only of paper, they have not been found generally useful in book-printing houses, which have to print upon many sizes of paper from different sizes and numbers of pages. The rotary press compels the use of a sheet (after it has been cut from the web) no longer or shorter than the circumference of its cylinder.

Nothing more seems to be needed in the speed of modern printing machinery but improvements are needed in printing-ink, printing-paper, and improved methods of preparing type for printing, known under the pressman's phrase of 'making-ready'.

Type-setting and type-making machinery received great improvements during the last half of the century. In 1853 William H. Mitchel invented a typesetting machine which was used for many years in the office of the late John F. Trow. It failed to meet general approval because of the inventor's inability to produce an equally good type-distributing machine. After Mitchel, came not less than a score of inventors, who devised machines of greater or less merit. The machine most in favour at the present time, most largely used by newspapers, is the Mergenthaler or Linotype, which does the work of many men. Without this machine, which has cheapened typesetting, our newspapers could not afford to furnish so great an amount of reading-matter.

During the last ten years new fashions in typography have appeared. For more than three hundred years each generation of printers followed more or less faithfully in the paths made by their predecessors without attempting to create new forms of letters or new styles in typography. When Bodoni of Italy at the close of the last century made types with sharp lines, and when good French and English engravers began to imitate copper-plate methods on wood-cuts, every tendency toward a greater delicacy of print was sedulously cultivated by publishers, engravers, and type-founders. This feminine style of typography reached its highest development in 1870. Then came the rebound. Not long after, Andrew Tuer of London began to reprint old English chap-books that were noticeable for rudeness, blackness, and uncouthness. In 1890 William Morris of London established the Kelmscott Press for the reproduction of old books in mediæval style. He made for his exclusive use Roman and Gothic types of new forms and great blackness, which he graced with initials and borders after monastic designs. This revival of a thoroughly masculine style of typography had many features of high merit which were properly admired, but unfortunately it has met with imitators who copied its form and missed its spirit. Amateurs in typography have been encouraged to attempt imitations of coarse styles of printing done in the sixteenth and seventeenth centuries. Type-founders, following in their steps, have recently produced letters and decorations more uncouth than those of the printers of any age or country. The good models made by able men for four centuries have been supplanted for advertising purposes by the clumsy letters of school-boys. This affectation of clownish simplicity, which plunges letter-designing in a pit of slovenliness, is but a passing fashion.

The nineteenth has been a century of wonderful achievement in every branch of printing. The Fourdrinier paper-making machine, the Bruce type-caster, the Linotype type-casting and type-setting machine, and other mechanical type-setters of merit, composition inking-rollers, the cylinder press, the web press, and mechanisms of many kinds for the rapid printing of the smallest label or the largest sheet, in black or many colours; machines for folding, sewing, and binding books; the arts of stereotype, electrotype, and photo-engraving – all these are its outgrowth, and the more important have been invented or made practicable within the memory of men now living. It is a summary of which the printing trade may be proud; but whether printers have made the best use of their great advantages is another question not to be answered too confidently. Printing was never done better and never done worse; never was cheaper, never was dearer, than it is today. It has never been furnished in so large a quantity at so small a price. For two or more cents can be had a newspaper with more reading matter than would fill a stout

octavo volume. Yet books are made and sold in limited editions to eager subscribers at prices ranging from five to fifty dollars a volume. There is much difference of opinion concerning the quality of printing now done. William Morris
maintained that printing had gone steadily from bad to worse, until he revived its
best features. Many publishers maintain, with more reason, that books of real
value for instruction or amusement, were never better fitted than they are now for
usefulness to all classes of readers.

T. L. De Vinne (1828–1914), *Printing in the Nineteenth
Century*, New York, 1924. (First published 1901).

Century Schoolbook

ABCDEFGHIJKLMN
OPQRSTUVWXYZ&
$ 1 2 3 4 5 6 7 8 9 0
a b c d e f g h i j k l m n o p q
r s t u v w x y z . , - : ; ! ? ' '
fi ff fl ffi ffl

ABCDEFGHIJKLMN
OPQRSTUVWXYZ&
$ 1 2 3 4 5 6 7 8 9 0
a b c d e f g h i j k l m n o p q
r s t u v w x y z . , - : ; ! ? ' '
fi ff fl ffi ffl

Century Schoolbook, commissioned by De Vinne for the *Century Magazine*, 1895.

Thomas James Sanderson *(as he was born) was one of those rare human beings who think for themselves. He actually attempted to put his ideals into practice in his daily life. This led him to give up, first, a career in the Church, and then, in the Law; but it was not until he met Annie Cobden that he found the way to overcome doubts and take up the activities, for which he is known, of, first, bookbinding and then printing. When he married Annie Cobden in 1882 (he was then aged forty-two) he added her name to his to become Cobden-Sanderson.*

He was an extraordinary man, whose importance to his friends and those who worked with him is shown in the tribute written by Edward Johnston (p.57).

He set up his own Doves Bindery in 1893 with four employees, one of whom was Douglas Cockerell, in a house called The Nook, almost opposite the Kelmscott Press in the Upper Mall at Hammersmith. Morris had thought of buying the house as an extension for his Press and invited Cobden-Sanderson to be his tenant. The Cobden-Sandersons wisely decided to buy the house for themselves and Morris became their tenant, but they asked him to leave within a year.

When Cobden-Sanderson founded the Doves Press in 1900 (Morris had died in 1896) he was on the one hand inspired by the Kelmscott Press, but on the other determined to challenge Morris's ideas on book design.

The Doves Press pages are the most devastating criticism ever made of the Kelmscott Press. It was the Doves Press, not Kelmscott, that showed the world of printing the path which, at that time, book design should take. Cobden-Sanderson did what Morris, the born decorator, could not do: he made plain typography noble.

The Doves Press books were never illustrated. The only decorations were coloured initials – sometimes very prominent – by Edward Johnston or Graily Hewitt. No one who has seen the opening text page of the Doves Press Bible, with a flaming red initial 'T' running down the left-hand margin, will ever forget it.

Approximately 50 publications were issued by the Doves Press before its demise in 1916. Cobden-Sanderson then threw all the Doves Press type into the river Thames from Hammersmith Bridge, in direct contradiction of a promise made to his partner, Emery Walker. The episode is fully described in C. Volmer Nordlunde's book mentioned below.

See T. J. Cobden-Sanderson, Catalogue Raisonné of Books Printed and Published at the Doves Press 1900–1916, *Doves Press, 1916; and C. Volmer Nordlunde,* Thomas James Cobden-Sanderson, Bookbinder and Printer, *Copenhagen 1957.*

THE WHOLE DUTY OF TYPOGRAPHY

The whole duty of Typography, as of Calligraphy, is to communicate to the imagination, without loss by the way, the thought or image intended to be communicated by the Author. And the whole duty of beautiful typography is not to substitute for the beauty or interest of the thing thought and intended to be conveyed by the symbol, a beauty or interest of its own, but, on the one hand, to win access for that communication by the clearness and beauty of the vehicle, and on the other hand, to take advantage of every pause or stage in that communication to interpose some characteristic and restful beauty in its own art. We thus have a reason for the clearness and beauty of the text as a whole, for the especial beauty of the first or introductory page and of the title, and for the especial beauty of the headings of chapters, capital or initial letters, and so on, and an opening for the illustrator as we shall see by and by.

Further, in the case of Poetry, verse, in my opinion, appeals by its form to the eye, as well as to the ear, and should be placed on the page so that its structure may be taken in at a glance and distinctively appreciated, and anything which interferes with this swiftness of apprehension and appreciation, however beautiful in itself, is in relation to the book as a whole a typographical inpertinence.

> T. J. Cobden-Sanderson (1840–1922), *The Ideal Book
> or Book Beautiful*, Doves Press, 1900.

I do not believe in the doctrine of William Morris. I do not believe that pleasure in one's work produces ornament. Nor do I believe that ornament has any special privilege in the production of happiness. Ornament is born of faculty, and may or may not be preceded, accompanied, or followed by happiness.

> T. J. Cobden-Sanderson, 2 October 1902, *The Journals of
> Thomas James Cobden-Sanderson 1879-1922*, Richard
> Cobden-Sanderson, London, 1926.

B RUCE ROGERS, *after being impressed by some Kelmscott Press books a little after 1890, became in effect the world's first professional freelance typographer; but he had originally intended to be an illustrator. His ability in drawing was linked with consummate craftmanship, and when he turned to typography it was expressed in exquisitely drawn printer's symbols and devices, in bookplate designs, in typeface design, of which he did more than is generally realised, and in the occasional making of model ships.*

The Kelmscott books were shown to Rogers, to whom they came as a revelation, in Indianapolis by J. M. Bowles, founder of a quarterly, Modern Art, which in Frederic Warde's words was 'one of the first American reflections of the new Arts and Crafts movement'. Again to quote Warde, 'Modern Art gained popularity and lost money until it was subsidised by a wealthy firm of "art publishers", L. Prang & Co. of Boston, who in 1895 persuaded Mr Bowles to edit the quarterly in that city'.[1] Rogers followed Bowles to Boston and was soon noticed by the directors of the Riverside Press, which he was invited to join and where he began to design and produce books. From 1900 he was given the opportunity to design fine limited editions, which made his name.

In 1916 Rogers came on a second visit to England to work on a publishing project with Emery Walker. This resulted in a single, but important book, Dürer's Of the Just Shaping of Letters, *and in the invitation to become typographical adviser to the University Press at Cambridge, then in poor shape, typographically speaking. In fact, Beatrice Warde, referring to the distinguished typeface 'Centaur' which Rogers had begun to design before leaving the United States, said 'B.R. had had a chance to kick up his heels in the Centaur's paddock; he now found himself in something like an augean stable'. At the request of Cambridge University Press, Rogers wrote a Report: his words on the first page 'I might go even farther and say that a book ought almost to be identified in the dark, merely by the feel or sound of it' must have stunned the Syndics. The Report was never made public until 1950, when Brooke Crutchley, then the University Printer, published it in a limited edition in honour of Bruce Roger's eightieth birthday. The whole Report (of which this extract represents the first four out of 33 pages) was adopted and implemented in due course – despite, as Crutchley points out, the war situation and appearance of imminent disaster in 1917. Rogers returned to the United States in 1919.*

The literature by and about Bruce Rogers is considerable. See Frederic Warde, Bruce Rogers, Designer of Books, *Harvard University Press, 1925, reprinted 'with a few alterations' from an article in the fourth number of* The Fleuron, *which includes some fine examples of Rogers' drawing not shown in Warde's book;* The Work of Bruce Rogers: Jack of all trades: master of one, *New York, Oxford University Press, 1939; and* Paragraphs on Printing *'elicited from Bruce Rogers in talks with James Hendrickson on the functions of the book designer', New York, William E. Rudge's Sons, 1943, also particularly well illustrated.*

1. F. Warde, Bruce Rogers, Designer of Books, Harvard University Press, 1925.

THE TYPOGRAPHY OF THE CAMBRIDGE UNIVERSITY PRESS

A distinctive style in book-making is now quite as difficult of attainment as it ever has been, if not more so. When printers were their own type-founders, ink-makers, and sometimes paper-makers, the products of various presses were easily distinguished and were, in a sense that we have now nearly lost, a much closer reflection of the printers' individual tastes and capabilities.

To-day the majority of types in current use are much easier of acquisition by all presses, large or small, and are therefore more widely distributed; the output of a multitude of printing-houses has enormously increased; and the growing use of type-casting and type-setting machines tends to bring about still greater uniformity amongst the products of many printing presses. The same conditions hold good in the selection and distribution of papers and inks: nearly all are 'standard' or 'stock' products, ready for the use of printers everywhere and the public generally.

It is assumed in the following rough notes that the object of the Managers of the University Press is the production of books which shall bear, in some degree at least, the unmistakable stamp of having been issued from this Press and from no other. In other words, to infuse enough of that elusive quality called *style* into its work so that (as with almost any Pickering* book for instance) a glance at a perfectly plain type-page shall serve to identify it, without recourse to either the title-page or the imprint. I might go even farther and say that a book ought almost to be identified in the dark, merely by the feel or sound of it.

* William Pickering (1796–1854), London publisher.

There are several general factors in the method of procedure by which distinction in printing may be accomplished, but none of them will serve if taken alone. They must be combined in varying degrees, according to the particular object in view. (a) The acquirement of special materials – types, papers, inks, ornaments – either made particularly for the Press, or at least according to its specifications; and differing in some particulars from the stock products supplied to the general trade. (b) The admission of no other materials into the manufacture of any book issued from the Press; in other words, standardising within certain limits the raw materials used by the Press. But (c) Special materials will be of little avail unless employed in the combinations and arrangements best suited to their special character and to the particular objects for which they are chosen.

It follows, also, that the converse of (c) is almost inevitably true; commonplace materials of book-making may be arranged in the most faultless manner, yet the result will always be commonplace – good perhaps, even excellent, but without real distinction, just as a new brick wall may be quite without flaw yet if the bricks are characterless, machine-made ones, no skill of masonry, no pattern of bonding, will make it interesting and beautiful. Combinations and arrangements of type are impossible to prescribe in general terms with any degree of exactitude, varying so much as they do with varying tastes and requirements and conditions. It is only possible to give a sort of consensus of opinion of various printers of acknowledged standing, both old and modern ones, as manifested in their works, and this is what I have aimed to present instead of my personal preferences in the following strictures on certain types and papers, and commendations of others. Where preferences are my own, I indicate it.

I am aware of the danger of making sweeping statements and, if the next one seems too condemnatory, it is only because in a brief report I cannot make the necessary qualifications of it without going too much into details, nor can I note many exceptions. But, broadly speaking, the present equipment of the Press as to types and papers (and, I think, most of the inks) is a very inferior one, quite unworthy of the standing of such an establishment. I am aware of the difficulty – almost the impossibility – of making many radical reforms in that equipment during the present interrupted condition of business affairs, but a few at least could be accomplished with a moderate expenditure. Even in ordinary times any serious improvement in the product of the Press could be made only by a considerable expenditure of money as well as of time and care.

But, with judgement, this additional expenditure could be first applied only to such undertakings as would show a decided improvement in their results, and it need not be distributed over the whole product of the Press. I mean that for books on theology, on the various sciences or technical subjects generally, clearness and accuracy are the first requirements; and these are, I believe, fairly well met at present. But works on literature (*belles lettres*) and the arts, have generally a wider appeal amongst people of aesthetic tastes, and these should be concentrated upon and issued from the Press in the very best style of which it is capable, even if at a financial loss, for a time at least. The Press, as I understand, makes many sacrifices in the service of science and scholarship. It might now include art in that list, and the most immediate art with which it could begin is the art of printing.

Reprints of the classics, in particular, should be given the utmost attention and the best materials possible, for it is this branch of book-making that undergoes the closest scrutiny and receives the keenest criticism. Eventually, of course, the ideal would be to bring all the output of the Press to an approximate level, but its reputation could be increased much more quickly and effectively by improvements in its books on the liberal arts rather than in its scientific or technical publications, these already being on a high plane.

Before taking up details of technical matters, I would like to say a word about privately printed volumes done at the Press. In most of these, it seems to me, the client has too large a hand in the physical make-up of the book. Many authors seem to have the conviction that by reason of their literary attainments, they also become skilled printers, whereas the opposite is far more likely to be true. At any rate, the fact that a man pays for a book should not give him the absolute right to dictate how that book should be made – at a first-rate printing house. At least the book should not go out with that house's imprint upon it. As the public are generally unaware of the inside history of the production of the volume, they naturally hold the printing house responsible for all the vagaries the client may impose upon it, and rightly so if it bear that press's imprint.

The author's taste should, of course, be considered, and his wishes followed so long as they do not directly oppose the canons of the Press, but it should always be understood that in matters of vital importance the Press should have the deciding voice; just as, I suppose, it would have in matters of eccentric spelling. I believe that commissions which could not be thus treated should be declined entirely; not treated thus, they are a continual menace to the reputation of the Press and, in the end, much more costly than would be the possible loss of a few printing commissions. The theory and practice should be that no outsider can use the Press merely as a manufacturing agent to suit his own designs.

Bruce Rogers (1870–1957), *Report on the Typography of Cambridge University Press*, prepared by Bruce Rogers in 1917, and printed in honour of BR's eightieth birthday by Brooke Crutchley, University Printer, Christmas 1950.

Device by Bruce Rogers

JOSEPH THORP'S Printing for Business, published in 1919, had as its sub-title 'A Manual of Printing Practice in non-technical idiom' – and was dedicated to Emery Walker, 'a pioneer of printing revival in Europe and America'. The real but hidden subject of the book was design, or typography: Thorp wrote it not for professional designers (of whom there were then very few) or printers or publishers, but for laymen who would be dealing with printers and buying printing without knowing anything about it – until they read his book, when they would find, he hoped, what an intensely interesting and enjoyable subject it was. Thorp writes, towards the end of his book, 'Men of business who must needs use printing little know what they miss by merely considering it an inevitable expense connected with salesmanship...I owe countless happy and crowded hours of a not unamusing life to my connection with what I can't help feeling to be, perhaps, after house making, the noblest and most essential of the crafts. Perhaps to be quite fair we ought to put cooking and tailoring before it. But I'll make no further concessions.'

Beatrice Warde has recorded how on her first day in her first job, as assistant librarian to Henry Lewis Bullen in the American Type Founders Library, Bullen handed her a duster and asked her to dust the 14,000 books, and said, 'I don't mind if you stop and read the books'. She pulled down (because she had to dust it) Thorp's Printing for Business and 'a whole new universe opened for me'. The book is still worth perusing and is particularly well illustrated.

Thorp was a Jesuit for ten early years, studied theology at Oscott, and then, under the wing of Wilfrid and Alice Meynell, became involved in printing. He worked for a time in the Art & Book Company, which became the Arden Press, then joined W. H. Smith & Son as a printer's traveller and, later, consultant.

He was also consultant to the Curwen Press, a founder member of the Double Crown Club, a contributor to Punch (for whom he became dramatic critic), and author of various books, including Eric Gill, Cape, 1920, the most beautiful book on Gill ever made, with 40 superb collotype plates by the Chiswick Press. He also wrote an important memoir on Bernard Newdigate, Scholar-printer, for Basil Blackwell, 1950.

THE NOBLEST AND MOST ESSENTIAL OF THE CRAFTS
Chapter 1. Introductory and explanatory

Men of business, secretaries of political and professional organisations, of learned and entirely unlearned societies, church and school authorities, officials of all manner of clubs, publishers and authors – a veritable host of responsible folk – are constantly using printed matter in the normal course of their work.

A very little knowledge of printing processes and the best tradition of printing practice would enable them to make much more effective use of this indispensable servant.

A working knowledge

It is the object of this volume to give an elementary knowledge of printing, of the working arrangements of a printing office, of paper and type, and engraving processes, which will enable more knowledge to be readily acquired by the mere routine connection with the production of printed matter. Without some such first general survey much that would be readily intelligible is entirely missed. It may safely be said that such knowledge enormously increases the interest of one's work in this direction and turns a piece of tiresome extra business into an interesting interlude.

The truth is that the buyer of printing has always, from the nature of the case, to co-operate with the printer in the process of manufacture. Printed matter is rarely if ever made precisely to sample. It is usually freshly planned. A good deal of printed matter is designed deliberately to attract favourable attention; a good deal more of it, I mean, than is explicitly recognised under the term of advertising matter. All of it *ought* to be so designed.

Customer and Printer partners

The fact is – the fact which is the real begetter of this volume – that the non-printer, the intelligent layman, may with a very little training and guidance become an effective, even a predominant partner in the production of his printed matter. I mean that if, as frequently happens, he is a man of natural good taste and appreciation of beauty and seemliness, say in furniture, or house decoration, or architecture, or dress, he may, by the simple process of having his eyes turned in the right direction towards the excellent examples and the characteristic precepts which are the privileged possession of every craft, be enabled to use those excellent qualities in this direction of printing.

And, lest I be suspected of being about to ride a hobby too furiously, let me say that I propose to keep a frankly utilitarian end in view – so that business men shall get more business, the secretary more members or subscribers, the official be more efficient and appreciated.

The so-much per 1,000 view

I will certainly promise that the buyer of printing who has this amount of knowledge at his command will be better served by his printer than ever before. The keen printer's representative of the right kind, who suddenly finds a customer who has the intelligence and knowledge to be *interested*, becomes your devoted servant. You need never bother with the other kind of representative who looks upon printing as the manufacture of so many parcels at so much per 1000 – because that it emphatically is NOT.

As for method; assuming the natural reluctance of healthily-minded men to plunge into the dismal and dismaying complexities of technical explanations, I propose to carry such explanations no farther than is absolutely necessary; to make no attempt to be complete or thorough, which would defeat the end I have in view by discouraging and confusing the reader; to explain enough, but not all terms; to make repetitions rather than to send him hunting about the volume; in fact to coax the reader instead of supposing him to be bursting with desire to get to the bottom of the whole wide craft. Thus he may be led a useful way down into it.

Proof-correction without tears

As an instance one may take the scheme of printers' marks for proof-correcting which is passed down by tradition. That is well enough for the printer's reader or the frequent author, but the layman shies at it; the man of business does not need it at all, and the first general view of it anyway is so discouraging that he turns aside to more amusing things. It can be simplified with advantage, and anyone with a little good will and energy can master it at a glance and entirely 'without tears'.

Again, all healthy folk prefer explanatory pictures to explanatory text. I commend the intelligent diagrams in this volume to the reader with the promise that they contain with their notes a great deal of information and suggestion in a small compass.

Chapter 2. Human relations: also Prefatory, but not without significance

Between printer and customer two attitudes are possible, and both are found in current practice. The first is that of mutual distrust – leading to close and often not by any means quite honest beating down of price on the part of the customer with, on the printer's part, an endeavour to get back some of his own by some little piece of sharp practice made possible by his customer's ignorance.

There's a sort of defence set up for this sort of relation. This kind of buyer thinks it legitimate to bluff on price, as it is up to the printer to refuse the work if he doesn't want it. And moreover, he looks upon the buying of printing as he would on the buying of any other commodity, such as rolls of galvanised wire netting. In the first of these assumptions he must be his own judge. In the second he is unquestionably wrong.

Kindliness and self-interest

To get the best printed matter for one's purpose the buyer needs to be in a decent personal relation with the printer or his representative, because only by an intelligent co-operation between them is the best result possible. Printers are human; and it is only natural to put more energy and devoted service into work for a decent fellow than for the other kind. Apart from this, too, there's a cruder, more substantial reason. A traveller isn't only a traveller, he's also a man. He meets with other men; may have considerable influence. The tobacconist who was the first man of business to treat a certain printer's traveller in his first very difficult and largely unsuccessful weeks with courtesy, to give him a chair, to provide him with the best possible of cigarettes, to let him tell his story and (convinced) to give him a modest order, must owe many pounds of direct and still more indirect orders to that kindly interview.

The biter bit

On the other hand that scallawag in quite another trade who, later, putting the same traveller to considerable trouble in estimating, in interviews and dummy-making, finally used the ideas, copied to the best of his ability (which was not excessive) the design and printed the work elsewhere, must have lost a good deal more than the difference in price if sincere de-recommendations are of any avail helped by the destruction of that offending catalogue wherever it has been met with by the traveller aforesaid in hotels. Happily business men are not commonly so unfair nor travellers, perhaps, so vindictive! But *'make the traveller your friend'* is no bad maxim. Nor is another, of American origin – to see every man at least once, judge him acutely in that interview and issue orders accordingly. It is well not to leave all the discretion in these matters to the office boy or clerk who is apt to be quite unduly impressed by spats.

There are many reasons for considerate treatment of the printer. No manufacture, I think literally none, is so consistently complex. There are, broadly, no patterns. Every job is a fresh job. A score of accidents may happen to mar the work at any stage. Impossible things are expected of the printer in regard to time, and he is often bullied into promising the impossible.

A knowledge of printing processes, and of those points where special difficulties occur, some idea of the time taken by various operations, will, while informing the customer, materially help the printer. In any case there's nothing gained by the making of mysteries. Speaking as a printer I should say that the more the outsider knows the more intelligent will be his co-operation; and in general the more sympathetic and considerate he will be, the more appreciative of a loyal service.

Here, then, is the second and more mutually profitable relationship between customer and printer, the antithesis of the antagonistic theory.

Co-operators or antagonists

The more intelligent and well-informed customers there are, the more the trade – and the customers – will benefit. Interesting experiments will be made and paid for. It need not be denied that the printer, pre-occupied with the extraordinarily burdensome and exacting detail of his craft, is not too keenly on the look-out for new ways. Honestly, it is hardly to be expected, though in rare cases it is found. But clever, exigent men of business, advertising men, organisers and the like, by the demands they make and the problems they propose lift the general level of accomplishment in the trade. They will make more and more reasonable and practicable demands the more they know. Inspiration, that is to say, is necessarily largely from without. It should be welcomed by the printer, not resented. We very much need such liftings. Our grooves need filling up and cutting anew.

These notes about printing and its allied processes are, I hope, fitly preceded by these few words on the human relationship between the printer and the customer. As is usual in failures of mutual appreciation, the cause is largely mutual misunderstanding.

Joseph Thorp (1873–1962), *Printing for Business*,
London, 1919.

Hand Ink roller.

'THE ACCOMPANYING EXTRACTS *from the Transactions of the Society of Calligraphers' (wrote Dwiggins in 1919 in a Note prefacing the extracts printed here) 'are published with the approval of the Society.' The Society in fact never existed, except in the heads of Dwiggins and his cousin Laurance Siegfried – but Dwiggins designed distinguished stationery for it, and in 1925 issued a leaflet awarding Honorary Membership to twenty-two friends, including D. B. Updike, Stanley Morison, and Beatrice Becker (later Warde). The 'extracts' are reprinted here (not for the first time) because they are nearly as true and certainly as readable as they were when first published. They are still not, as far as I know, currently available in print anywhere else.*

Dwiggins was illustrator, decorator, typeface designer, typographer, carpenter, puppeteer, author; brilliant in every one of those activities, and in a few more besides. In 1928 Beatrice Warde wrote in The Fleuron, vol.6, that Dwiggins 'is almost alone in his country in championing modernism in printing, and in rejecting...traditional motives of decoration'. In 1935 Philip Hofer wrote, in Dolphin 2, that Dwiggins was 'America's one truly modern typographer'. Dwiggins indeed looked forward, without, however, denying the past; his work is as modern as that of Imre Reiner or Jan Tschichold, but quite different, and stamped with his own personality – which, incidentally, Tschichold in his early days would have condemned.

Dwiggins was the author of Layout in Advertising, (Harper, New York, 1928), one of the best handbooks on the subject, and also of works of poetic science fiction. When he wrote about any aspect of typographic design, it was always with devastating common sense. There is no biography; Dwight Agner's The Books of WAD (Press of the Night Owl, Louisiana, 1974) is a useful but incomplete biography. A good introduction to him as a man is in Postscripts to Dwiggins, Typophiles Chapbooks 35 and 36, 1960, edited by Paul Bennett, with contributions by some fourteen people who knew and loved him, and many fine illustrations. In Boston Public Library (the old building, not the new) there are two 'Dwiggins Rooms' – possibly the only rooms in the world where the output of a single designer can be studied and actually touched by students. His puppets are celebrated and described by Dorothy Abbe, with superb photographs, in a remarkable book, The Dwiggins Marionettes (Harry N. Abrams, New York, 1970).

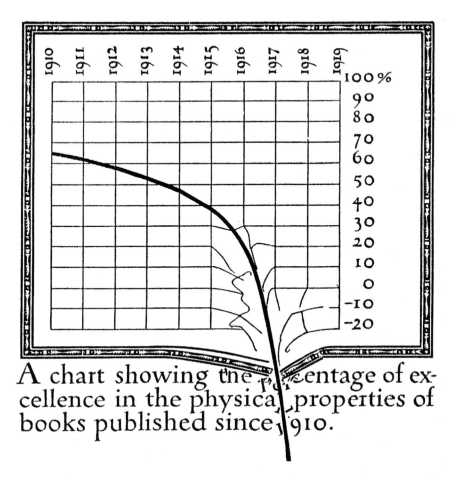

A chart showing the percentage of excellence in the physical properties of books published since 1910.

AN INVESTIGATION INTO THE PHYSICAL PROPERTIES OF BOOKS

1. Mr B.

Q. Mr. B——, will you please tell the committee why you printed this book on cardboard?

A. To make it the right thickness. It had to be one inch thick.

– Why that thick, particularly?

– Because otherwise it would not sell. If a book isn't one inch thick it won't sell.

– Do you mean to say that people who buy books select them with a foot rule?

– They have to have some standard of selection.

– So that it is your practice to stretch out the text if it is too short by printing it on egg-box stock?

– Not my practice, particularly. All publishers do it. We are obliged to use this and other means to bring the book up to a proper thickness. You must remember that our prices are not based on the contents of a book but on its size.

– You mention other methods. Would you mind telling us what other methods you use?

– We can expand the letter-press judiciously. We limit the matter to seven words on a page, say, and so get a greater number of pages. We can use large type and can lead considerably.

– But does not that practice hurt the appearance of the page? Make a poor-looking page?

– I am afraid I do not get your meaning.

– I mean to say, is not the page ugly and illegible when you expand the matter to that extent?

– You don't consider the look of a page in making a book. That is a thing that doesn't enter into the production of a book. If I understand you correctly, do you mean to say that it matters how a book looks?

– That was the thought in my mind.

– That's a new idea in book publishing!

★ ★ ★

– You were speaking of the pressure of industrial conditions since the war. Under these conditions what percentage of the traditions of the craft can you preserve, would you say?

– The traditions of what craft?

– The craft of printing, obviously. What I am trying to get at is this:– There are certain precise and matured standards of workmanship in the printing craft; these standards are the result of experiment through nearly five hundred years. How far are these standards effective under your present-day conditions?

– Those standards, so far as I know anything about them, are what you would call academic. In the first place, book-manufacturing is not a craft, it is a business. As for standards of workmanship – I can understand the term in connection with cabinet-making, for example, or tailoring, but I should not apply the expression to books. You do not talk about the 'standards of workmanship' in making soap, do you?

– Then in your mind there does not linger any atmosphere of an art about the making of books?

– When you talk about 'atmosphere' you have me out of my depth. There isn't any atmosphere of art lingering about making soap, is there?

– You would class soap-making with book-making?

– I can see no reason why not.

– May I ask you why you were selected by ———— Company to manage their manufacturing department?

– Really, I must say you overstep the borders –

– Please do not misinterpret my question. It is really pertinent to the inquiry.

– It should certainly be obvious why a man is chosen for a given position. I am employed to earn a satisfactory return on the share-holders' investment. Is that the information you want?

– I think that is what we want. Would you then consider yourself as happily employed in making soap as in making books?

– Quite as well employed, if making soap paid the dividend.

★ ★ ★

– While we're on this subject, may I ask you how you choose the artists who make your illustrations?

– My practice is to select an illustrator whose name is well known.

– Is that the only point you consider?

– I should say, yes. I am not aware of any other reason for spending money on this feature. It is always an uncertain detail and this way of making a choice puts the matter on a safe basis.

– It is sometimes assumed that the illustrations should have a sympathetic bearing on the story. Does not that consideration have some weight with you in choosing your artist?

– None, I should say. You see, the pictures are not really a necessary part of the book. They are a kind of frill that the public has got in the way of expecting, and we have to put them in. Illustrations as a rule stand us as a dead loss unless they are made by a well-known artist. Then, of course, they help sell the book.

II. Mr McG.

A. The gentlemen of the committee must remember that the book-publishing business is a gamble. Each new issue, particularly in the department of fiction, is a highly adventurous risk. Our percentage of blanks would astonish you if we dared to state it. But any book may turn out a best-seller. This hope keeps us going. It is absolutely a gamble, as I say. You can see that under these conditions we cannot spend very much money on non-essentials. We have to strip the books down to the barest necessities.

Personally I should like to see the firm put out nothing that is not well designed and well printed. But as an agent of the firm I have to set aside my personal preferences. The directors are very much down on what they call art.

– Has the firm ever looked into the question of good workmanship as a possible aid to sales?

– Not under the present management. The founder looked at good work as more or less a marketing advantage.

– What do you think caused the present management to change from that opinion?

– They haven't changed. They never had it. They get at the matter from another angle altogether. Their policy is to reduce the production cost to the minimum. The minimum in theory would be reached when the public complained. The public hasn't complained, so you can't tell when to stop cheapening.

You see the directors don't look at a book as a fabricated thing at all. Books are merely something to sell – merchandise. Our management – and all the rest of them for that matter – come from the selling side of the business and do not have any pride in the product. Old Mr ———— was a publisher because he liked books. That made an entirely different policy in the old firm, of course.

– To get back to the question of good workmanship helping sales:– Here are two books published abroad to be sold at 50 cents and 80 cents. They can very well be called works of art. Do you not think that these well-designed paper covers would stand out among other books and invite customers to themselves?

– Undoubtedly they would.

– Have you ever tried the experiment of putting out editions in paper covers of attractive design?

– Never. It couldn't be done. People wouldn't buy them.

– But you said a moment ago –

– —Moreover the difference of cost between cheap cloth sides and paper covers of the kind you have there is so slight that it wouldn't pay to try the experiment. People want stiff board covers. It doesn't much matter what is inside, but they insist on board covers.

– How do you arrive at that fact?

– Through our salesmen.

– And you say that paper covers have never been tried?

– Never. None of our travellers would go out on the road with a sample in paper covers.

★ ★ ★

– A little while ago you said something about your salesmen helping you to an understanding of the public taste. I infer that you get considerable help from this source?

– Most valuable help indeed. We depend entirely on the reports the sales force turns in in these matters. The salesmen are in direct contact with the retailers and are naturally in a position to feel the public pulse, so to speak. Their help is invaluable. They can anticipate the demand very often.

– I had reference more particularly to the way books are made.

– Oh, on that point too. We never make a final decision on a cover design, for instance, without showing it to the salesmen. They very often make valuable suggestions as to changes of colour, etc. They run largely to red.

– It would seem, then, that the designing of books is very much in the hands of the salesmen?

– Quite in their hands.

– Are the office-boys often called into consultation?

– Mr ——— finds his stenographer a very great help in passing upon certain points – illustrations, etc.

– Does it appear to you that the sales department would be the one best qualified to pass on points of design?

– Well, there, you see – the books have to be sold – that is what we make them for – and the sales department is the one in closest touch with the people that buy the books – that knows just what they want.

– The standards of quality, then, are set by the people who buy the books?

– Oh, absolutely so. How else would you move the books? It is a merchandising proposition, you must remember.

– But do you not think that people would buy decently made books as willingly as poorly made books?

– At the same price, yes. No question about it. The book-buying public doesn't worry its head about the way books are made. It doesn't know anything about it. And well made books cost more. The trade is committed to a dollar-and-a-half article and can't risk going above it.

– Your opinion is that the price of a well made book would be so high as to prevent its sale?

– In the case of fiction, yes. The price has become almost a fixture.

– We shall have to go outside of fiction, then, to look for well made books?

– It amounts to that.

– You have said that certain unproductive factors prevent you from spending what you otherwise might on good workmanship. What specific factors would you mention?

– Plates – electros. We plate everything on the chance of its running into several printings. 80 per cent of the books are not reprinted. You can see that the money tied up in plates is a very considerable sum, and, as I say, 80 per cent of it is dead loss. We are obliged to take the chance, however.

– Has any remedy occurred to you?

– If stereotyping could be revived as an accurate process it might help us out. It would cost much less to make and to store paper matrices than to make electrotypes. The difficulty here is that no one knows how to make good stereotypes, and the stereotype plates at their best are more trouble to make ready. Trouble with the press-room, you see.

– Is it possible under good conditions to get satisfactory results from stereotype plates?

– Unquestionably. The books printed from this kind of plates in the first days of the invention are entirely satisfactory.

III. Mr L.

Q. Can a trade-edition book be well made and sell for $1.50?

– That depends on how high you set your standard.

– Well, let us not be too rigorous. Can it be made better, say, than this book?

– Beyond question. It will all depend on whether or not the printer has a few lingering memories of the standards of printing.

– But should not the setting of standards come from the publisher?

– Oh yes, under ideal conditions. Both printer and publisher should have a hand in it.

– How would you make a book of fiction to be sold for $1.50?

– Well, such a book could have a good title-page as cheaply as a bad one – and the whole typographic scheme would cost no more if it were logically done instead of crudely strung together. By logically done I mean with well proportioned, practicable margins and legible headings, etc. The press-work on books is reasonably good but the 'lay-out' or design is entirely neglected. It calls for a little planning, of course, but no more than should be available in any reputable plant, It isn't so much that these books are badly planned as it is that they are not planned at all.

– But most printing firms have a planning department, do they not?

– The planning in most presses is concerned with the handling of material, not with the *designing* of material. This is no doubt due to the fact that the Taylor System has not yet got around to Aesthetic Efficiency.

– Are not the typographical unions concerned to train their men on these points of design that you mention?

– The unions have only one idea – and it is not concerned with the improvement of printing.

– Are there any trade schools that teach these things? Are not the employers' associations promoting schools to train men in the craft?

– The employers' associations have one idea – a little different from the idea of the unions, perhaps, but not concerned with the improvement of printing. There are trade schools but they teach only the mechanics of the craft.

– Apparently, then, there is no place in this country where one can learn how to design printing?

– You can safely say that there is no such place.

IV. MR A.

Q. What is your own opinion on the subject of illustrations in books?

– In what particular do you mean?

– I mean, do you think that illustrations help or hinder the quality of a book?

– The question is too general to be answered easily. May I ask you to be more specific?

– For example, here is a 'best-seller' with several – five or six – half-tone illustrations. Do you consider that these pictures make the book a more complete thing as a specimen of book-making?

– Most certainly not.

– Then would you say that illustrations in such books were a detraction?

– Illustrations such as these, yes. Though it would be hard to detract from this particular book.

– It is a standard book – a standard type of book.

– I fear that it is.

– What kind of illustrations would you favour?

– For many books, none at all. In these books of current fiction the pictures are either futile or else detrimental to the development of the plot. They give the game away, so to speak, when the author may wish to hold the story in suspense. The effort to avoid this disaster accounts for the multitude of undramatic pictures you see in books.

– Your theory of no pictures should appeal to the publishers but I doubt if the illustrators will stand with you.

– Illustration is a trade as well as an art.

– True. But we are trying to limit the inquiry to the artistic side at present. When, then, according to your deductions, would illustrations be called for?

– When they can make a stage-setting for the story. When they ornament it or suggest it, perhaps, instead of reveal it. Impressions and 'atmosphere' instead of literal diagrams with a cross marking the spot where, etc.

– But perhaps people like the cross marking the spot where.

– We are limiting the discussion to the artistic side, are we not?

– What about the half-tone process of engraving?

– The process is a way of doing things that cannot be done cheaply by any other means.

– Do you consider it a process that adds to the artistic possibilities of book printing?

– You mean according to the standards that prevailed in the earlier days of the craft?

– I do. Yes.

– According to those standards it seems to me that half-tones will always have to be considered as necessities forced upon the book-printer. They demand a kind of paper that is never a satisfactory book-paper. In the case of the kind of books we are talking about the relief line methods have always given the most artistic results, because they are so closely related to the character of the type.

One regrets, however, to give up the chances for tonal designs that the half-tone process provides. Probably the designers and printers will work out a satisfactory relation between half-tones and type when the craze for photographic detail passes a little. As things stand, I should say that the best results are to be had with uncoated book-papers and with line plates. It is true books are rarely illustrated this way – current fiction, I mean – but the method might be used to produce a very attractive and unusual result.

– Then you would condemn the use of half-tones in this kind of books?

– If you mean the usual kind of half-tones printed separately and inserted, I do. But if you are making a book of travel, for example, the half-tones from photographs explain and justify themselves.

But on this whole subject of book illustration it strikes me that if you are to make the design from the start you might as well make it in harmony with the kind of paper and printing you are planning to use, and get all the artistic advantage of fitting your means to your limitations.

★ ★ ★

– Are you familiar with the Christy-Holbein Test?

– Yes. That is to say, I have heard of your applying it, and remember that the percentages were very much against Holbein.

– Ninety-three to seven, on an average. How do you explain such a crudity of taste in these groups of people otherwise well educated?

– By the deduction that they are not educated. That is to say that these people, cultivated in other ways, react precisely like savages when confronted with pictures or drawings. They 'go for' the tinsel and glitter and are opaque to the higher and more civilised values. They get the most pleasure from drawings that they think they could make themselves. This is the basis of the Eight-year-old Formula widely applied in the department of newspaper comics: 'Make your drawing so that it can be understood by a child eight years old'.

All of this is clearly lack of training, because their taste is good in other matters – music, for example, and house furnishings.

– You would deduce, then, that the periodical and book-publishing industry has failed to train the taste of its public in such matters?

– It has done worse: it has depraved that taste. Because there was, not very long ago, a fine tradition in this country in the line of illustration.

– Why should the publishers find any advantage in depraving the taste of the public – as you say they have done?

– Because they turned their backs on the standards of the publishing business and became merchandisers solely. They had to sell the goods and they had to 'sell' a big new public. The quickest way to this public – through flash-and-crash tactics – they adopted. And naturally ran themselves and the public downhill.

– May there not be other sides to it, too? May it not be that the art schools are not now producing draughtsmen of a calibre to support the fine tradition you mention?

– That may have something to do with it. But even that is mixed up with the other. I think that the chief difficulty is with the publishers.

– And the public?

– The public will follow if the publishers lead.

v. MR S.

A. Are you not making the mistake of keeping too close to the publishers? It seems to me that you will not get at all the facts behind the situation until you get in touch with the people we sell the books to. *They* are the factors that bring about the conditions you object to. The publisher is merely a machine for selling the public what it wants.

– Then the publisher has no selective function?

– Absolutely none.

– How does the public bring about the condition we object to?

– Obviously by buying the books.

– I mean to say, how does the public prevail upon you to sell it trashy books instead of well made books?

– The public is entirely uneducated on the subject of books, in your sense. People know nothing at all about paper or printing or pictures or things of that sort. One book is as good as another to any educated man so long as he can read it. He doesn't know that there is any such thing as good printing or bad printing or good or bad taste in making books. Under these conditions we should be fools to spend money on features that do not have any bearing on sales. It's a simple business proposition.

– Would the public that you are discussing buy well made books as willingly as trashy books?

– Oh, absolutely. It's the books they are interested in – what they contain, not how they are made. They wouldn't know the difference.

VI. MR G.

A. What's the use of talking about standards in connection with things like these? These are not books. They aren't fit to wad a gun with. I wouldn't have them in the house. Nobody pays any attention to stuff like that.

There isn't what you would call a book on the table, except this one, perhaps. That's printed in England and sent over in sheets and bound on this side. But that one is set in a bastard Caslon. It isn't the original Caslon but a revision with the descenders cut off. See how he's got his O upside down!

Those others – what's the use of talking about them at all? It reminds me of the story about the Chinaman –

– But, Mr———, do you not think it possible to get up this class of books in a manner that would suit you better?

– You can't hope to get anything like a decent book until you do away with the damnable cheap paper and the vile types. And then you will have to start in and teach the printer how to print. There aren't more than half a dozen presses in the country that know how to print. Most printing looks like it had been done with apple-butter on a hay-press –

– What you say is unhappily true. What we are trying to find out are the causes of this state of things.

– The causes are everywhere – all through the rattle-trap, cheap-jack, shoddy work that is being done in every kind of trade. Nobody cares for making decent things any more.

The only cure is to get back to decent standards of workmanship in everything again. But the case seems to me to be hopeless. I try to do printing up to a decent standard – and that is about all any of us can do. I don't believe you can hope to do much good through your societies and investigations. I believe in each one doing his own job in the best way he knows how. That's the only way you can raise the standard. It's the work you turn out that counts.

W. A. Dwiggins (1880–1956), *An Investigation into the Physical Properties of Books*, 1919.

Drawing by W. A. Dwiggins on cover of the *Investigation*.

Bernard Newdigate *was a scholar-printer in the highest tradition. He also wrote elegantly and amusingly. He never wrote a book, which he might well have done, but from 1920 to the beginning of the Second World War he wrote regular Book Production Notes in the* London Mercury *(whose editor for most of that period was Sir John Squire). The Notes from 1920 to 1925 have been reprinted, with their original illustrations, in a fine limited edition by Philip Kerrigan at his Tabard Private Press in 1986, from which the quotations here have been taken.*

'On printing poetry' is one of the most sensible passages that has ever been written on the subject, and makes an intriguing contrast with Francis Meynell's dictum that poetry should always be printed in italic 'to slow the reader down'.

The second piece 'About type-design' expresses views, e.g. on the 'heavy leading' in Goudy's The Alphabet, *with which some would find it difficult to agree today – but it is otherwise authoritative. The third piece, about the future of offset-printing, is characteristic of Newdigate's vision and prescience – he looked ahead, as well as back.*

The fourth piece 'A BLUE BOOK...' is worth reprinting if only for its first sentence.

See Joseph Thorp, B. H. Newdigate, Scholar-Printer 1869–1944, *Basil Blackwell, Oxford, 1950, and* Book Production Notes, *Tabard Private Press, 1986.*

ON PRINTING POETRY

The printer who would make a comely page and at the same time make the poet's message as clear as possible to the eye, and through the eye to the mind, is beset with special problems. He may not run his lines on – else how should we know them for poetry? – & long lines and short play havoc with his margins. A couple of four-line stanzas of tetrameters may have to face a page of alexandrines, or, say, Mr Vachel Lindsay's 'Bryan, Bryan, Bryan, Bryan!': how in such a case can the 'opening' be the 'unit'? The shape of some poems seems to defy all effort to bring them into relation with the proportions of the page: Pegasus jibs at being so harnessed. Take the sonnet for instance – the single sonnet, not a sequence of them. William Morris likened the sonnet to a bloody brick.

To a printer who cares what his pages look like, these very difficulties offer a delight not comparable with any other make-up; just because each page, or rather pair of pages, calls for its own special treatment. Nevertheless, if the book is to be a book at all, there are certain conditions which will govern the setting of all the pages, however varied the length, metre, rhythm, rhyme or reason of the poems which they present. The pages must at any rate be all of the same size, and the poems must all be printed in the same type. The first things to choose, then, are the size of the page and the type.

The page is best wide in proportion to its length, so that the vessel may have plenty of beam for carrying its mixed cargo. For a wide page will take the short lines and the long lines too, and 'turned' lines should be as few as possible. As for the type, let it be as big and as clear as the page will admit, lest eye-strain be added to mind-strain.

As for margins, it might be thought that these need not trouble the printer much; for whatever margins he may propose, his poets by the varying lengths and measures of their lines and of their poems will dispose them otherwise. He must, however, determine the make-up of his pages in width and depth just as he would if they were to be solid prose, except that, if wise, he will allow for a wider & deeper page than he would choose for prose. The greater width will allow him room enough for the longest lines of the longest metres; & the greater depth will allow him greater freedom in fitting the stanzas to the page. For stanzas should not be broken at the foot of a page, unless their length makes the break inevitable. If they are broken, not only will the flow of the verse be interrupted, but the symmetry of the facing pages will be lost. The printer will not, however, so make up most of his pages that the print will cover the page to its full depth. His margins will be variable.

A chief problem in printing poetry is to make facing pages balance one another as well as the versification will allow. It will help to solve this problem of balance if we remember that every written or printed poem, however irregular the length of its lines, has what we may call its meridian, represented by an imaginary perpendicular line dividing the poem into approximately equal halves...

May 1920

ABOUT TYPE-DESIGN

Good letter alone does not give good printing. Tolerably good printing may even be done with letter weak in character or design. Bodoni, of Parma, for instance, the 'sweltering hideousness' of whose type established towards the end of the eighteenth century a vogue which we have not yet wholly put off, was in many ways an excellent printer. On the other hand, intolerably bad printing often comes from the misuse of quite good letter. Good work depends on the use made of means and materials rather than on themselves. Nevertheless, letter fine in design and well cut & well cast is needed for the finest printing.

If the type used by modern printers is inferior to that used by the earliest printers, the defect is in the design and in the size and proportions of the letter rather than in the quality of the type-founding. In many points of merely technical and mechanical excellence – in alignment, for instance, in the refinement & exactness of his line, in the quality and temper of his metal – the modern type-founder is better than his early predecessors. It is possible that such perfection has indirectly contributed to the uglifying of modern type; for it has made type-founding a business of manual and mechanical skill rather than a search for beautiful form. Even the better wearing quality of modern case type has made for deterioration in design; for the constant need for renewal must have sent the early type-founders back to the fine models which they found in contemporary book-hands. There are no modern book-hands to which type-founders can go; and most of those who seek to replace or improve upon established shapes of letter set out upon their adventure with neither tradition nor good taste to guide them. That is what makes a modern type-founder's specimen book the ugliest thing on earth, except a municipal cemetery. Good taste in general is not enough: painters and sculptors who design their own letter are often guilty of the worst atrocities of all.

I have referred before in these Notes to the good type-design which of late years has been done in America. There has recently reached me from New York a copy of a thin but handsome quarto on *The Alphabet*, written by Mr F. W. Goudy, & printed under his direction in the 'Kennerley' type, which he designed. Even apart from its subject the book is an interesting specimen of book production. The Kennerley type itself is perhaps the most attractive letter which has been placed within the reach of British and American printers in modern times. The size used in this book is large – 12 point – and the line is seven inches long, which happens to be just about the length used by Jenson for his Pliny.... The Kennerley type, like most of the good types which have come to us of late years, owes much to Jensen; & Mr Goudy shows us in his book a small specimen of his 'Goudy Antique', which follows Jenson's type even more closely & promises to surpass even the Kennerley type in beauty. Jenson's Pliny is close set, with no more space between the lines than is required by the generous dimensions of ascending or descending strokes of such letters as b, d, h, g, j, p. Mr Goudy's Kennerley pages are heavily leaded, and are much more widely spaced than Jenson's. They are much weakened thereby. His ascenders and descenders are shorter than Jenson's.

The most valuable part of the book is the series of twenty-seven large plates reproducing each of the letters of the alphabet in a variety of forms. I reproduce the key to the plates, which shows the letter D as presented in the plate for that letter, but reduced to about a third of its height and breadth, so that it loses much of its value for comparative study. No. 1, the large letter in the middle, is copied from the letter in the Trajan Column, that *locus classicus* of fine roman letter. No. 2 is a pen form, and 3 and 4 are Gothic and Lombardic developments of the letter. No. 8 is copied from Jenson's roman type, and Nos 9 & 12 are from Mr Goudy's Kennerley

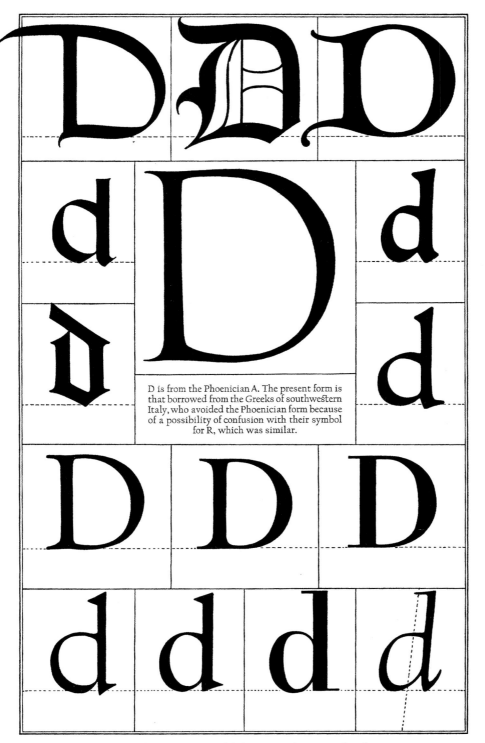

D is from the Phoenician A. The present form is that borrowed from the Greeks of southwestern Italy, who avoided the Phoenician form because of a possibility of confusion with their symbol for R, which was similar.

Page from Goudy's *The Alphabet*, New York, 1922. Reduced.

type. Nos 10 and 13 are based on the famous letter designed and cut by William Caslon about the year 1720, which is even more in favour to-day than at any earlier period of its career. Nos 11 & 14 show types by Bodoni, of Parma, denounced by William Morris and Emery Walker as the leader of that 'luckless change which first produced letters that are *positively* ugly, and... are dazzling to the eye owing to the clumsy thickening & thinning of the lines,' as compared with 'the seventeenth-century letters, which are at least pure and simple in line'. (*Arts and Crafts Essays: Printing*, Longmans 1903)

These plates cannot fail to bring home to the student of lettering & of printing the essence of the details of fine letter, whether written or printed. Yet he must not overlook the wholesome warning given by Mr Edward Johnston, who by his teaching and by his admirable book on *Writing & Illuminating* has done more for the revival of fine lettering than any other living man: 'Alphabets wrested from their original places in MSS and inscriptions (and printed books) are in danger of becoming mere "copies", or crystallisations, that may breed literal copies & inscriptions without spirit.' A course of fine writing on the lines taught by Mr Johnston & his followers would be the best preliminary training for gaining that appreciation & command of letter-forms which is needed for good type-design.

OFFSET PRINTING AND ILLUSTRATION

Of late years the method of printing known as litho-offset has, with the help of photography, been making great strides in the way of improvement; and one by one the difficulties which beset its infancy seem to be yielding to research, experiment, & practical skill. Its latest development is due to the astonishing enterprise of the owners of a north-country bi-weekly newspaper, the *Blackpool Times*, who opened the present year by printing their paper entirely by offset. Their venture seems likely to prove the first step towards a revolution in newspaper printing. The copies of the newspaper which I have before me suggest also that offset will in time supplant many of our present ways of printing and illustrating books.

★ ★ ★

Instead of the coarse screen used for most newspaper illustration, that used for the offset method is so fine as to be invisible. The printing is not uniformly good; but improvement may come with practice.

If a cheap country newspaper can be printed so well by photo-litho offset, it needs little imagination to foresee that before long the same method will be used for the printing of illustrated books, enabling photographs to be reproduced and printed with the text on rough paper of strong fibre instead of those coated 'art' papers which alone take impressions of half-tone blocks with the fullest brilliancy. It is possible, too, that photo-litho offset may in time supersede stereotyping for reprints of books.

May 1922

A BLUE BOOK ON GOOD PRINTING

Good printing is sane printing; and sane printing is plain printing. That is the lesson taught by example & by printed examples even better than by precept in the remarkable Blue Book on type faces and type display for Government Printing which has lately issued from the Stationery Office. The Committee appointed some two years since 'to select the best faces of type and modes of type display for Government printing having regard to appearance, ease in reading, and economy', reports guardedly and tactfully that 'the general standard of Government printing has not always been as high as it should be'.

'There can be little doubt that a well-printed book is not only more legible, but also more saleable than a book which is ill printed; and on general grounds Government printing in a country which can claim so many of the great printers of the past ought to be as good as possible consistently with economy. The Government should set the highest standard practicable in the various classes of its own productions and so help to improve the public taste. This should indeed be the natural corollary of the policy it has advisedly adopted in aiding & maintaining Schools of Arts and Crafts throughout the country, and in establishing the Victoria & Albert Museum at South Kensington, where printing and bookbinding are among the crafts represented.'

After remarking upon the beneficent influence which the State printing presses of foreign nations had upon the commercial printing done in their several countries, the Report continues: 'The Government is in a position to exercise a great influence for good upon the printing craft, partly by achieving a high standard in its own work and partly by requiring the same high standard in work put out to contract.'

Borrowing in the main from Morris's famous 'Note' on the aims of the Kelmscott Press, the Report considers some of the many factors which go to make a type face that is at once legible and simple: 'The letters should be as simple in form as possible. They should be broad in the face rather than compressed, & should avoid both undue thickening & thinning of the serifs and strokes or of (sic) reducing the whites between them. The faces should be so proportioned that leading between the lines should not be necessary for legibility.'

The Committee gives, with specimens of each, a 'Schedule of Suitable Type Faces', handset, monotype or linotype, which they have approved as conforming to their canon. Some of the specimens, indeed, rather flagrantly violate it; but the selection as a whole will serve as a useful guide to the printer in the choice of his founts, and these examples, shown in juxtaposition, should help our type-designers and typefounders to a better idea of what makes for good letter. In a later issue of *The London Mercury* I hope to discuss the Committee's selection of approved types in more detail.

Besides discussing & showing type faces the Report lays down rules for margins, for setting tables of figures, and for title pages, the arrangement of which 'should be as simple as may be'. Some good examples of these simplified title pages are given. There is also a series of model Blue Book covers, beside each of which is pilloried the ugly and far less legible cover which the improved setting should supplant.

ASCENDING AND DESCENDING FIGURES

The Report recommends that figures for tabular matter should be wider than those most in vogue: they should be of the width of two thick spaces, like some of those cast by Messrs Shanks, instead of an 'en' only, which is the usual width. The Committee would like to refer the whole question of the best figures to use for different kinds of tables to the Medical Research Council. I doubt whether such enquiry would be found to support the provisional recommendation of the Committee that 'modern' figures, which all 'ascend' like capital letters

1 2 3 4 5 6 7 8 9 0

are really more readable in tables than the older forms, of which some 'ascend', others 'descend', and others do neither:

1 2 3 4 5 6 7 8 9 0

The very differences between the several figures make them easier to distinguish and so make for clearness, just as words printed in lower case letters are easier to read than those printed in 'ascending' capitals.

September 1922

Bernard Newdigate (1869–1944), *Book Production Notes* (from *The London Mercury*, 1920–1922), Tabard Private Press, 1986.

THE TEXT PRINTED HERE is Francis Meynell's introduction to Typography, 1923, which can be compared with Joseph Thorp's Printing for Business, published four years earlier (cf.p.17). Meynell, like Thorp, was, in his own words, making an attempt 'to assist the amateur to a right appreciation of type-forms, and to direct him towards the beautiful and the useful rather than to the "curious". In fact, Typography is a brilliant promotion for the Pelican Press which Meynell had founded in 1916. It is probably the most elaborate and beautiful printer's specimen book ever produced, and perhaps the only one with a title-page which folds out and becomes a poster. There are forty pages of text in which Meynell states his precepts in book design and typography overall, followed by thirty pages of type and border settings printed in several colours, including another fold-out plate of Pelican symbols.

When he later founded the Nonesuch Press, Meynell linked the private press movement with general publishing. The Nonesuch limited editions were all books of literature which had good reason for existing; but it is sometimes forgotten that Nonesuch also published an excellent series of non-limited 'compendious' editions (Blake, Byron, Lewis Carroll, Coleridge, etc.) and also that brilliant best-selling anthology, the Week-end Book, which came out in a succession of editions with illustrations by different artists.

See Francis Meynell's autobiography My Lives, Bodley Head, London, 1971, and John Dreyfus, A History of the Nonesuch Press, 1981.

A ⋆ B ⋆ C ⋆ D ⋆ E ⋆ F ⋆ G ⋆ H
I ⋆ J ⋆ K ⋆ L ⋆ M ⋆ N ⋆ O ⋆ P
Q ⋆ R ⋆ S ⋆ T ⋆ U
V ⋆ W ⋆ X
Y ⋆ Z

'WITH TWENTY-FIVE SOLDIERS OF LEAD I HAVE CONQUERED THE WORLD'

That dramatic statement is French in origin, and (as they say) of a certain age – which means, here as always, of an uncertain age. Who said it, and when? Was it a village-bound boaster with a sudden and wonderful revelation of the dramatic spirit? Or was it in very truth a conqueror of men's minds?

Let those who know forbear to tell us. Let the birthplace of his aunt, the recollections of his schoolmaster, the intrigues which gave him his first start in life , let his habits in face of the bottle (to which he was wont to ascribe so much of his success or failure), his taste in cigars, or sword-hilts, or politics, or religion – let all be left unknown and ungathered. For whoever he was, however he prospered, he said and he did (I'll be bound) nothing else that could justify the sublime arrogance of that declaration –'with twenty-five soldiers of lead I have conquered the world'. Anything more of his were a derogation from that assertion, or a flat denial, or (worst of all) a jest thrown at it – a very profanation of his moment of divinity.

One thing only shall be allowed. You who like 'internal evidence' – a pleasant relic of school-days and Skeat – may consider the number 25. Does that date the phrase? In the mid-17th century the W was added to the 25; and the 25 itself was promoted from 24 only a decade or two earlier by the establishment of J. Therefore, if you wish to put a date to Cæsar-Shakespeare, I am prepared to agree to 1640. But my side of the bargain is this: that you do now, and with so much, rest content, and leave unopened the dictionary of phrases, where, doubtless, the thing is indexed, dated, annotated, ascribed, analysed, historified, and stripped naked for the confusion of all our theory.

With 25 soldiers of lead.... If it is not individually it is at least generally true. All the heights and depths and breadths of tangible and natural things – landscapes, sunsets, the scent of hay, the hum of bees, the beauty which belongs to eyelids (and is falsely ascribed to eyes); all the immeasurable emotions and motions of the human mind, to which there seems no bound; ugly and terrible and mysterious thoughts and things, as well as beautiful – all are compassed, restrained, ordered in a trifling jumble of letters. Twenty-six signs! The complete equipment of my child of six – and of Shakespeare. Two dozen scratches so chosen and so arranged as to make King Lear and the Sonnets! They are common to the greatest, and to us. They are the key to eternity. They are the stepping-stones to the stars. And we use them, one to split his infinitives, one to forge a cheque, one to write betting-slips, one to compose an article which will consist of just so many words as fulfil the order to write such an Introduction as this.

Pause, gentle reader. Come back from the edge of this profound pool of sentiment and truth. Consider this in mitigation of the wonder. As literature is thus contained by a group of symbols, so life is controlled by another and shorter series. I make bold to declare that with eleven soldiers of lead – eleven, no more – I could conquer the universe. You doubt it? But first behold them:

9 8 7 6 5 4 3 2 1 0 £

The following simple summary of the history of type-forms, of their uses and of their technology, is addressed to the buyer of printing (be he author, merchant, secretary of a learned society, or publicity agent) who is at the same time a lover of the craft – an amateur of letters no less than of literature. There are plenty of learned, and it is to be feared pedantic, books for the professional bibliophile; and for the less expert and more open-minded a simpler and a more familiar method may be found of use. In the following pages, then, an attempt is made to assist the amateur to a right appreciation of type-forms, and to direct him towards the beautiful and the useful rather than to the 'curious'. That it is the work of a printer, and that its material is of necessity a display of his own wares, a well-furbished and furnished shop-window, should not detract, even in an age sensitive to (because governed by) advertisement, from whatever merit it possesses; indeed, it should add thereto. For, whatever this book amounts to, it is realistic, it is representative, it shows what can be commanded into his service by any buyer of printing; and it attempts to demonstrate what a commercial press can do to enrich the craft by ransacking the treasure houses of the past and breathing into old bodies the living spirit of our own day.

Francis Meynell (1891–1975), *Typography*, Pelican Press, 1923.

Device for The Nonesuch Press by Stephen Gooden. Later redrawn version, 1932.

'T HAT I HAVE made enough of a success of printing' wrote Updike in 1930 'to be proper-ly asked to contribute something to this book [a recruiting book for the Boy Scouts of America], I neither affirm nor deny. But there is one encouraging thing to be learned from what I have done – that starting with no education, not much health, little money, and a generally poor and unpractical training for life, and being pushed by necessity into printing, a work that I hated, by studying that work and persistently keeping at it, I have succeeded in it better than some men, and, in spite of many handicaps, made myself over, through it...I became a printer by accident. If I have become a good printer – not more – it is through intention and determina-tion, and the intention has got hold of me to such an extent that printing has become to me – with one exception – the most interesting thing in the world.'

Updike later wrote a more accurate and amusing account of how he entered printing, start-ing as an office boy with Houghton, Mifflin & Company in Boston in 1880 and then moving to the Riverside Press in Cambridge under Mr Mifflin. In 1893 he set up on his own, first as plain Mr D. B. Updike and soon as the Merrymount Press. (The curious reasons for calling it 'Merrymount' are discussed by Carl Purington Rollins in his essay in Updike: American Printer.)

The first book issued by the Merrymount Press was an Altar Book, designed for Updike by Bertram Grosvenor Goodhue in the Kelmscott style, and set in Merrymount type. Goodhue, an architect, also designed the Cheltenham typeface.

If Updike ever developed his own style in typographic design it would be hard to define. His books were soon noted for their dignity, elegance and simplicity. A word used by Frederic Warde was 'allusive', meaning probably 'suggestive of the period of the text'. In his essay on Bruce Rogers he wrote 'Allusive typography in its more brilliant and subtle forms was, after all, a new thing then. One suspects Mr Updike, if not of having invented it, at least of having found it in the nursery and left it in the drawing-room. There can be no doubt of the influence of the Merrymount Press and its brilliant director upon Mr Rogers....'

Updike was one of these rare typographers who could not draw. He once boasted that he could not sharpen a pencil. But he was a perfectionist, for whom no trouble was too great to get things right. The motto on his bookplate was Optimum vix satis – 'the best is hardly enough'. He was also an excellent writer, with a sense of humour, as can be seen in his great book Printing Types, one of the most enjoyable works on typography ever written – and in the brief extracts from other works chosen for these pages. He never wrote an autobiography (it is incon-ceivable that he would even have tried) but a convincing picture of the man can be traced in the writings of those who knew him, and perhaps most attractively in the letters he wrote to Stanley Morison, happily published in 1980.

'The Seven Champions of Typography' is the third and last piece from In the Day's Work, a modest summing-up of Updike's printing philosophy, published when he was sixty-four. The two other pieces in that book are entitled 'On the planning of printing' and 'Style in the use of *type'. No one has written more sensibly on these subjects than D. B. Updike.*

A recommended reading list is: D. B. Updike, Printing Types: their history, forms and use, a study in survivals, 2 vols, Harvard University Press, 1922, 2nd edn, 1937, Republished by Dover Publications, New York, 1980; Updike: American Printer and his Merrymount Press, American Institute of Graphic Arts, New York, 1947; G. P. Winship, Daniel Berkeley Updike and the Merrymount Press, Rochester, New York, 1947; Daniel B. Bianchi, D. B. Updike & John Bianchi, Society of Printers, Boston, 1965; Daniel B. Bianchi, Some Recollections of the Merrymount Press, G. L. Harding & R. Levenson, California, 1976; David McKitterick, ed., Stanley Morison & D. B. Updike, Selected Correspondence, Scolar Press, London, 1980; and Daniel Berkeley Bianchi, The Merrymount Press. A centenary keepsake, Bridgewater, Connecticut, 1993.

THE SEVEN CHAMPIONS OF TYPOGRAPHY

There was once upon a time a curate, whose cast of thought ran to symbolism, and who became so fascinated by the mystical meanings of the number seven, that one day, being called upon unexpectedly to preach, he inflicted on his congregation all that he could for the moment remember of seven-fold numbers occurring in the Old and New Testaments – the days of creation, the gifts of the Spirit, the seven churches of Asia, etc.; but like many extempore speakers before and since, he suddenly became confused and ended his phrase precipitately with the surprising words, 'And we all remember, dear brethren, that there were seven apostles – plus five!'

When I entitled this paper The Seven Champions of Typography I had in mind (being a lay person) the seven champions of Christendom, the seven wonders of the world, the seven seas, stars, deadly sins, liberal arts, and some other 'sevens'. But on counting up my champions, I was disconcerted to discover that there were but six – thus (like the curate) finding myself suddenly at sixes and sevens in more senses than one. Yet why spoil a good title for a mere detail! That royal and unpleasant spinster called Good Queen Bess or the Virgin Queen – who appears according to the best modern authorities to have been neither – is said to have considered a lie to be merely an intellectual way of getting over a difficulty. Perhaps so: but, even then, remembering the precept of St Francis de Sales, 'Little things for little people,' we have our little scruples. So I propose to make my title good by adding to six Champions of Typography – Spacing, Leading, Indentation, Ink, Paper, and Imposition – one more – the most important of all, without which (as is alleged of charity) the rest profiteth nothing. That Seventh Champion, dear Reader, is You. And it all depends on how seriously you take the following pages, whether my title turns out to be truth or falsehood! I assume for it no further responsibility.

No matter how admirably we plan our work, nor how fine in design are the types we select, its appearance when printed depends on good composition, – the combination of type into words, the arrangement of words in lines, and the assemblage of lines to make pages. And composition falls into three divisions, spacing, leading, and proper indentation – all factors in the effect of a type-page. Furthermore, the successful presentation of our printing depends upon three things more – ink, colour of paper, and proper imposition on that paper. On these six points – for I shall not bore the reader and myself by continuing the 'champion' nomenclature – the successful effect of our plans for printing and the use of good typeforms must rely.

I. Spacing is a term used in connection with composition to describe the space between the words in a line of type, or the lateral distance of one word from another. It plays an extremely important part in composition. Everybody knows that there must be space between words, but the problem for the printer is its proper adjustment. This is effected by the discriminating use of spaces of different thickness, just as leading – the proper adjustment of space between lines – requires the intelligent use of leads.

The spaces between words in a line should be apparently uniform. If they were *exactly* uniform, they would not seem so to the eye; more space being required between two ascending lower-case letters such as 'l', which may end one word and begin another (as occurs in 'medical libraries'), than between a 'y' and an 'a' (as occurs in 'any author'). 'In good printing,' said William Morris, in his paper on 'Printing' in *Arts and Crafts Essays*, 'the spaces between the words should be as near possible equal (it is impossible that they should be quite equal except in lines of poetry); modern printers understand this, but it is only practised in the very best establishments. But another point which they should attend to they almost always disregard; this is the tendency to the formation of ugly meandering white lines or 'rivers' in the page, a blemish which can be nearly, though not wholly, avoided by care and forethought, the desirable thing being 'the breaking of the line' as in bonding masonry or brickwork, thus:

The general *solidity* of a page is much to be sought for: modern printers generally overdo the 'whites' in the spacing, a defect probably forced on them by the characterless quality of the letters. For where these are boldly and carefully designed, and each letter is thoroughly individual in form, the words may be set much closer together, without loss of clearness. No definite rules, however, except the avoidance of 'rivers'* and excess of white, can be given for the spacing, which requires the constant exercise of judgement and taste on the part of the printer.' On looking at the page of Mr Morris's essay about proper spacing, we find the enemy has sown tares in the field, for in derision of Mr Morris's own theories, a large white 'river' runs across the very phrase in which he deplores them! The book was issued under the auspices of the London Society of Arts and Crafts – an example of how much easier it is to tell people that work should be done 'so that our commonest things are beautiful,' than it is to put the precept into practice!

While I cannot agree with much that has been said about the folly of close spacing and pages of type set solid (i.e. without leading), as if it were merely an affected return to archaic methods and a perverse desire to make books unreadable, some modern printers, in their efforts to obtain 'colour' in a page, have undoubtedly forgotten that the spacing of a line must be sufficient to make a distinct separation between words and one sufficient to be readily apparent to the eye. A good test of spacing is to hold a printed page upside down, when, the sense of the words not being caught, the eye more readily perceives whether the spacing of the page is even or not.

An old and rather ignorant prejudice against the breaking of words makes against good spacing. It is better not to break words if one can help it, but often they must be broken, if good spacing is to be maintained. Many printers who may be willing to break single words consider that two consecutive lines should not end with hyphens; but hyphens at the end of two, three, or even four successive lines, while undesirable, are not so ugly as matter unevenly spaced to avoid them.* The problem is to space evenly in spite of these difficulties. Then again bad spacing may often be as a result of corrections. Sometimes replacing one letter by another makes no change in the proper spacing of a line; but when words are replaced by longer or shorter ones, or when whole phrases are inserted, serious difficulties occur. Useless and expensive changes are often ordered by an author because he does not know the tedious process by which they are effected, or realize that the substitution of one word for another may necessitate carrying over words or parts of words for several lines. Yet if, to avoid expense, this is not done, the result is uneven, and therefore bad, spacing.

The principles of good spacing which have been stated are of equal application to machine-set type. If by the use of type-setting machines printers cannot follow this 'counsel of perfection,' it would appear to show that, as yet, the best hand composition is better.

* 'Dog's-teeth,' or as Moxon called them, 'pigeon-holes.'

* Entire books have been printed without a single broken word. An example of this is Marcellin Brun's Manuel pratique et abrégé de la Typographie française – the first edition printed by Didot père et fils at Paris in 1825, and the second by Vroom of Brussels in 1826. The latter is a 12mo volume of two hundred and forty pages, and is set in 8-point type, with notes in a still smaller size.

II. The excessive indentation of paragraphs, and em width spaces between sentences, are usually unneccessary. In an early printed book the paragraphs were indented to allow a paragraph mark to be put in by hand. Often the paragraph marks were never filled in, and this led to the discovery that the eye could pick out beginnings of paragraphs by blanks almost as well as by paragraph marks. While a paragraph mark preserved more or less the desirable regularity of outline of the page, whereas a blank space broke it, for clearness it was necessary that it should be broken; but not to such an extent as it often is by modern indentation.

Again, the conventional use of an em quad at the beginning of a new sentence is unnecessary and makes 'holes' in the composition of pages. In most cases, the same spacing used between other words in the line, together with the period at the end of one sentence and the capital letter at the beginning of the next, make a sufficient break.

III. Leading is to lines what spacing is to words; and the introduction of leads between lines of type has a great deal to do with the effect of a page. Type set solid is usually hard to read, and slight leading improves its legibility. When to lead and how much to lead is a matter of taste and judgement. For with the same type the colour of a page can be increased or decreased by its leading. Nor does every type demand the same amount of leading. Blackletter, although in early times occasionally leaded for purposes of manuscript interlineation, should normally never be leaded, and should be closely spaced: for leading of blackletter makes a 'striped' page; open spacing, a page full of holes. On the other hand, light faces of roman type almost always look better leaded, and sometimes require slightly open spacing. So it will be seen that the effect of printed pages often depends on leading and spacing as well as on the face of type employed. The leading of the same kind of type in a given book should be uniform throughout. There is no more wretched product in typography than a book in which, for reasons of economy or convenience, pages which should have the same leading or the same size of type throughout are set with less leading or in a smaller type to 'get the matter in'.

An unbroken type-page when held at a little distance should make a perfectly defined block of even tint. This impression on paper of a definite parallelogram which is practically uniform in tone is a chief factor in the beauty of a printed book. Early books were remarkable for the even colour of their pages, and that is one reason that they give the eye a sense of satisfaction. This was arrived at by the use of types which were masculine in design and fairly uniform in weight of line, set solid, and close spaced. 'Experience proves,' says Day, 'that the eye is best satisfied by a tolerably uniform distribution of the letters, Roman, Gothic, or whatever their character, over it [the page], so that they give at first sight the impression of a fairly even surface, distinguished from the surrounding surface (that is, the margin) more by a difference of tint than by any appreciable letter-forms within the mass.'*

* Day's Lettering in Ornament, London, 1902, p. 20.

What about machine composition and typefaces for machine-work, some one may ask? To answer this very proper question I must make a digression. The introduction of a linotype or monotype into a printing-office is open to no objection, provided the machine is operated with the same care that is taken with the best hand-setting, in which case the cost is often, I fear, much the same as if set by hand; for the proper justification of the lines of type reduces the rapidity of their product. Usually machines have not been carefully worked, and to judge them by their ordinary product is not fair. Then again machines can be desirably employed only in printing-houses which have enough work of the kind that can be *well done* upon such machines. They cannot always readily or quickly perform certain sorts of composition, in spite of the ingenious exhibits of this sort of type-setting which are shown as specimens of their work.

The collection of matrices from which types are cast, on both linotype and monotype machines, has been, until lately, unworthy of their pretensions, and it is difficult to see on what principle such a variety of mean types, differing so slightly from one another, were for many years 'the only wear'. Nowadays they are enormously improved, and the best of them have been used for book-work with marked success.

On the other hand, it is absurd to be prejudiced by a machine or machine-work because it is mechanical; the results obtained are what really count. Some ultra-conservative men are (or have been) foolish enough to shy at new inventions in machinery – for type-setting, for instance. They feel that somehow a 'modern spirit' is in the machinery, and that in some sly and malign way it will defeat artistic excellence! This is quite childish. The problem is to determine how work can be done best. If for some typography the old method (incidentally endeared to the lover of early printing by historical associations) produces a better result than a modern machine, then the old method may be adhered to. If a modern machine does other classes of printing better and quicker than the old method and more conveniently for the workmen, it is to be adopted. The tendency about us, it is true, is to glorify speed, wthout paying attention to the details of the result. 'This machine,' says the seller, 'can turn out so many ems per hour'; but one must regard only *how many ems properly set up* such a machine can turn out, and not be beguiled by speed, which is an attribute of excellence in automobiles, but not the sole question in type-setting! To judge between the sentimentalist who believes that all virtue resides in the hand, and the commercialist who thinks that salvation is obtained by a machine, is not easy. I prefer good machine work to bad hand work and vice versa. If one is as good as the other, – incidentally I have my doubts, – I take the quickest and cheapest. But I quote without comment the statement of a distinguished colleague – whose name is withheld for what we are nowadays pleased to call prudential reasons – 'The machine is like a jungle animal, more or less obedient under the whip, but always a wild animal'.

IV. To show good type-setting (whether set by machine or by hand) to advantage, the inking of a page must be even. Composition, no matter how careful, is dependent on good ink and the right amount of it. The letters in a printed page, if not well inked, show, when examined through a magnifying glass, little specks of white through the black, and the effect of type, as a whole, is lifeless and faded. The result of using too much ink is so obvious that it is needless to say anything about it.

Furthermore, ink must be black. A great deal of the so-called black ink used in modern books has a brown, green, pink, or blue tinge. If a good black ink is compared with inks commonly employed, it will be found that there is little that is really black. It is cheaper to make ink of materials that give it disagreeable tinges than to use the proper ingredients. But no page will be effective or lively except when printed in pure black ink.

V. Though ink must be black, paper should not always be white. The somewhat irregular Caslon type (and some 'period' and transitional types) appears much more agreeably when printed on a slightly rough paper of a cream tint. Caslon's types in his day were printed on wet paper, which thickened their lines and roughened the paper, so that we get more nearly the effect that he meant them to have when we print them on toned, rough paper. If smooth white paper is used for old style types, it exposes their slight crudities of form in a disagreeable way, and accents too much the shape of individual letters. This is understood by some typefounders, who for that reason often display their old style types on toned paper. Many people prefer a smooth and pure white paper (or think they do) because they look at the paper alone, and do not realize that its colour makes any difference in the effect of printing. Some of the lighter modern-faced types look well on a paper that is nearly white; for they are more clean cut, more regular in shape, and have not the irregularities which such a paper reveals. For these types the paper should *look* white. There are, fortunately, few absolutely white printing papers.

VI. And finally, there is imposition. A page of type, however well set, well spaced, well inked, and printed on suitable paper, may be a complete failure unless well 'imposed'. 'It is no less effective than it is logical,' says Morris, 'to consider two pages of the open book as one area on which to plant, as it were, two columns of print. A very considerable reduction of the inner margins, as compared with the outer and the upper and lower, has this effect; and it is perhaps the most satisfactory way of imposing the page – if only the binder were to be depended upon. Unless the folding of the sheets is perfect, the two patches of print do not range, and the closer they come together the more obtrusive is the fault; it is not so easily detected when there is a broad space of white between.' A well-imposed page, which is to show off the type properly, must have margins widest at the bottom, narrower at the outside, narrower still at the top, and narrowest of all on the inside. If type-pages are imposed in the centre of a paper page, the margins appear less at the bottom than at the top, and the combined inside margins of pages thus imposed, in an open book seem so wide that the print appears to be falling out of it! I believe that there are various *formulae* that are intended to effect perfect imposition; but they are not infallible in their results.

To sum up, therefore, pages of type – however fine in design – must be carefully spaced, tastefully leaded, moderately indented, thoroughly inked, printed on paper suited to their design, and properly imposed. Neglect one of these requirements, and the result is failure. But – and it is the eternal 'but' of the half-hearted printer – why should one adopt a style of printing which involves much more labour and little more return? The answer is that these simple but laborious requirements have always been met in the best printing; and that all this is merely typographical truth. It would be easier, no doubt, to believe that there is something wrong about the idea. But there isn't.

Nor is there anything that is new in all this; for in principle it would be admitted by most printers. Yet what men often mean when they talk of principles is a mere theory of conduct upon which they have never acted. The theory becomes a principle only when practised. And thus it depends on *You* whether you will be the Seventh Champion of good typography or not....

D. B. Updike (1860–1941), *In the Day's Work*, Harvard University Press, 1924.

B ORN IN LEIPZIG IN 1902, *the son of a traditional sign painter and lettering artist, Jan Tschichold was trained in lettering and calligraphy from the beginning: he became interested in book design as soon as he could read. He was born with strong artistic gifts and it is significant that at first he wanted to become an artist; but his parents persuaded him to choose a safer career and become a teacher of drawing. The training that this required led him into calligraphy and type design, and in his spare time he devoured Edward Johnston's Writing & Illuminating, & Lettering, which had been translated into German by Anna Simons. In 1921, aged nineteen, he was appointed by the director of Leipzig Academy (Walter Tiemann, type designer) to be assistant in charge of evening classes in lettering. His career was now started: but the spark that really fired him was a visit to the first Bauhaus exhibition in Weimar in August 1923. There for the first time he saw modern art and design by Moholy-Nagy, El Lissitzky and others of that inspiring group. However, their typography was in itself an art form rather than a means of communication: Herbert Bayer, its leading practitioner, to the end of his life thought capital letters were not necessary. Tschichold was never a member of the Bauhaus, but he was the first to rationalise and formulate their new ideas into a system which made sense in everyday printing.*

His first book was Die neue Typographie, 1928, from which the first passage below is quoted; the second passage is from his sixth book, Typographische Gestaltung, 1935. Both books are well worth reading to-day. He later modified some of his more dogmatic assertions, for example that sanserif type was the only face suitable for modern use; but his basic philosophy remains valid.

Tschichold was an artist in everything he did; as a calligrapher, lettering artist, symbol and type designer, typographer, even as a repairer of early manuscripts. All his life he did nothing but practise, teach and write about typographic design; perhaps his only hobby was the study of Chinese calligraphy. He was happily married, with a quiet sense of humour; but on typography he was single-mindedly serious: it was for him the core of his life.

No biography of Tschichold has yet appeared. For accounts of his life and work see Jan Tschichold Typographer by Ruari McLean, Lund Humphries/David Godine, 1975, and Leben und Werk des Typographen Jan Tschichold, Verlag der Kunst, Dresden, 1977. See also The new typography (Die neue Typographie), transl. R. McLean, University of California Press, 1995, and The Form of the Book, essays on the morality of good design by Jan Tschichold, edited with an introduction by Robert Bringhurst, transl. by Hajo Hadeler, Hartley & Marks/Lund Humphries, 1992.

THE PRINCIPLES OF THE NEW TYPOGRAPHY

Modern man has to absorb every day a mass of printed matter which, whether he has asked for it or not, is delivered through his letterbox or confronts him everywhere out of doors. At first, today's printing differed from that of previous times less in form than in quantity. But as the quantity increased, the form also began to change: the speed with which the modern consumer of printing has to absorb it means that the form of printing also must adapt itself to the conditions of modern life. As a rule we no longer read quietly line by line, but glance quickly over the whole, and only if our interest is awakened do we study it in detail.

The old typography both in feeling and form was adapted to the needs of its readers, who had plenty of time to read line by line in a leisurely manner. For them, function could not yet play any significant role. For this reason the old typography concerned itself less with function than with what was called 'beauty' or 'art'. Problems of formal aesthetics (choice of type, mixture of typefaces and ornament) dominated considerations of form. It is for this reason that the history of typography since Manutius is not so much a development towards clarity of appearance (the only exception being the period of Didot, Bodoni, Baskerville and Walbaum) as an embodiment of the development of historical typefaces and ornaments.

It was left to our age to find a natural attitude to the problem of 'form' or design. While up to now form was considered as something external, a product of the 'artistic imagination', today we have moved considerably closer to the recognition of its essence through the renewed study of nature and more especially of technology (which is only a special kind of nature). Both nature and technology teach us that 'form' is not independent, but grows out of function (purpose), out of the materials used (organic or technical) and out of how they are used. This was how the marvellous forms of nature and the equally marvellous forms of technology originated. We can describe the forms of technology as just as 'organic' (in an intellectual sense) as those of nature. But as a rule most people see only the superficial forms of technology, they admire their 'beauty' – of aeroplanes, cars or ships – instead of recognising that their perfection of appearance is due to the precise and economic expression of their function. In the process of giving form, both technology and nature use the same laws of economy, precision, minimum friction and so on. Technology by its very nature can never be an end in itself, only a means to an end, and can therefore be a part of man's spiritual life only indirectly, while the remaining fields of human creativity rise above the purely functional or technical forms. But they too, following the laws of nature, are drawn towards greater clarity and purity of appearance. Thus architecture discards the ornamental façade and decorated furniture and develops its forms from the function of the building – no longer from the outside inwards, as determined by the façade-orientation of previous days, but from the inside outwards, the natural way. So too typography is liberated from its present superficial and formalistic shapes, and its so-called 'traditional' designs which are long since fossilised. To us, the succession of historic styles, reactions against the Jugendstil or 'Art Nouveau', are nothing but proof of creative incompetence. It cannot and must not be our aim today to follow the extreme inflexibility of the typography of previous centuries, itself conditioned by its own time. Our age, with its very different aims, its often different ways and means and highly developed techniques, must dictate new and different external forms. Though its significance remains undeniable, to think today that the Gutenberg Bible represents an achievement that can never again be reached is both naive and romantic rubbish. If we want to 'prove ourselves worthy' of the clearly significant achievements of the past, we must set our own achievements beside them born out of our own time. They can only become 'classic' if they are unhistoric.

The essence of the New Typography is Clarity. This puts it into deliberate opposition to the old typography whose aim was 'beauty' and whose clarity did not attain the high level we require today. This utmost clarity is necessary today because of the manifold claims for our attention made by the extraordinary amount of print, which demands the greatest economy of expression.

Jan Tschichold (1902–1974), *The new typography*,
University of California Press, 1995. Translated by
Ruari McLean from *Die neue Typographie*, Berlin, 1928.

THE WORD

The correctly set word is the starting-point of all typography. The letters themselves we have to accept – they are shaped by the type cutter or the type designer. The relationship of the letters is the job of the dresser in the foundry. He has to achieve the right regularity and rhythm and his work is as important as the engraver's. Many good types have recently been spoiled by tight dressing. This forces the compositor to make good the larger sizes with letter spaces. Apart from this, letter-spacing is always harmful. The letter-spacing of capitals, although technically the same, is not considered as letter-spacing in this sense. A normally set word is always the most legible; letter-spacing only reduces its legibility. The unspaced, evenly flowing word is also the most beautiful. It is a compact shape, an essential requirement in the new typography. It is also more economical – letter-spacing takes time, is expensive and weakens the word-shape. For all of these reasons it is unacceptable in the new typography. It should not be used to artificially alter the length of a word just to fill a specific space, nor for emphasis in ordinary text setting.

Jan Tschichold (1902–1974), *Asymmetric Typography*,
New York, 1967, translated by Ruari McLean from
Typographische Gestaltung, Basle, 1935.

THE FOLLOWING PIECE *is a perceptive statement on decoration in typography, taken from a book (a very handsome one, designed by Warde) whose purpose was to advertise products of the Lanston Monotype Corporation.*

It is a spectacular demonstration of the possibilities of 'Monotype' printers' ornaments used for book pages and other commercial purposes. It is a remarkable tour-de-force, and probably Warde's masterpiece in terms of book design.

Warde was born in the United States and travelled, designed, and discussed design, in England, France, Germany, and Holland, as well as in the States. Many of the books he designed were small and intrinsically unimportant, but extremely pretty. For the Limited Editions Club of New York, however, he designed Walt Whitman's Leaves of Grass, the club's second title. About this book George Macy (the LEC's Director) later wrote: 'I made two serious mistakes in the planning of this book. The first was that I prepared an inadequate text.... The second was that I asked Fred Warde to design the book; and now I know that Fred was not the man to translate Walt into type: the binding and the pages of type are very pretty, and that is the trouble, the barbaric yawp of Walt Whitman is hushed by the meticulous, delicate, charming and inappropriate typography of Fred Warde.' Warde later designed five other books for the Limited Editions Club, including Alice in Wonderland ('Warde made an exquisite book of it' said Macy).

Warde also designed the Arrighi italic to accompany Bruce Rogers's Centaur, which had no italic. A good account of this beautiful face is given in 'Some notes on Frederic Warde and the story of his Arrighi type' by Herbert Johnson in Fine Print, 12, 3, 1986.

PRINTERS ORNAMENTS

A good typographer is one who can arrange type so as to produce a graceful and orderly page that puts no strain on the eye. This is the first and last fundamental requisite of book design, and like most simple operations it is a matter of years of training. But beyond this essential problem of type arrangement is another field for the printer-designer which is less austere and richer in opportunities for invention, namely the decoration or embellishment of the type message. Here is the little added touch that goes beyond the bare essentials of taste into the realms of fantasy. For this reason the ornamentation of printing is at once the most charming and the most dangerous diversion that the typographer can find; charming because of its power to add beauty to the strict simplicity of type; dangerous because all matters of decoration call upon the utmost discretion and sense of fitness for their effective use. There are also many ways of beautifying a page. Before and during the early days of printing illuminators carried over their arts into the printed page, and since then woodcuts, intaglio engraving and lithography have all been used.

But it is a question whether any method can be so happily combined with type as can 'printer's flowers' which have been in use since the sixteenth century. These small decorative units – the smaller and simpler the better for use in combination – have the immense typographic advantage of having been recently re-cut in steel and cast just as type is cut and cast, and therefore can be printed with the text at the same operation. For this reason, however quaint or delicate their outline may be they are of the very family of printing types rather than having the nature of an alien process; they can be demurely and inoffensively pleasing only because of this family tie. In fact the line between letters and ornaments is so arbitrary that it is quite possible to use such types as section-marks or even graceful italic letters, in combinations forming patterns, for decorating a page, whilst certain initial letters, especially of the fanciful sorts, are ornaments in themselves.

The art of the designer is expressed in the creation of patterns, that is, of units or groups of units arranged so as to give the eye a sense of deliberate rhythm, either static, as in the case of a simple repeated pattern, or dynamic, as with a form implying natural growth. In the first case alone the possibilities of combination of one or two simple motifs are practically endless: and in the case of dynamic patterns Nature herself has never found a limit to ingenuity. The fascination of experimenting with combining, reversing, spacing-out and alternating the simplest unit is indescribable.

This book is presented to designers of printing as the merest suggestion of what these possibilities can offer, rather than as any manual of principles of ornamentation. There are no principles; there are only the units themselves, small and willing, amazingly able to take on new appearances upside-down or back-to-back yet always retaining that subtle relation to the printed surface that makes them so valuable.

Frederic Warde (1894–1939), *Printers Ornaments on the 'Monotype'*, London, Lanston Monotype Corporation, 1928.

IT HAS BEEN SAID (by the American calligrapher Paul Standard) that there are two books which belong in every working printer's library: Updike's Printing Types, and Johnston's Writing & Illuminating, & Lettering. Johnston's book, first published in 1906, and still in print, was also called (by Sydney Cockerell) 'the best handbook on any subject'. It is clearly and wisely worded, and beautifully illustrated: the drawings by Noel Rooke of the calligrapher's hands are especially remarkable.

Johnston's essay about Cobden-Sanderson has been chosen here because it tells us as much about Johnston as about his subject. After his death, his life was written by his daughter Priscilla Johnston. His skill at making and repairing things is a recurrent theme, as in 'Edward stayed with the Peplers whenever he spent a night in Town. After one such visit, when he had been teaching the boys to make darts, David remarked to his father "if there hadn't been flying machines Mr Johnston would have made one". Gerard Meynell seems to have agreed for he wrote Edward a postcard saying "Dear Sir, I am sending two sardine tins. Please make me a motor bicycle and a telescope".'

In Modern Book Design, 1958, I wrote: 'Edward Johnston was a great man, declared to have been a saint by those who knew him, a claim not contradicted by study of his face in the few photographs of him that survive. When a pupil said to him that he did not believe in perfection, Edward Johnston replied "I believe in the Book of Kells".'

See Edward Johnston and English Lettering by Anna Simons, Heintze & Blanckertz, Berlin/Leipzig n.d., c. 1937; Tributes to Edward Johnston, calligrapher, The Society of Scribes and Illuminators, Maidstone, 1948; and Edward Johnston by Priscilla Johnston, Faber & Faber, London, 1959.

ON A MASTER CRAFTSMAN BY A SCRIBE WHO WORKED FOR HIM

We first met when Mr T. J. Cobden-Sanderson was acting as secretary to the Arts and Crafts Exhibition Society at the New Gallery in 1899. I had come to the secretary's table to ask some question – probably a tiresome one, such as exhibitors bother secretaries with – and he, softening his refusal, told me the story of a previous secretary who had been asked by an old lady whether he had fed the goldfish (the secretary, a tall and very shy poet, had drawn himself up to his full height, and had answered: 'Madam, the man who feeds the goldfish is another man').

On December 11, 1898, the entry in Cobden-Sanderson's journal (just published – October, 1926) reads: 'I must, before I die, create the type for today of The Book Beautiful, and actualise it – paper, ink, printing, writing, ornament, and binding. I will learn to write, to print, and to decorate.'

And on February 3, 1900, the entry is: 'Last Thursday night, February 1st, I joined the Calligraphic Class at the Central School of Arts and Crafts'.

This was the class in 'Writing, Illuminating and Lettering' – probably the first of its kind – which, in some fear and trembling, I had undertaken to conduct in the previous autumn. It was held at the old London County Council Central School in Regent Street. Mr Cobden-Sanderson attended it only a few times – there was but little which he could get out of it – but he was much interested in the characterisation of letter forms by means of the pen. His son and daughter also attended, and I remember one evening when he sat beside me watching me write, with his son beside him. He said in a characteristically whimsical way: 'It is like watching some strange bird' (to the embarrassment of his son, who said in a loud whisper, 'Don't, Daddy, don't!'). In the spring of that year he gave me the commission of writing out his *Tract on the Ideal Book or Book Beautiful*. This tract was printed by The Doves Press that autumn and published in February, 1901. It was the second book published (the Tacitus was published in January) and it constitutes a key to the work of the Press. I suppose that no one has ever written with such insight, or so eloquently, of *The Book Beautiful*, and this brief comprehensive vision might well be taken to heart by all honest printers.

When we moved to No.3 Hammersmith Terrace – only two doors from the Press – he frequently brought me small commissions to draw initial letters, headings and the like, which were afterwards engraved on wood.

Of the technical and typographic work of The Doves Press I shall not presume to speak: but we can all appreciate its works, as readers – if we are so fortunate as to possess, or be able to borrow, any of them, and we shall find them an admirable exponent of a master mind. I believe that these books were at once the plainest and the most idealistic ever produced by any of the 'Private Presses'; they recall the words, 'Whose adorning, let it not be that outward adorning. . .but let it be. . .the ornament of a meek and quiet spirit': they depend not upon ornament, nor even upon conventional 'decorative treatment', but upon their utter legibility and high quality. They fulfil the principle laid down by him: 'The whole duty of Typography is to communicate to the imagination, without loss by the way, the thought or image intended to be conveyed by the Author'. And here, in view of the reckless 'book decoration' now so common, I am constrained to quote from his journal for 1899: 'Pattern must be articulate. Its parts seen, that is to say, in some way to belong to another. Then pattern must be like the imprint of tender fingertips, touching or caressing what it loves. All other pattern is soulless and dead, and the book had better be plain and untouched – lettered only.'

To those who knew him well, he himself showed the qualities of legibility – simplicity, distinctiveness, and proportion. He had mastery and reverence combined

with a quaint whimsicality, and he had an almost childlike way in his statement –
whether in a public lecture or his writings – of the overpowering emotions inspired
in him by the beauty of the earth, by the mystery of the cosmos and of being, and
by visions of untold human possibility. (He would have exclaimed with the Hebrew
Prince, 'I have said, ye are gods; and all of you are children of the Most High'.) This
statement, of thoughts which most men do not think about in their working hours,
or do not think it good form to mention in public, even led to his being misunder-
stood by many who did not know him, or knew him but little. Even one or two
friends of mine were among these – in the attitude of the world to a prophet. Even
some of the people 'of his own country' (of arts and crafts) admired his work but
failed to understand him. His mind approached things by the ideal, theirs by the
practical. Yet few craftsmen would vie with the perfect technique of his work, and
everything he touched he beautified.

All his visible material environment in all its smallest details, his work, his
house, and his use and wont in both work and home, were made to harmonise to
the best of his power – and he had a prophet's eye and a craftsman's skill – with
the divine beauty of the universe.

And like the universe itself, he had many sides – a keen sense of humour keeping wrath and impatience in check – and this gentlest and most fastidious of
craftsmen confessed to me once, when we were comparing notes on the difficulty
of the too-obedient student (who depended too much on his teacher and wondered
all the time if he were doing what he ought) that he wished that he could put up a
notice over the door of his workroom, saying, 'For God's sake do something
damned careless!'

In connection with my work I was brought into frequent contact with him, and
saw much of him in the course of his ordinary life and affairs. And he knew me
well enough to 'pitch into' me if what I had done was not up to time or standard. I
subscribed all my notes written to him, 'Your Faithful Scribe'. But when I had been
'pitched into', or was conscious of deserving it, marked my repentance by the sub-
scription, 'Your sometimes Faithful Scribe'. He probably always regarded me as
'some strange bird', with a kind of affectionate and amused appreciation: a feeling
which I paid him back, under reverence.

He was a seeker all his life to the end. This is the dominant note of his journals.
It might be said of him that 'He searched the scriptures – of the cosmos – for in
them he thought we have eternal life and that they testify of God'. He found much,
as we know from by his works, and I believe that 'in some distant star' he is still
finding.

I close this brief tribute to a Prophet and a Master Craftsman, with an extract from an exordium characteristically printed by him in a catalogue of the books of The Doves Press: 'Greater than all that we can imagine, is the Reality of Life from its Beginning – IN THE BEGINNING GOD CREATED THE HEAVENS AND THE EARTH – in the infinitudes of Time and Space, amid which, whether as a fact or as an idea, we still live today; greater than all we can imagine is Reality, and Man's life as part of it, and it is this which, in the language of the compositor, we must "compose", and in the language of the publisher, "publish".'

Quondam Scriba Fidelis,
EDWARD JOHNSTON

Edward Johnston (1872–1944), from John Henry Nash, ed., *Cobden-Sanderson and the Doves Press*, San Francisco, 1929.

Fig. 41 in Edward Johnston's *Writing & Illuminating, & Lettering*, drawn by Noel Rooke.

Morison's famous essay, *from which the following passages are taken, first appeared in the seventh and last volume of The Fleuron, 1930, and then in book form from Cambridge University Press in 1936. Right from the beginning it was noticed (by Brooke Crutchley) that the title should more correctly have been 'First Principles of Book Typography': but it was so important and useful a statement at the time that many people in the world of printing learned it almost by heart; and it has retained nearly biblical authority ever since. It can however now be seen to have several important limitations.*

Morison was an extraordinary character. He started from humble beginnings: his first job, on leaving school aged 14, was as an office boy at six shillings a week. In September 1912 he happened to see The Printing Supplement just put out by The Times, and was projected, in the words of his biographer Nicolas Barker, 'suddenly, if not violently, into a new and quite unfamiliar path, whose course he was to change more radically than anyone for over a hundred years'. Via a new periodical called The Imprint, the Pelican Press and then the Cloister Press, and the Monotype Corporation, he became a man of ever-growing dominance in British printing. In 1925 he was appointed typographic advisor to the Cambridge University Press and in 1929 he joined the staff of The Times. Within three years, The Times was being printed in the new type he introduced for it, which as 'Times New Roman' soon became world-famous. Three years after that, the first volume of Morison's History of the Times was published, completed by 1952 in five volumes.

Morison was a strong character, dogmatic, witty, widely read and with interests that extended to railway engines, postage stamps, champagne and liturgy. One of his virtues was that he was not afraid of rushing into print; his prolific writings are catalogued in a 140-page bibliography compiled and published by Tony Appleton in 1976. One of his failings was a reluctance to admit the significance of 'modern typography' or indeed the modern movement in art. But he was a great man. Laurence Irving, a director of The Times and a long-time friend, wrote of him after his death: 'He wore no social mask; he was immune to flattery; he was incapable of pretence and he reacted intuitively and sardonically to humbug; his deep compassion for the pretensions and follies of his fellow men invited an intimacy that transcended the formalities of friendship'. (Times News, Nov.-Dec.1967).

See Nicolas Barker, Stanley Morison, Macmillan, London, 1972. Also The Monotype Recorder, vol. 43, no. 3, Autumn 1968; James Moran, Stanley Morison His typographical achievement, Lund Humphries, London, 1971; Herbert Jones, Stanley Morison displayed. An examination of his early typographic work, Frederic Muller, London, 1976; and Appleton's Bibliography already cited.

FIRST PRINCIPLES OF TYPOGRAPHY

I

Typography may be defined as the craft of rightly disposing printing material in accordance with specific purpose; of so arranging letters, distributing the space and controlling the type as to aid to the maximum the reader's comprehension of the text. Typography is the efficient means to an essentially utilitarian and only accidentally aesthetic end, for enjoyment of patterns is rarely the reader's chief aim. Therefore, any disposition of printing material which, whatever the intention, has the effect of coming between author and reader is wrong. It follows that in the printing of books meant to be read there is little room for 'bright' typography. Even dullness and monotony in the typesetting are far less vicious to a reader than typographical eccentricity or pleasantry. Cunning of this sort is desirable, even essential, in the typography of propaganda, whether for commerce, politics, or religon, because in such printing only the freshest survives inattention. But the typography of books, apart from the category of narrowly limited editions, requires an obedience to convention which is almost absolute – and with reason.

Since printing is essentially a means of multiplying, it must not only be good in itself – but be good for a common purpose. The wider that purpose, the stricter are the limitations imposed upon the printer. He may try an experiment in a tract printed in an edition of 50 copies, but he shows little common sense if he experiments to the same degree in the tract having a run of 50,000. Again, a novelty, fitly introduced into a 16-page pamphlet, will be highly undesirable in a 160-page book. It is of the essence of typography and of the nature of the printed book qua book, that it perform a public service. For single or individual purpose there remains the manuscript, the codex; so there is something ridiculous in the unique copy of a printed book, though the number of copies printed may justifiably be limited when a book is the medium of typographical experiment. It is always desirable that experiments be made, and it is a pity that such 'laboratory' pieces are so limited in number and in courage. Typography today does not so much need Inspiration or Revival as Investigation. It is proposed here to formulate some of the principles already known to book-printers, which investigation confirms and which non-printers may like to consider for themselves.

II

The laws governing the typography of books intended for general circulation are based first upon the essential nature of alphabetical writing, and secondly upon the traditions, explicit or implicit, prevailing in the society for which the printer is working. While a universal character or typography applicable to all books produced in a given national area is practicable, to impose a universal detailed formula upon all books printed in roman types is not. National tradition expresses itself in the varying separation of the book into prelims, chapters, etc., no less than in the design of the type. But at least there are physical rules of linear composition which are obeyed by all printers who know their job. Let us see what these rules mean.

The normal roman type (in simple form without special sorts, etc.) consists of

A B C D E F G H I J K L M N O P Q R S T U V W X Y Z &

A B C D E F G H I J K L M N O P Q R S T U V W X Y Z

a b c d e f g h i j k l m n o p q r s t u v w x y z

A B C D E F G H I J K L M N O P Q R S T U V W X Y Z &

a b c d e f g h i j k l m n o p q r s t u v w x y z

The printer needs to be very careful in choosing his type, realising that the more often he is going to use it, the more closely its design must approximate to the general idea held in the mind of the reader who is accustomed to the normal magazine, newspaper and book. It does no harm to print a Christmas card in **black letter**, but who nowadays would set a book in that type? I may believe, as I do, that black letter is in design more homogeneous, more picturesque, more lively a type than the grey round roman we use, but I do not now expect people to a read a book in it. Aldus' and Caslon's are both relatively feeble types, but they represent the forms accepted by the community; and the printer, as a servant of the community, must use them, or one of their variants. No printer should say, 'I am an artist, therefore I am not to be dictated to. I will create my own letter forms', for, in this humble job, such individualism is not helpful to an audience of any size. It is no longer possible, as it was in the infancy of the craft, to persuade society into the acceptance of strongly marked and highly individualistic types – because literate society is so much greater in mass and correspondingly slower in movement. Type design moves at the pace of the most conservative reader. The good type-designer therefore realises that, for a new fount to be successful, it has to be so good that only very few recognise its novelty. If readers do not notice the consummate reticence and rare discipline of a new type it is probably a good letter. But if my friends think that the tail of my lower-case r or the lip of my lower-case e is rather jolly, you may know that the fount would have been better had neither been made. A type which is to have anything like a present, let alone a future, will neither be very 'different' nor very 'jolly'.

So much for Type. The printer possesses also Spaces and Leads as a normal part of his typographical material, straight lines of metal known as rules, braces, and finally a more or less indiscriminate collection of ornaments – head and tailpieces, flowers, decorated initial letters, vignettes and flourishes. Another decorative medium at his option lies in his command of colour; red is, with sound instinct, the most frequently used. For emphasis, heavy faces are used. White space is an important item of composing-room equipment – margins, blanks, etc., being filled in with what are known as 'quotations'. The selecting and arranging of these elements is known as Composition. Imposition is the placing of the composed matter upon the sheet. Printing includes impressing in due order, perfecting the sheet in due register (backing up), regulating the inking, and achieving a crisp type-page. Finally the tone, weight and texture of the paper are important factors entering into the completed result.

Typography, therefore, controls the composition, imposition, impression and paper. Of paper, it is at least necessary to demand that it be capable of expressing the value of the composition; of imposition, that the margins be proportionate to the area of the text, affording decent space for thumbs and fingers at the side and bottom of the page. The old-style margins are handsome in themselves and agreeable to the purpose of a certain kind of book, but are obviously not convenient in books where the page dimension is unavoidably small or narrow, or the purpose of the book is to be carried in the pocket. For these and other kinds of book, the type may be centred on the measure of the page, and slightly raised above ocular centre.

Imposition is the most important element in typography – for no page, however well composed in detail, can be admired if the *mise-en-page* is careless or ill considered. In practical printing to-day, these details of imposition are on the whole adequately cared for; so that it is possible to report that the mass of books presents a tolerable appearance. Even a badly composed work may give a good appearance if it is well imposed – good imposition redeeming bad composition, while a good composition would be effectively ruined by bad imposition....

V

Here we may pause to counter an objection. It will be contended that whatever the value of our preceding conclusions, their adoption must mean an increase in standardisation – all very well for those who have an economic objective, but very monotonous and dull for those whose aim is that books shall possess more 'life'. This means that the objectors want more variety, more 'differentness', more decoration. The craving to decorate is natural,and only if it is allowed the freedom of the text-pages shall we look upon it as a passion to be resisted. The decoration of title-pages is one thing – that of a fount to be employed in books is another. Our contention, in this respect, is that the necessities of a mass-production book and the limited edition differ neither in kind nor in degree, since all printing is essentially a means of the multiplication of a text set in an alphabetical code of conventional symbols. To disallow 'variety' in the vital details of the composition is not to insist upon uniformity in display. As already pointed out the preliminary pages offer scope for the utmost typographical ingenuity. Yet even here, a word of caution may be in place, so soon do we forget, in arranging any piece of display (above all, a title-page), the supreme importance of sense. Every character, every word, every line should be seen with maximum clearness. Words should not be broken except unavoidably, and in title-pages and other compositions of centred matter, lines should hardly begin with such feeble parts of speech as prepositions and conjunctions. It is more reasonable, as assisting the reader's immediacy of comprehension, to keep these to the ends of lines or to centre them in smaller type and so bring out the salient lines in a relatively conspicuous size.

No printer, in safeguarding himself from the charge of monotony in his composition, should admit, against his better judgement, any typographical distraction doing violence to logic and lucidity in the supposed interests of decoration. To twist his text into a triangle, squeeze it into a box, torture it into the shape of an hour-glass or a diamond is an offence requiring greater justification than the existence either of Italian and French precedents of the fifteenth and sixteenth centuries, or of an ambition to do something new in the twentieth. In truth, these are the easiest tricks of all, and we have seen so much of them during the late 'revival of printing' that we now need rather a revival of restraint. In all permanent forms of typography, whether publicly or privately printed, the typographer's only purpose is to express, not himself, but his author. There are, admittedly, other purposes which enter into the composition of advertisement, publicity and sales matter; and there is, of course, a very great deal common to both book and advertisement composition. But it is not allowable to the printer to relax his zeal for the reader's comfort in order to satisfy an ambition to decorate or to illustrate. Rather than run this risk the printer should strive to express himself by the use of this or that small decorative unit, either of common design supplied by the typefounders or drawn for his office by an artist. It is quite true that to an inventive printer decoration is not often necessary. In commercial printing, however, it seems to be a necessity, because the complexity of our civilisation demands an infinite number of styles and characters. Publishers and other buyers of printing, by insisting upon a setting which shall express their business, their goods, their books and nobody else's goods or business or books, demand an individuality which pure typography can never hope to supply. But book-printers, concerned with the permanently convenient rather than with the sensational or the fashionable in printing, should be on their guard against title-page borders, vignettes and devices invented to ease their difficulties. There is no easy way with most title-pages; and the printer's task is rendered more difficult by the average publisher's and author's incompetence to draft a title or to organise the preliminaries in reasonable sequence.

VI

Those who would like to lessen or vary the tendency towards standardisation in day-to-day book production have a field for their activity in the last-mentioned pages. Their positions on the page and their relation to each other are not essentially invariable. Nevertheless, as it is well for printers and publishers to have rules, and the same rules, it may be suggested that the headings to Preface, Table of Contents, Introduction, etc., should be in the same size and fount as the chapter heads; and should be dropped if they are dropped. The order of the preliminaries remains to be settled. With the exception of the copyright notice, which may be set on the verso of the title-page, all should begin on a recto. The logical order of the preliminary pages is Half-title or Dedication (I see no reason for including both), Title, Contents, Preface, Introduction. The certificate of 'limitation', in the case of books of that class, may face the title where there is no frontispiece, be incorporated with the half-title, or be taken to the end of the volume. This order is applicable to most categories of books. Novels need neither Table of Contents nor List of Chapters, though one or the other is too often printed. If it is decided to retain either, it would be reasonable to print it on the back of the half-title and facing the title-page, so that the structure, scope and nature of the book will be almost completely indicated to the reader at a single opening. Where the volume is made up of a few short stories, their titles can be listed in the otherwise blank centre of the title-page.

VII

Fiction, Belles-Lettres and Educational books are habitually first published in portable, but not pocketable, formats; crown octavo (5 by 7   in.) being the invariable rule for novels published as such. The novel in the form of Biography will be published as a Biography, demy octavo (5^1 by 8^i in.), the size also for History, Political Study, Archaeology, Science, Art and almost everything but fiction. Novels are only promoted to this format when they have become famous and 'standard'; when they are popular rather than famous they are composed in the pocket (4   by 6^i in.) editions. Size, therefore, is the most manifest difference between the categories of books.

Another obvious difference is bulk, calculated in accordance with the publisher's notion, first, of the general sense of trade expectation, and, secondly, of the purchasing psychology of a public habituated to certain selling prices vaguely related to number of pages and thickness of volume (inconsistently enough, weight does not enter into these expectations). These habits of mind have consequences in the typography; they affect the choice of fount and size of type, and may necessitate the adoption of devices for 'driving out', i.e. making the setting take up as much room as possible. By putting the running headline between rules or rows of ornaments; introducing unnecessary blanks between chapters; contracting the measure; exaggerating the spaces between the words and the lines; excessively indenting paragraphs; isolating quoted matter with areas of white space; inserting wholly unnecessary sectional titles in the text and surrounding them with space; contriving to drive a chapter ending to the top of a recto page so that the rest of it and its verso may be blank; using thick paper; increasing the depth of chapter beginnings and inserting very large versals thereto; and so on, the volume can be inflated to an extra sixteen pages and sometimes more – which is a feat the able typographer is expected to accomplish without showing his hand.

Limited editions of standard authors, or of authors whose publishers desire them to rank as such, are commonly given a rubricated title or some other feature not strictly necessary. A dreadful example of overdone rubrication is to be found in a recent edition of Thomas Hardy's verse, in which the running heads throughout the book are in red – the production of a firm which desired to make an impression on the purchaser in view of the price asked for the edition. This could have been better done by reserving colour for the initial letters. Handmade paper is generally used for éditions de luxe, and none but the brave among publishers will disregard the superstitious love of the book-buying classes for its untrimmed, ugly and dirt-gathering edges. That most of the public prefer to have it so is because a trimmed book looks 'ordinary' to them. Any book which is 'different' from the 'ordinary' in one superficial way or another is apt to impress those lacking trade experience. And there has been a notable increase during recent years in the category of books, generally illustrated, known to the trade as *fine printing*, *éditions de luxe*, *press-books*, *limited editions*, *collectors' books* etc. Hence, it is hoped that the above setting out of the first principles of typography may give the discriminating reader some sort of yardstick which he can apply not only to the entries catalogued by the booksellers as limited editions, but to the output of publishers responsible for printing the literary and scientific books which are more necessary to society, and are often designed with greater intelligence.

Stanley Morison (1889-1967), *First Principles of Typography*, Cambridge University Press, 1936, but first published in *The Fleuron*, 1930.

Morison wrote (in section III of *First Principles*, here omitted): 'As lower-case is a necessary evil, which we should do well to subordinate since we cannot suppress, it should be avoided when it is at its least rational and least attractive - in large sizes'. However, it appears in a large size, for the title, on the cover of his book in 1936.

Harry graham carter's *essay on sanserif types is a model of typographic analysis. It appeared in* The Curwen Press Miscellany *in 1931. This was a year after his monumental translation of Fournier's* Manuel Typographique *(still well worth reading) and three years after Jan Tschichold's* Die neue Typographie, *1928, which has so much in it about sanserif types that I believe Carter would have mentioned it if he had read it; but few if any copies of that work had by then percolated into England. One of Carter's other monumental works was his translation of Herodotus'* Histories, *published (in over 600 pages) by the Limited Editions Club in 1958 with illustrations by Edward Bawden. Carter was among other things a remarkable linguist: Latin and Greek before he went to school at Bedales, virtually perfect in French, and fluent in German, Spanish, Dutch and Russian. His son Matthew says he must have learned some Arabic and Hebrew while working in Jerusalem during the Second World War, although he denied it. He had a prejudice against Italian.*

After getting a degree in history at Oxford and training as a barrister, he became 'passionately' interested in printing (the adverb is used by Oliver Simon, writing about Carter in Printer and Playground). *After being a learner at the Monotype works in 1928-9, he became production manager of the Kynoch Press, under Herbert Simon, from 1929 to 1937, where he designed two outstanding type specimen books and a series of imaginative Kynoch Press Diaries with illustrations by Edward Bawden, Eric Ravilious and others. He then joined the Nonesuch Press to work, for a year, for Francis Meynell, who called him 'my Nonesuch understudy - sometimes indeed my overstudy'.*

After spending 1939-1945 in the army (which did not prevent him from designing a Hebrew type, for which he cut the punches by hand) he was chosen by Francis Meynell to head the newly-formed layout department of Her Majesty's Stationery Office. In 1954 he returned to Oxford to become Archivist to the University Press and to begin writing the History of the Press; only the first volume, to the year 1780, was published, in 1975.

As well as the Hebrew type already mentioned (which never got beyond a proof) Carter also drew innovative numerals for Green Line Bus timetables in 1937, a condensed version of Edward Johnston's Underground sanserif for the route-blinds of London buses, a Russian type made by Monotype, said to be one of the best cyrillics, and a bible type cut by Monotype for an OUP small-format Bible.

He was also an essentially modest and even private person, with a particularly lovable wife.

SANSERIF TYPES

The name 'sanserif' conveys to a printer a kind of type not merely lacking serifs, but also without contrasting thick and thin strokes. It is the natural form of letter to anyone who writes otherwise than with a pen or a brush. There is some reason to think that this style of letter was imported into printing from inscriptional sources, and was at first used for display work to which it was intended to give a monumental air. But a printer having become acquainted with these types would value them for their durability, for they have no serifs or hair-lines to break or become thick in wear; which quality, no doubt, goes as as far as a printer's partiality can towards accounting for their popularity.

Sanserif types made their appearance in England between 1820 and 1830, to which decade indeed we may trace the rise of 'jobbing faces' as a class. Johnson in his *Typographia* (1824) testifies to this efflorescence: 'Upon the gradual improvement of metal types, our Founders (emulating each other) in addition to their plain two-line letters, commenced cutting open letters of almost every size: yet here their exertions did not end, they have now taken [nearly] the whole range of Fancy, in bringing forward ornamented letters of every size and description, together with a new character which they term Egyptian; this latter is all the rage at present, particularly in placards, jobs, etc.' England may justly claim to be the cradle of this letter, variously called sanserif, sans-surryphs, grotesque, Doric, block, or Gothic; and it found its way into British Type-specimens in 1832. In that year Figgins showed it in 5-line pica and 2-line great primer, while Thorowgood had one size only – a 14-line. In 1835 Figgins included a complete range of it, announced as 'A large, and elegant assortment, of the most modern job letter'. There is a certain *quality* in Figgins's sanserif due to bad cutting, but as these types as a class were perfected from a technical point of view, so they increased in dullness. Their association with the inscriptions on nineteenth-century granite tombstones and obelisks may be partly responsible for their depressing effect on the mind. The sanserif was cut in many different styles, condensed, extended, elongated, heavy, light, and open, but always in the 'modern' fashion as regards the proportions of the letters and the curvature of the strokes. Thus, the B, E, L, S, Y, are comparatively wide, and the H, M, N, are narrow; the J and R have the 'modern' curves.

In course of time a lower-case was cut. It is very difficult to design a satisfactory set of minuscule letters without thick and thin strokes. The traditional roman lower-case is essentially pen-made. In a letter of ordinary weight the thickening of the hair-lines results in distorted counters and a disturbance of the even colour of the page. The designers of the nineteenth-century sanserifs resorted to a subterfuge and half-thinned some lines, such as the crossbars of 'a' and 'e', which is not elegant. The attempt to dispense with hair-lines reveals their efficacy in providing a compromise between legibility and economy of space, which means quick reading.

The nineteenth-century sanserif won itself a permanent place in every composing-room. Its earlier monumental associations were discarded as it came to be increasingly used for the humblest purposes. Its legibility and durability in wear fitted it for the printing of cartons, wrappers, labels, and similar trade purposes, and thus it earned a certain discredit among those who cared for fine printing and fine types.

As the teaching of William Morris penetrated business houses, how many printers emptied their cases of Gothics and Grotesques, in various degrees of extension and condensation, and sold the contents as scrap! How many afterwards regretted doing so when they saw the havoc done to their fragile book-types by rougher kinds of commercial jobs!

The sturdy virtues of the sanserif only awaited intelligent exploitation by clever designers to bring them into favour with the new generation of printers. The modern mechanical methods of type-making are especially well adapted for this purely logical style of letter. The credit for the regeneration of the sans is due to the genius of three men: Mr Gerard Meynell, of the Westminster Press; Mr Frank Pick, then Publicity Manager to the Underground Railways, and Mr Edward Johnston. It was Mr Meynell who suggested that the Underground should have a type by Edward Johnston, and Mr Pick, with an artistic audacity rare in industrial magnates, gave the designer a free hand. The 'Underground' Sans, which made its appearance in 1918, proved that the technical advantages of the block letter may be associated with a kind of beauty that is much appreciated by living critics of the applied arts. With regard to the objects of our daily use we like to feel that form has been dictated by functional considerations: let them be so designed as to serve their purpose with maximum efficiency and to proclaim themselves for what they are. Ornament, the appearance of costliness, are no longer prized. Thus modern sentiment has singled out the sans from Victorian job-founts for preservation and condemned all the rest.

Mr Johnston's 'Underground' Sanserif, which is of great beauty, was the first of the twentieth-century variety. It is a member of the old-face family of types. Based on the Roman inscriptional models, the essential form of letters is the same as Jenson's or Caslon's: only the fashion of them has been dictated by function. The absence of serifs and hair-lines is natural and proper in letters of a large size to be used for a few isolated words and at a distance. Hair-lines are useful where economy of space is a paramount consideration, and serifs help the eye to isolate and follow one line in a maze of reading matter: they are both aids to quick reading. But neither is a help to sure reading, and both are inappropriate in a short legend commanding ample space for its display. These are two of the reasons why we instinctively acclaim the Underground block letters as apt and agreeable. They have other virtues: they are easily distinguished by the eye from the types used for surrounding advertisements, they break with the literary tradition, and therefore sort well with the starkly mechanical associations of an electric railway, yet their essentially Roman forms link them with classical culture.

Not long after the adoption of the new letter by the Underground a delegation of German artists engaged in advertising came to London and saw it. Prepossessed in its favour by the repute of Edward Johnston in their country, and inevitably delighted by the good taste of the advertisements in which it figured, these *Gebrauchsgraphiker* went home and made the fullest use of this new convention in lettering. The typefounders had no option but to cut sanserif types following the old-face proportions. Modern German versions of the new sans are now very many, but most remarkable are Bauer's Futura and Klingspor's Cable. Futura is audaciously modernist, but very successful, while Professor Koch's Cable is, to the writer, almost as good as Johnston's Sans, and is thought by many to be better. It has an exceedingly good lower-case, which is a unique distinction. In its rigid adherence to the geometrical bases of the roman letter-design in its purest form it may even be a little faddy.

Monotype Gill Sans, a sober and satisfactory display type, has the stark economy of the modern machine. In design it resembles the Johnston design closely, but it is lighter in colour, a quality which makes it more useful for full pages and less so for a caption of few words. Well designed, the Gill letter has been excellently founded, so that it has a wider range of usefulness in typography than any other sanserif has had.

Three very good sanserif types are now on the market. Had they been available thirty years ago Mr Harold Curwen might never have brought his block-type into being. With an origin quite independent of, and indeed earlier than the other modern sanserifs, it was conceived at a time when Mr Curwen was studying lettering under Edward Johnston. It was quite natural that they should both solve the problem of a simplified roman letter in the same way, for both took the Trajan column as a model of good lettering. The 'Curwen' block capitals were first used for a letter-heading in 1912. They were the result of following the best Roman models with a big round-pointed lettering nib. Soon afterwards, when Messrs Crittall were seeking for a distinctive letter for their publicity, they found what they wanted in these capitals that Mr Curwen had drawn. For several years they were printed from line-blocks, but after a while reasons of economy prompted their being made into type. Messrs Bannerman, of Wood Green, engraved the matrices. Recently Mr Curwen has drawn a lower-case and has had one fount made, in 24-point.

The Curwen Sans is bold in colour and the strokes are of precisely equal thickness throughout. It is unconventional in several respects, and even open to criticisms from a purist in type-design. Yet it has great vigour and charm and is suitable for long-range display, especially of an open character.

A great virtue in this new type is that, being of the pure breed of twentieth-century sanserifs and almost primitive in its regeneracy, it comes at a time when the class as a whole is showing signs of a decline through wrong use. The block letter is not a book hand: it is unsuitable for close matter. It should not be used in conjunction with ornament. A simplified thing in itself, in order to appear to best advantage it needs studiously simple, perhaps rather precious, treatment. Its novelty to the advertising world is resulting in its indiscriminate use, and this in turn leads to injudicious purchasing, so that some antiquated and bad gothics in thin disguise are being resuscitated by the founders.

Those who handle these types should attend to De Vinne's warning. No types need more careful setting than these. The capitals always need thoughtful interspacing: the set which the founder has given them is a mean which calls for adjustment in particular combinations of letters. Sanserifs also need generous interlinear spacing.

Harry Carter (1901–1982), in *The Curwen Press
Miscellany*, 1931.

JOHNSTON SANSERIF

CURWEN SANSERIF TYPE
DESIGNED BY HAROLD CURWEN

THIS IS SET IN CABLE
DESIGNED BY RUDOLPH KOCH. CUT BY KLINGSPOR

'THE CRYSTAL GOBLET' *was originally an address given to the British Typographers Guild at the St Bride Institute, London, in 1932. It was later published, in a book of Beatrice Warde's essays under the same title, in 1955. It is a very good example of her ability to hammer in nails, using poetic language, on her own subject, the importance of which she epitomised in her famous and poetic 'This is a printing office' poster.*

Beatrice was born in the United States, the daughter of May Lamberton Becker, a noted journalist, and a father who was 'a professional musician, pianist and musical pedagogue, with a curious bent toward verbal communication or the equivalent of it through music'. No wonder she became a great communicator — in her own words, above all a vocal communicator. 'There is not a paragraph I have ever written which has not been re-written three or four times. What I'm really good at is standing up in front of an audience with no preparation at all, then for 50 minutes refusing to let them even wriggle an ankle.'

She came to England in 1925, and became publicity manager for the Monotype Corporation. From 1927 she edited their house magazine the Monotype Recorder, turning it into a periodical of international typographic importance. Each issue was produced by a different printer (always a Monotype customer) and contained an important article, beautifully designed, usually by Stanley Morison. She herself, researching in Paris, discovered that some types previously thought to be by Garamond had actually been copied from Garamond by Jean Jannon, and published her findings in The Fleuron under the pen-name of Paul Beaujon (to avoid confusion with the work of her husband Frederic Warde).

She was a beautiful woman, the model for many drawings by Eric Gill, including in 1929 two wood-engravings of 'La Belle Sauvage', made as a colophon for the publishing house of Cassell (whose history had started in the old Belle Sauvage inn in London).

See 'I am a communicator', an interview with John Dreyfus published as her memorial in The Monotype Recorder, vol.44, no.1, Autumn 1970.

THE CRYSTAL GOBLET
OR
PRINTING SHOULD BE INVISIBLE

Imagine that you have before you a flagon of wine. You may choose your own favourite vintage for this imaginary demonstration, so that it be a deep shimmering crimson in colour. You have two goblets before you. One is of solid gold, wrought in the most exquisite patterns. The other is of crystal-clear glass, thin as a bubble, and as transparent. Pour and drink; and according to your choice of goblet, I shall know whether or not you are a connoisseur of wine. For if you have no feelings about wine one way or the other, you will want the sensation of drinking the stuff out of a vessel that may have cost thousands of pounds; but if you are a member of that vanishing tribe, the amateurs of fine vintages, you will choose the crystal, because everything about it is calculated to *reveal* rather than hide the beautiful thing which it was meant to *contain*.

Bear with me in this long-winded and fragrant metaphor; for you will find that almost all the virtues of the perfect wine-glass have a parallel in typography. There is the long, thin stem that obviates fingerprints on the bowl. Why? Because no cloud must come between your eyes and the fiery heart of the liquid. Are not the margins on book pages similarly meant to obviate the necessity of fingering the type-page? Again: the glass is colourless or at the most only faintly tinged in the bowl, because the connoisseur judges wine partly by its colour and is impatient of anything that alters it. There are a thousand mannerisms in typography that are as impudent and arbitrary as putting port in tumblers of red or green glass! When a goblet has a base that looks too small for security, it does not matter how cleverly it is weighted; you feel nervous lest it should tip over. There are ways of setting lines of type which may work well enough, and yet keep the reader subconsciously worried by the fear of 'doubling' lines, reading three words as one, and so forth.

Now the man who first chose glass instead of clay or metal to hold his wine was a 'modernist' in the sense in which I am going to use that term. That is, the first thing he asked of his particular object was not *'How should it look?'* but *'What must it do?'* and to that extent all good typography is modernist.

Wine is so strange and potent a thing that it has been used in the central ritual of religion in one place and time, and attacked by a virago with a hatchet in another. There is only one thing in the world that is capable of stirring and altering men's minds to the same extent, and that is the coherent expression of thought. That is man's chief miracle, unique to man. There is no 'explanation' whatever of the fact that I can make arbitrary sounds which will lead a total stranger to think my own thought. It is sheer magic that I should be able to hold a one-sided conversation by means of black marks on paper with an unknown person half-way across the world. Talking, broadcasting, writing, and printing are all quite literally forms of *thought transference*, and it is the ability and eagerness to transfer and receive the contents of the mind that is almost alone responsible for human civilization.

If you agree with this, you will agree with my one main idea, i.e. that the most important thing about printing is that it conveys thought, ideas, images, from one mind to other minds. This statement is what you might call the front door of the science of typography. Within lie hundreds of rooms; but unless you start by assuming that *printing is meant to convey specific and coherent ideas*, it is very easy to find yourself in the wrong house altogether.

Before asking what this statement leads to, let us see what it does not necesssar-ily lead to. If books are printed in order to be read, we must distinguish readability from what the optician would call legibility. A page set in 14-pt Bold Sans is, according to the laboratory tests, more 'legible' than one set in 11-pt Baskerville. A public speaker is more 'audible' in that sense when he bellows. But a good speak-ing voice is one which is inaudible *as* a voice. It is the transparent goblet again! I need not warn you that if you begin listening to the inflections and speaking rhythms of a voice from a platform, you are falling asleep. When you listen to a song in a language you do not understand, part of your mind actually does fall asleep, leaving your quite separate aesthetic sensibilities to enjoy themselves unim-peded by your reasoning faculties. The fine arts do that; but that is not the purpose of printing. Type well used is invisible *as* type, just as the perfect talking voice is the unnoticed vehicle for the transmission of words, ideas.

We may say, therefore, that printing may be delightful for many reasons, but that it is important, first and foremost, as a means of doing something. That is why it is mischievous to call any printed piece a work of art, especially fine art: because that would imply that its first purpose was to exist as an expression of beauty for its own sake and for the delectation of the senses. Calligraphy can almost be considered a fine art nowadays, because its primary economic and edu-cational purpose has been taken away; but printing in English will not qualify as an art until the present English language no longer conveys ideas to future genera-tions, and until printing itself hands it usefulness to some yet unimagined succes-sor.

There is no end to the maze of practices in typography, and this idea of printing as a conveyor is, at least in the minds of all the great typographers with whom I have had the privilege of talking, the one clue that can guide you through the maze. Without this essential humility of mind, I have seen ardent designers go more hopelessly wrong, make more ludicrous mistakes out of an excessive enthusiasm, than I could have thought possible. And with this clue, this purposiveness in the back of your mind, it is possible to do the most unheard-of things, and find that they justify you triumphantly. It is not a waste of time to go to the simple funda-mentals and reason from them. In the flurry of your individual problems, I think you will not mind spending half an hour on one broad and simple set of ideas involving abstract principles.

I once was talking to a man who designed a very pleasing advertising type which undoubtedly all of you have used. I said something about what artists think about a certain problem, and he replied with a beautiful gesture: 'Ah, madam, we artists do not think – we *feel!*' That same day I quoted that remark to another designer of my acquaintance, and he, being less poetically inclined, murmured: 'I'm not *feeling* very well today, I *think!*' He was right, he did think; he was the thinking sort; and that is why he is not so good a painter, and to my mind ten times better as a typographer and type designer than the man who instinctively avoided anything as coherent as a reason.

I always suspect the typographic enthusiast who takes a printed page from a book and frames it to hang on the wall, for I believe that in order to gratify a sensory delight he has mutilated something infinitely more important. I remember that T. M. Cleland, the famous American typographer, once showed me a very beautiful layout for a Cadillac booklet involving decorations in colour. He did not have the actual text to work with in drawing up his specimen pages, so he had set the lines in Latin. This was not only for the reason that you will all think of, if you have seen the old typefoundries' famous *Quousque Tandem* copy (i.e. that Latin has few descenders and thus gives a remarkably even line). No, he told me that originally he had set up the dullest 'wording' that he could find (I dare say it was from *Hansard*), and yet he discovered that the man to whom he submitted it would start reading and making comments on the text. I made some remark on the mentality of Boards of Directors, but Mr Cleland said, 'No: you're wrong; if the reader had not been practically forced to read – if he had not seen those words suddenly imbued with glamour and significance – then the layout would have been a failure. Setting it in Italian or Latin is only an easy way of saying "This is not the text as it will appear".'

Let me start my specific conclusions with book typography, because that contains all the fundamentals, and then go on to a few points about advertising.

The book typographer has the job of erecting a window between the reader inside the room and that landscape which is the author's words. He may put up a stained-glass window of marvellous beauty, but a failure as a window; that is, he may use some rich superb type like text gothic that is something to be looked at, not *through*. Or he may work in what I call transparent or invisible typography. I have a book at home, of which I have no visual recollection whatever as far as its typography goes; when I think of it, all I see is the Three Musketeers and their comrades swaggering up and down the streets of Paris. The third type of window is one in which the glass is broken into relatively small leaded panes; and this corresponds to what is called 'fine printing' today, in that you are at least conscious that there is a window there, and that someone has enjoyed building it. That is not objectionable, because of a very important fact which has to do with the psychology of the subconscious mind. That is that the mental eye focuses *through* type and not *upon* it. The type which, through any arbitrary warping of design or excess of 'colour', gets in the way of the mental picture to be conveyed, is a bad type. Our subconsciousness is always afraid of blunders (which illogical setting, tight spacing and too-wide unleaded lines can trick us into), of boredom, and of officiousness. The running headline that keeps shouting at us, the line that looks like one long word, the capitals jammed together without hair-spaces – these mean subconscious squinting and loss of mental focus.

And if what I have said is true of book printing, even of the most exquisite limited editions, it is fifty times more obvious in advertising, where the one and only justification for the purchase of space is that you are conveying a message – that you are implanting a desire, straight into the mind of the reader. It is tragically easy to throw away half the reader-interest of an advertisement by setting the simple and compelling argument in a face which is uncomfortably alien to the classic reasonableness of the book-face. Get attention as you will by your headline, and make any pretty type pictures you like if you are sure that the copy is useless as a means of selling goods; but if you are happy enough to have really good copy to work with, I beg you to remember that thousands of people pay hard-earned money for the privilege of reading quietly set book-pages, and that only your wildest ingenuity can stop people from reading a really interesting text.

Printing demands a humility of mind, for the lack of which many of the fine arts are even now floundering in self-conscious and maudlin experiments. There is nothing simple or dull in achieving the transparent page. Vulgar ostentation is twice as easy as discipline. When you realise that ugly typography never effaces itself, you will be able to capture beauty as the wise men capture happiness by aiming at something else. The 'stunt typographer' learns the fickleness of rich men who hate to read. Not for them are long breaths held over serif and kern, they will not appreciate your splitting of hair-spaces. Nobody (save the other craftsmen) will appreciate half your skill. But you may spend endless years of happy experiment in devising that crystalline goblet which is worthy to hold the vintage of the human mind.

Beatrice Warde (1900–1969), *The Crystal Goblet*,
London, 1955, originally an address given in 1932.

THIS IS
A PRINTING OFFICE

CROSSROADS OF CIVILIZATION

REFUGE OF ALL THE ARTS
AGAINST THE RAVAGES OF TIME

ARMOURY OF FEARLESS TRUTH
AGAINST WHISPERING RUMOUR

INCESSANT TRUMPET OF TRADE

FROM THIS PLACE WORDS MAY FLY ABROAD

NOT TO PERISH ON WAVES OF SOUND

NOT TO VARY WITH THE WRITER'S HAND

BUT FIXED IN TIME HAVING BEEN VERIFIED IN PROOF

FRIEND YOU STAND ON SACRED GROUND

THIS IS A PRINTING OFFICE

Broadsheet by Beatrice Warde, June 1940,
set in Monotype Perpetua titling, printed in
black and red (reduced).

ADLER WAS BORN IN 1884. Joseph Blumenthal in The Printed Book in America, 1977, writes of him: 'Adler was a designer, a printer, a collector, an editor, a teacher, a curator, and a publisher. In each of these careers he retained the curiosity and enthusiasm of the amateur with the acquired competence of the professional.'

As a young man he entered his family's clothing business in Rochester, New York, and eventually became advertising manager. But he also became a collector of prints and drawings and books about printing, and in 1922, aged thirty-eight, he left the family business to set up a press in New York, which he named Pynson Printers after the early London printer. Pynson Printers produced such distinguished work that in 1924 the publisher of the New York Times invited Adler to move his Press into the new Times building on 43rd Street, in the belief that a fine printing office would add prestige to a huge newspaper plant. The new Pynson offices were designed by Lucien Bernhard. A room was provided with a large refectory table where Adler held weekly seminars on bookmaking. To quote Blumenthal again: 'Adler gave famous teas on Thursday afternoons. He invited artists, writers, publishers, printers, collectors – only friends and celebrities of whom he approved. This was during the era of Prohibition when teacups frequently contained alcoholic refreshment. But to Adler, who neither smoked nor drank, and who had fastidious criteria to people and their ways, tea was tea.'

Adler designed The American Mercury for Knopf in 1923, a literary periodical edited by George Jean Nathan and H. L. Mencken (who wrote to Knopf that Adler's designs 'look somewhat whorish...I shall follow them'); and in 1930 Adler started The Colophon; a Book Collector's Quarterly, which ran for twenty issues until 1935. Each issue was bound in decorated paper boards and an outstanding feature was that nearly every article was printed by a different fine printer (which made normal pagination impossible). Issue 4, for example, contained an article by A. W. Pollard designed by Bruce Rogers and printed by Oxford University Press, and in addition a famous article by Francis Meynell, 'Some Collectors read', printed by the Curwen Press, with 13 actual Nonesuch pages tipped in. Issue 6, with a dramatic cover drawn by T. M. Cleland, had 6 pages from Stanley Morison, printed by the Cambridge University Press. The Colophon remains a very great achievement.

Before he died in 1961, Adler founded, with official support and private help, a Museum of the Book in San Juan, Puerto Rico. An excellent account of his varied life and achievements is given in Elmer Adler in the World of Books, edited by Paul Bennett and published in 1964 by The Typophiles in New York.

THE MAKING OF A BOOK

If the individual designing the physical structure of a book could ignore all responsibilities other than the making of a beautiful volume, his task would be much simplified. In other fields there are examples of form with almost a total absence of substance. For instance, it is told that in the early days of the Mormon Church, the leaders, often for hours at a time, stood before their congregations making sounds and gesturing. They were making sounds, however, that resembled no words understood by the crowds. The orators were said to have 'the gift of tongues', and although no one got any specific idea from what he heard, all the auditors were tremendously impressed and emotionally moved. Each of these demonstrations was a good example of perfected medium. The audience was so completely under the spell of form that it was not conscious of a lack of substance.

But the job of the bookmaker starts with substance; it is substance already created and which is to be put into a form available to many others. Furthermore, this form should appear to have been developed with little or no resistance, and to function with the highest degree of efficiency.

When a reader is made more conscious of the form of the book than of its subject matter, the work of designing is badly done. The projector of such a book might have qualified on a Utah platform, but he is not likely to make any real contribution to the art of the book. The bookmaker's main tool, type, is a medium of expression and all the mediums have a common quality: the greater art exercised, the lesser realisation of labour.

The telling orally of stories of adventure had gone on for thousand of years before symbols were developed to present the records in some visual or permanent manner. And it is important to remember that when man, in a comparatively recent time, devised symbols for the visual presentation of ideas, these symbols for the most part represented the sounds in which ideas were originally expressed.

Even the nomenclature applied to the visual forms is adapted from the oral. We ask 'what tongue' or 'what language' does he use? There is no special word for the written language. We virtually call it symbolised sound. Almost all devices for the written or printed forms of expression are derived from the oral; commas, periods, paragraphs are simply degrees of pauses in imitation of vocal presentations. Not only is the vocal form of literature the original, but it also continues to be the most natural. Doubtless, most authors write by arranging words as they sound to the ear. The visual form adapts; it does not create.

Elmer Adler (1884–1961), in The Dolphin, No. 2,
New York, 1935.

THESE PASSAGES ARE TAKEN *from an address given to the Society of Printers in Boston in 1936. They give a highly perceptive view of the early impact of Kelmscott on Boston, Massachusetts, and an amusing description of the later progress of printing. This includes an early warning about offset printing, which later turned out to be a main road after all – but no warning of the dangers of the New Typography, then already on the horizon in Germany.*

Rollins was born in 1880, and became fascinated by printing before he was twelve. After three years at Harvard, and working as a journalist on a small country newspaper in Massachusetts, he applied for a job at the Merrymount Press under D. B. Updike. Updike offered to take him on, but made a condition that if he accepted, he would agree not to go out and start a printing office of his own. Rollins declined, and as his wife wrote in Carl Rollins at Montague, 'I think it is a tribute to both Carl and Updike that Carl could conclude his account of the episode with the sentence "My long friendship with Daniel Berkeley Updike began then".'

So he went to Boston's second-best printer, Carl Heintzemann, where he worked and learned, but he did not like living in a city. He moved to the country outside Boston and worked in a Utopian community in Montague for a while. At some point he lost the sight of one eye, perhaps due to a detached retina, for which there was then no remedy, and was advised to give up printing. However in 1907 he returned to Montague, bought an old mill, and set up the Montague Press. Here he had a notable collaboration with his friend Bruce Rogers, including two books, one of which was Maurice de Guérin's The Centaur, in 1915. Of Rollins, Rogers wrote in Paragraphs on Printing, 1943: 'I cannot refrain from occasional memoirs of the men whom I have known best; and of these Carl Rollins easily comes first as the master craftsman. Besides furniture and all sorts of gadgets in wood and iron he has built two pleasant houses; and he rebuilt his famous Dyke Mill at Montague almost annually (I should say) over a long period of years. When his energies were transferred to Yale his propensities for hand-work entered the larger field without diminution... all the printing of the Yale University Press still bears that desirable, indefinable quality of having come out of the work-shop rather than off the drawing board.'

Of the Montague Press his wife wrote: 'It did not do too badly financially – it was out of the red now and then – but as the first world war wore on, the demands for fine printing began to dry up'. But in 1918, Yale University Press asked him to take charge of their printing. Rollins took his type and presses to New Haven, and a year later was formally appointed Printer to Yale University with the rank of Professor. He stayed at Yale for thirty years and produced a large number of memorable books. He died in 1960.

WHITHER NOW, TYPOGRAPHER?

I used to spend occasional evenings at the Boston Public Library, reading, partly for

the pleasure of the contents, partly for the exhilaration of the printing, the books
which William Morris had printed at the Kelmscott Press. This was only five or six
years after the close of that establishment, and those who have not the necessary
years to their credit or discredit, cannot possibly realise the effect of that virile
printing on the English-speaking world of that day. But its effect on Boston – and
Cambridge – was peculiarly and particularly fortunate. It is true, and, looked at in
perspective, a bit amusing, that the first repercussion was imitative. Mr Rogers
produced such books as the *Song of Roland* and Raleigh's *Last Fight of the Revenge at
Sea*, beautiful and magnificent books, both of them, yet showing very clear evi-
dences of the Morris influence; while Mr Updike succumbed to the spell of
Kelmscott by printing the *Altar Book*; and Joe Bowles's *Modern Art*, the University
Press's edition of Louise Guiney's *Nine Sonnets* written at Oxford, the *Masters in Art*
series, and other books, tried valiantly to catch the mood of Morris printing with
that respectable but hardly distinguished Antique Old Style type. But Boston printing, which had such sound traditions as Henry O. Houghton had maintained at the
Riverside press, after bowing temporarily to the strong blast from Upper Mall,
Hammersmith, righted itself, found its true course again, and proceeded to take
the Kelmscott lesson to heart with an intelligent sanity.

The first fruits of the Morris influence were those beautiful little books of Stone
& Kimball's, based rather more on the work of the Chiswick Press than on that of
Kelmscott, but which nevertheless would hardly have been born but for the work of
the latter. Stone & Kimball made use of Caslon type as well as the Modernised Old
Style; their influence on current typography was probably very great, as may be evidenced by the work of their contemporaries and successors. And when the typographers came on the scene, Mr Rogers and Mr Updike and Mr Heintzemann and
others, they had the good sense to use the best of the traditional types, but they
used them with a freer hand than anyone had done in America for a hundred years.
(I do not forget Mr De Vinne, but while he did use the traditional types, he did not
use them with a free hand, and he had no such aesthetic judgement as the Boston
printers in the selection of the better of the existing types.)...

...A study of the past does not mean that one must try to print like John Day or
Christopher Plantin or Bodoni, but it does mean that if one is trying to do good
printing he must have a head full of memories of how good printers in the past
have printed. More than that, he must have a feeling for books of the best kind,
their size and shape and the paper they are printed on, of how the type fits the
page, and how the title pages are displayed. He must regard books not as models
to be followed implicitly, but as food for the printer's mind, ideas to pack away in

that storehouse of the memory which is, after all, the prime equipment for a printer. He must not be unduly concerned with the work of his contemporaries because imitation of imitations, like half tones of half tones quickly lose their freshness and sparkle.

The great printer's highway out of the past into the future is not a boulevard, with high visibility and easy banked curves and clover-leaf crossings. It winds, and it is obscure in some places: it resembles more an English or a New England country road than a Route Nationale. As I have travelled it I have been impressed by the many detours, branch roads, dangerous precipices, and muddy bottoms along the way. Once I remember, I came on a magnificent six-lane macadam highway which swung off at such an easy angle that one could hardly resist the temptation to take it. At the intersection stood a cylindrical gentleman in what looked like a state policeman's uniform, and he advised all of us to go up the new road, which had a gaudy sign, slightly blurred at the edges, marked 'Offset Way'. Most of us had our doubts, and as we got along a little farther, the new road was seen to stop short a few hundred feet from the main highway, and to dwindle into a mere rutted cart path. True, much farther along it began to improve, and to parallel our road, but so far the dream of the cylindrical gentleman (whose uniform it afterwards turned out was merely that of a bellhop) that his grandiose boulevard should become the main highway has not come true.

There are numerous hot-dog stands and roller coasters and especially motion picture houses along the roadside, where sooner or later nearly everyone stops for a moment at least. I have seen some otherwise very respectable printers succumb to the fascination of an Ultra Bologna sausage or of the peep show of a shady type face. Of course there are the stolid wayfarers who plod along as near the middle of the path as possible, with never an eye for the allurements of the roadside stands. Most of them are accompanied by a disreputable, mangy dog who answers to the name of 'Old Style Number One'.

Of the wayfarers on the printer's highway, some have left us for a handful of silver, some for a ribbon to stick in the coat. But these are few in number. The most who have left the path have ventured into the byways and have remained there, some in abandoned Greek temples, some in old colonial houses, some in queer, angular buildings, and many have their quarters in the same building with banks and five-and-ten-cent stores – though I notice that in general the printing offices can hardly compare in appearance with their neighbours.

Along the highroad the company is good, and there is diversion. Down the road comes one like a centaur, without apparent care for the way, but never missing it, and singing as he goes

They gave me what I did not seek, I fed on roasted swan a week!
They pledged me in their malmsey, and they lined me warm with ale.
They sleeked my skin with red-deer pies, and all that runs and swims and flies...

There lumbering along at steady pace is a covered motor truck, and every now and then the back doors open, a benign figure appears on the tail board and scatters type and matrices and patterns to the crowd – when the door shuts, and the dial above moves a notch from 196 to 197. But now we have come to a place where the way is not clear. The mist envelops it, and the printers are at loss – some of them – whither to proceed. Curiosity leads one to an open-air fête at one side, just where a group of workmen, dressed along agate lines, are preparing to build a new road. The surface is of a curious substance, an imitation of an imitation of an imitation of vellum. Over this is smeared by compressed air a bright sheen of silver ink, which dries immediately on exposure to the air, and thus does not get tracked into the house by the pedestrian's feet. There seems to have been some deficiency in the planning of the road, for it has no general direction – only off. But you should see the fête champêtre! There are some French vaudeville actors, dressed in odd clothes – with names like Cochin and Astrée and Sphinx – accompanied by a Basque named Greco. There is a group of Germans, called the Totalitarians, a queer mixture, stout, beer-drinkers named Metropolis. Bold, gauzy reminiscences of the Berlin of postwar days called Eve and Eve Heavy, a group of nudists known as Kabel and Kabel Bold, a few naturalised Britishers, Perpetua and Granjon and Albertus, doing their tricks well but somewhat clumsily; while drawing back with considerable repulsion was a slightly lame man named Times Roman, ready to turn his back on it all.

I notice that while everyone is interested in this side show, and practically everyone stops to look at it, there is on the faces of many of the onlookers a reminiscent look, as if they had seen a show not unlike this somewhere before. And rather than assay the new and glittering road, aimlessly starting from the highway, these men press on into the mist, which, curiously, retreats before them as they advance into the future.

C. P. Rollins (1880–1960), extracts from 'Whither Now, Typographer?', a talk given to the Society of Printers, Boston, in 1936. From Off the Dead Bank. Addresses, Reviews and Verses by Carl Purington Rollins, New York: The Typophiles, 1949.

FREDERIC GOUDY *saw and absorbed the Trajan Column in Rome in 1910, when he was 45, and it influenced the rest of his life. Mitchell Kennerley, an Englishman in New York, published Goudy's The Alphabet in 1918. It is a wonderful book which includes 27 plates (the 26 letters and the ampersand, with the figures) in which a drawing of each capital (based on the Trajan letter) is surrounded by fourteen variants, in caps and small letters, of each capital shown. (A page is reproduced in the Newdigate article on p. 37).*

The book from which our excerpt is taken, called on the title-page The Capitals from the Trajan Column at Rome, but The Trajan Capitals on spine and cover, appeared in 1936: Goudy had looked at the Trajan letters with a craftsman's eye and wrote: 'Of all the majuscules inscribed in stone during the nineteen hundred years past, few equal and none surpass in beauty and dignity those drawn by an unknown artist on the Trajan Column in Rome'. He shows a photograph, followed by 'each letter in a size but slightly smaller than its original, exhibiting clearly all peculiarities or subtleties of form, and [I] have attempted to convey the impression one receives on viewing the tablet itself. The capitals have been printed from wood blocks, engraved by me from my original drawings.' They are cut in reverse (i.e. in white) and printed in olive-grey. The letters H J K U W Y Z, Goudy reminds us, do not appear in the inscription, so he has 'invented' them as he thought they might have been made had they been required. They repay careful study from all who care about letter forms and how they should be drawn.

Goudy was born in Bloomington, Illinois, of a family of Scottish blood. He was born with craftsman's fingers: Beilenson tells us 'his first ten dollars, earned at the age of fifteen, went for a lathe'. His earliest work was as a clerk and book-keeper in his father's office: he did not enter the world of printing until 1890. In 1896 he drew an alphabet of capital letters and sent them to the Dickinson Foundry in Boston asking if they were worth five dollars. Amazingly, back came a check for ten; and some months later the 'Camelot' capital, the first type Goudy ever designed, appeared in the American Type Founders specimen book.

After running a small printing firm, The Village Press, with his wife Bertha (who learned to set type by hand, and set The Alphabet), and suffering two disastrous fires, Goudy eventually became the world's first freelance type designer. Such a career was only possible after the inventions, all in the USA, of the Linotype and Monotype typesetting machines and the Benton punchcutting machine, in the last ten years of the nineteenth century. As Blumenthal wrote in The Printed Book in America, 1977, 'Goudy's love of type and typography was passionate, articulate, and indefatigable...Goudy's large accomplishments and his colourful personality were highly influential factors in the widespread concern with matters typographic in the first half of the present century'.

Goudy's best-known types, for example Goudy Modern, Deepdene and Deepdene Bold, are still in use today. An expert account of his achievement as a type designer is given in Walter Tracy's Letters of Credit, 1986. For Goudy's life and work, see A Half Century of Type Design & Typography, 1895-1945, edited by George L. Mackay, and The Story of Frederic

W. Goudy, by Peter Beilenson, both published by The Typophiles in New York. In another useful work, Twentieth century type designers, London, 1987; rev. edn Lund Humphries,
London; W. W. Norton, New York, 1995, Sebastian Carter writes of Goudy: 'Many of the types
are similar in conception, several are not very good, and some are so terrible that even their
author, inclined to view his own work with a favourable eye, did not reproduce them in A Half-
Century; but the ones that remain are enough to place Goudy among the handful of designers
who have changed the look of the types we read'.

THE TRAJAN CAPITALS

Nathaniel Hawthorne wrote of the Column erected in Trajan's Forum in Rome and
dedicated about 113AD, 'It is a great, solid fact of the Past, making old Rome actually visible to the touch and eye; and no study of history, nor force of thought, nor
magic of song, can so vitally assure us that Rome once existed, as this sturdy specimen of what its rulers and people wrought.'

The base of the Column forms a sepulchral chamber intended to receive the
Imperial remains, and it is believed by many that the ashes of the Emperor in their
golden urn are buried in front of the Column which was erected during his lifetime. It is not an improbable assumption since it was the custom in those days to
preserve the ashes of rulers in such an urn upon an altar in front of the Sepulchral
Chamber. When erected the Column* was surmounted by a statue of the Emperor
Trajan holding a gilt globe, but this was replaced later by the statue of St Peter.

The Column, one hundred and forty-seven feet high, composed of thirty-four blocks of marble, was erected by the Senate and people of Rome, and is covered by a spiral band of bas-reliefs illustrating the Dacian wars, almost the only record of these wars extant.

Over the doorway in the pedestal of the Column is a tablet bearing an inscription, the lettering of which is said to be the finest extant of the Imperial Era. Of the
inscription Edward F. Strange, the English writer and author of an authoritative
book, Alphabets, a Handbook of Lettering with Historical Critical and Practical Descriptions,
has said, 'No single designer, nor the aggregate influence of the generations since,
has been able to alter the form, add to the legibility, or improve the proportion of
any single lettter therein'.

The stone bearing the inscription is three feet nine inches high by nine feet and
three-fourths of an inch long. The inscription is composed of six lines of lettering
within a moulding, practically filling the free space. The letters forming the two
uppermost lines are four and one-half inches high; those in the next two lines are
four and three-eighths inches; in the fifth line, four and one-eighth inches; and in
the last line, but three and seven-eighths inches. The spaces between the lines vary
proportionately. These variations serve to counteract an optical illusion. As the
tablet is over the doorway in the pedestal of the Column, the observer must look up
and view it obliquely. Since each successive row from the bottom to the top is,

therefore, further from his eyes, the letters, in rows, would appear progressively smaller were they actually the same size. By making them progressively larger, the illusion is created that their height is uniform. By varying the spaces between the lines the uniformity of colour was secured.

The individual letters composing the Trajan inscription are primal; their essential forms have changed but little from that day to this. Their conception was not a matter of elaborate and conscious design, but came from the inevitable developments of earlier Greek forms, of which, however, individual letters were somewhat more primitive in idea.

Two thirds of the early Greek majuscules were composed largely of straight lines with a minimum of curves; more than half of the Roman capitals contain curves that complement the straight lines in them and supply also a touch of grace. Almost every letter of the Roman alphabet is distinctive and individual, and severely beautiful in combination.

I am frequently asked by students why Roman capitals of the first centuries of the Christian era show such ungainly contrasts in the widths of individual letters,

A B C D E G N O P R S

asserting that they do not appear to be correlated in true proportions.

My own explanation of the varying widths I have set forth briefly in my comments under the block showing the Trajan E, infra; at this time I wish merely to assert that, to my eye, the clear cut simplicity of the Trajan letters, their distinctiveness, their general effectiveness in mass, all are enhanced by the variations in letter widths, items that I feel add also to their legibility and beauty in combination.* These capitals present an essential alphabet that is superior to the alphabetic forms of any other people.

The severe simplicity of their forms is not due to paucity of imagination; on the contrary, rather, to restraint in the exercise of imagination. They present the simplicity that is the child of taste and measure, not, however, the bastard simplicity that is mere crudity of outline or the fruit of geometric logic.

There is also a profound consistency in the Roman majuscules as a whole, notwithstanding the fact that the shape of the same letter often varies in the same inscription, from which it would seem that each letter was drawn in artistic relation to the adjacent letters, rather than in conformity to any fixed standard.

The variety of width of line and of proportion was in no way made necessary by the material in which they were cut or by the cutting tool itself. The fact that the natural handling of a pen or brush will produce similar variations makes reason-

* 'It was felt that the nature of the shapes of B and S, for example, essentially required a narrower measure than the square which M clearly demands. The letter S extended to a square...., would have been regarded in classic times as a barbarity.' Stanley Morison in Fra Luca de Pacioli.

able an assumption that the use of reed-pen or brush strongly influenced the shaping of the lapidary letters.

The letters were probably designed *in situ* by a master writer or letter artist who was able to draw, or write, or paint rapidly in outline on the stone, leaving the actual cutting of the letters to be done by another workman. That the designer worked 'freehand' is clearly shown by the variations in colour and proportion of many of the repeated letters. The shapes and proportions are those of pen or brush-drawn letters, but the *character* is that of the cutting tool used to produce them.

The great merit of the Trajan Capitals lies in their simplicity – every useless or meaningless line has been eliminated. When curves are necessary they do not follow the precise mathematical lines that can be struck by compass or bow-pen, but are carefully considered quantities that impart to the forms of a character which no mechanical construction can provide. Even the straight stems which one might reasonably expect not to present any particular quality of interest, when carefully scrutinised will be seen to be defined by lines that are not perfectly straight, that is, as a straight-edge would rule them, but which curve in slightly above and below the centres as arcs of a large circle merging gently and gracefully into the straighter portions of stems and serifs.

The curves themselves are especially interesting. In an ordinary black and white rendering of letters, the swells invariably are made heavier or fatter than the straight stems, because optical illusion would make them seem less heavy or thinner if drawn of the same weight or equal width. This 'illusion' is corrected in the Trajan letters in another way. The early Greek builders knew that to make a column look straight the 'straight' edges defining the column must be slightly bowed. The Roman letter artist, realising that if he cut the swells of his B, C, D, G's, etc., thicker than the straight stems, the shadow cast by the upper portions of the swells would add to the apparent weight of the curves and make them seem too heavy, therefore deliberately cut them lighter than a black and white rendering would require.

From the fall of Rome to the end of the Dark Ages, Roman lettering, as an art, deteriorated. Its beauty was not completely recaptured until the Renaissance. The artists of the Italian Renaissance grasped the true spirit of classicism; indeed, their work often surpassed in refinement and delicacy the best of the earlier Roman examples. It is only just to say that this may have resulted, in part at least, from changed conditions and the use of different materials. Much of the later lettering was done on tombs and monuments where it could be seen at close range, and usually was cut in fine and close-grained marbles, rather than in the coarser stone used for high memorial arches, façades, columns, etc., on which the inscriptions of the earlier craftsmen were displayed. In 1497 Fra Luca Pacioli wrote, 'It is the custom of many upon such pillars to place letters arranged in various ways which tell and declare the purpose of (the building) in the beautiful style of the ancients, in all due proportion; and the same on the other summits of pillars, tablets and monuments which, beyond question make the work very beautiful'.

Writers of various times have written treatises on the shapes of the letters of classical inscriptions. Some have made diagrams for their construction, attempting to fix geometrically the measurements of the forms and the relations of widths to heights. As early as 1375, Giovanni Dondi, a friend of Petrarch, wrote of the 'splendour' of the Trajan inscription; other early writers have called attention to it and expatiated upon the nobility of its letters. However, the treatise by Felix Felicianus in 1473 is probably the earliest manuscript on the forms of letters. It is generally assumed that the passages treating of the geometric forms of letters, found in the appendix to the *Divina Proportione* by Luca Pacioli, and printed by Paganini at Venice in 1509, is the first printed work,* but the recent discovery of a book by Damianus Moyllus, printed in Parma some time between 1477 and 1483, gives priority of date to Moyllus. Others followed: Fanti in 1514, Vicentino in 1523, Albrecht Dürer's *Geometrica* in 1526, Geofroy Tory's *Champ Fleury* in 1529.

Moxon says of Roman letters that 'they were originally invented and contrived to be made and consist of circles, arches (arcs) of circles, and straight lines; therefore those letters that have their figures entire, or else properly mixt...may deserve the name of true shape'. It is my opinion that not all letters, although composed of straight lines, circles, and arcs of circles will necessarily submit to analysis or be reducible to set rules of formation, since subtlety of line is not a matter of geometry, but of feeling. Moreover, Stanley Morison has said in his work on Pacioli that 'He' (referring to Geofroy Tory) 'habitually uses the Compass and the Rule because he is convinced that they are the King and Queen respectively of instruments. It follows that Tory judges a Roman Letter by the *method of its construction and not by its appearance.*' (The italics are mine.)

Constructing a letter on a geometric basis precludes taking into account certain optical illusions in which the designer of taste discovers those fine and almost imperceptible qualities that mean so much to the appearance of lettering in the mass. Beauty in letters depends on the adaptation of each of its parts to every other part in a well proportioned manner, so that the presentation as a whole will satisfy the aethestic sense. Harmony, grace, beauty and symmetry are secured by blending the fine strokes, stems, and swells in their proper relations, and not by merely combining the approximate geometric quantities. Beauty is too illusive to be snared by geometry. And even the stone-cut inscriptions of today which employ

* An imposing volume of the art of Pacioli by Stanley Morison, designed by and printed under the supervision of Bruce Rogers at the University Press, Cambridge, England, has just been published for members of the Grolier Club, New York. A chapter from Dürer's Geometrica, and Tory's Champ Fleury printed under Mr Rogers' supervision from his designs and arrangement were previous publications of the Club.

freer forms, based on metal types or hand lettering, seem mean, trivial and lacking in dignity when compared with truly classic characters.

Through all the centuries since the first use of Roman capitals, the essential forms have persisted almost without change. Yet unhappily, much of our modern work fails to disclose the spirit of delight in fine craftsmanship that is so evident in the Trajan Capitals.

Frederic W Goudy (1865–1947), *The Capitals from the Trajan Column at Rome*, New York, 1936.

A B C D
E F G I L M
N O P Q R
S T V X

Carol Twombly of Adobe's interpretation of the Trajan Capitals
(also used on page 87).

E RIC GILL'S *An essay on typography was written in 1930, the same year in which Stanley Morison's essay* The first principles of typography *appeared in vol. 7 of* The Fleuron. *Both essays still deserve to be read, at least once, by thinking typographers; but as Francis Meynell pointed out when he reviewed Gill's essay; 'It isn't an essay at all. It is a collection of nine scarcely related essays of which the third is called 'typography'. A fair part of this essay is actually about typography...but an unfair part is about industrial ethics, which obtrudes also into all the other essays.' It should be added that Gill's essay, in its second edition, 1936, is a particularly pleasing small book to handle, not least because of the illustrations drawn and engraved by Gill, which are a lesson in typography and lettering by themselves.*

Our excerpt here is taken from the eighth chapter, 'The book', and is chosen for its plain common sense. It should be read in Gill's own typography. A sample page is here reproduced as an example.

Gill was many things: among them, a sculptor, an engraver, an illustrator, and a superb portrait draughtsman in pencil. A dominating activity all his life, however, was lettering, whether drawn or carved in wood or stone. In type design, he gave the world two of the most famous types of the century, Perpetua and Gill Sans (eventually available in twenty-four different series, one of which, an ultra-bold version, was advertised under the name of 'Kayo' (see Typography *1, Nov. 1936, inset between pp 36 and 37). It is sometimes forgotten that he also designed eleven other type faces: Felicity (1926-30), Solus (1929), Golden Cockerel (1930), Joanna (1930), Aries (1932), Jubilee (1934), Bunyan (1936), Floriated initials (1936), Perpetua Greek, a Hebrew and an Arabic.*

The finest printed illustrations of a selection of his sculptures, lettering and drawings are in Joseph Thorp's Eric Gill, *1929; also to be recommended, among the ever-increasing number of works on Gill, are Robert Harling's* The letter forms and type designs of Eric Gill, *Svensson & Westerham Press, 1976;* Eric Gill: his life and art, *Thomas Fisher Rare Book Library, University of Toronto, 1991; and, of course, the biography by Fiona MaCarthy,* Eric Gill, *Faber & Faber, London, 1989.*

A BOOK IS A THING TO BE READ

¶ A book is a thing to be read – we all start with that – and we will assume that the reader is a sensitive as well as a sensible person. Now, the first thing to be noticed is that it is the act of reading & the circumstances of that act which determine the size of the book and the kind of type used; the reading, not what is read. A good type is suitable for any and every book, and the size of a book is regulated not by what is in it but by the fact that it is read held in the hand (e.g. a novel), or at a table (e.g. books of history or reference with maps or other necessarily large illustrations), or at a desk or lectern (e.g. a missal or a choir book), or kept in the pocket (e.g. a prayer book or a travellers' dictionary). ¶ On the contrary some hold that size of book and style of type sh'ld be specially chosen for every book; that such & such a size is suitable for Shakespeare; such and such for Mr. Wells's novels, such and such for Mr. Eliot's poems; that the type suitable for one is not suitable for another; that elegant poetry should have elegant type, & the rough hacked style of Walt Whitman a rough hacked style of letter; that reprints of Malory should be printed in ‹Black Letter› and books of technology in ‹Sans-serif›. There is a certain plausibility in all this, & even a certain reasonableness. The undignified typography of the Daily Mail Year Book is certainly unsuitable for the Bible; a fine italic might be suitable for Milton but unsuitable for ‹Tono-Bungay›; sans-serif may be suitable for a translation of Jean Cocteau but might be unsuitable for a pocket prayer book. And as to size: it is impossible to print the Bible on too grand a scale, but third-rate verse might look and be absurd in a book requiring a lectern to hold it. Nevertheless, the reasonable producer of books starts with the principle that it is the reading, not the reading matter, which determines the size of book and style of type; the other considerations come in only as modifying influences. In planning a book the first questions are: who is going to read this, and under what circumstances?

¶ If then, there are normally four sizes of books, it would seem that there sh'ld be four sizes of type. A pocket book demands small type, say 8 point, for reasons of space. A book held in the hand demands type of about 10 or 12 point on account of the length of the human arm and the normal power of human eyesight, assuming a normally legible type. Table books & lectern books, normally read further from the eye, demand types of still larger sizes, say 14 or 18 point or over. But the sizes of types named here are not binding on anybody; it is only the principle we are concerned with. ¶ The proportions of books were formerly determined by the sizes of printing papers. These were always oblong in shape (probably because this was the shape most easily handled by the makers, or, perhaps, because the skins of animals used for writing on in medieval times are of this shape, and so books followed suit) & when folded in half and in half again and so on, made a narrow folio, a wide quarto, a narrow octavo, &c. But with the machine made papers now almost universally used these proportions are only retained by custom, the width of the web of paper and the direction of the grain being the only determining factors. Books printed on machine made paper can, these factors understood, be of any shape that pleases you. And thus the commercial book designer is, to a greater degree than his predecessor, released from the thraldom of any considerations but that of what will sell.

¶ As to what does or should sell, we may say that the things which should form the shape & proportions of the page are the hand and the eye; the hand because books of wide proportions are unwieldy to hold; and the eye because lines of more than 10-12 words are awkward to read. (With longer lines, set solid, i.e. without leads between them, there is difficulty in following from one line to the next, &, even if the type be leaded, a long line necessitates a distinctly felt muscular movement of the eye and, in extreme cases, of the head.) As to the height of a page, this is again governed by the needs of hand & eye; a very tall page necessitates either a distinct movement of the neck of the reader or a changing of the angle at which the book is held in the hand, & such things are simply a nuisance. It may be that there are other considerations than those of physical convenience which have helped to determine the normal octavo page; it may be that such a proportion is intrinsically pleasing to the human mind. It is, however, sufficient for us to see that there is a physical reasonableness in this proportion, and we may safely leave the discovery of other reasons to professional æstheticians.

¶ The shape of the page being given, it remains to discover the best proportions for the lines & mass of type printed upon it. Here again physical considerations are a sufficient guide. Two things are to be thought of: the type & the margins. Let us consider the margins first. The inner margin exists simply to separate a page from the one opposite to it, and need be no wider than is enough to keep the printed words clear of the bend of the paper where it is sewn in binding. The top margin, again, needs only to be sufficiently wide to isolate the type from the surrounding landscape of furniture and carpets (just as a 'mount' or frame is used by painters to isolate a picture from wall paper, &c.). On the other hand, the outer and bottom margins need more width than is required for mere isolation, for it is by these margins that the book is held in the hand; enough must be allowed for thumbs, and the bottom margins need more than the side or outer ones. These physical considerations being allowed for, we may now consider the margins in relation to one another, & it will be seen at once that, taking one page at a time, i.e. half the 'opening', slightly more must be allowed to the top margin than is required for mere isolation; for if you make the top and inner margins equally narrow, the outer margin wide and the bottom still wider, the text will appear to be being pushed off the top. We may say then that the general rule should be: a narrow inner margin, a slightly wider top margin, an outer margin at least double the inner, and a bottom slightly wider than the others; the exact proportions being left to the judgement of the printer. It is to be noted that unless the outer margin be at least double the inner the two inner margins, seen together when the book is opened, will appear to be pushing the text outwards off the page.

¶ With a normal octavo page of 5 inches wide and 7½ inches high, & supposing that we allow margins as follows: inner, ½ inch; top, ¾; outer 1; & bottom, 1⅙; we shall get a type page 3½ inches wide by 5⅔ inches high (i.e. 34 lines of pica type, 12 pt., set solid). This allows for a line of an average length of 10-12 words in pica, & pica is a good ordinary size for a book held in the hand. Obviously these dimensions may be varied slightly without destroying the rationality or normality of the page, & type slightly larger or smaller than pica (12 pt.) can be used without extravagance or loss of legibility; though it is obvious that, for reasons of physical convenience, a variation that entails a lengthening of the line to more than 12 or 13 words is a variation in a direction less commendable than one that entails a shortening of the line. The dimensions given may therefore be taken as a norm.

¶ The title page should be set in the same style of type as the book and preferably in the same size. The unfortunate printers who regard the title page as the only source of interest in an otherwise dull job are the miserable descendants of those scribes who knowing and even appreciating the glory of the books they wrote out naturally gave a glorious beginning to them. The title of a book is merely the thing to know it by; we have made of the title page a showing-off ground for the printers & publishers. A smart title page will not redeem a dully printed book any more than a smart cinema will redeem a slum...

Eric Gill (1882–1940), *An Essay on Typography*, second edition, London, 1936; reprinted with a new introduction by Christopher Skelton, Lund Humphries, London / David Godine, Boston, 1988.

THE SHAPES OF LETTERS

The shapes of letters do not derive their beauty from any sensual or sentimental reminiscences. No one can say that the O's roundness appeals to us only because it is like that of an apple or of a girl's breast or of the full moon. Letters are things, not pictures of things.

Eric Gill, *Autobiography*, Jonathan Cape, London, 1940; reprinted with an introduction by Fiona MacCarthy, Lund Humphries, London, 1992.

The Book   105

is that of materialist triumph tempered by fanciful-
ness and sloppiness, & that they are altogether without grace either in the physical or spiritual senses of
the word.

¶ A book is a thing to be read — we all start with
that — and we will assume that the reader is a sensitive as well as a sensible person. Now, the first
thing to be noticed is that it is the act of reading &
the circumstances of that act which determine the
size of the book and the kind of type used ; the reading, not what is read. A good type is suitable for any
and every book, and the size of a book is regulated
not by what is in it but by the fact that it is read held
in the hand (e.g. a novel), or at a table (e.g. books of
history or reference with maps or other necessarily
large illustrations), or at a desk or lectern (e.g. a missal or a choir book), or kept in the pocket (e.g. a
prayer book or a travellers' dictionary). ¶ On the
contrary some hold that size of book and style of
type sh'ld be specially chosen for every book ; that
such & such a size is suitable for Shakespeare ; such
and such for Mr. Wells's novels, such and such for
Mr. Eliot's poems ; that the type suitable for one is
not suitable for another ; that elegant poetry should
have elegant type, & the rough hacked style of Walt

A page from Gill's An
Essay on Typography,
2nd edition, 1936, set
in Joanna.

PETER BEILENSON *was a serious printer and publisher who was able to look at his work with a non-serious eye. The passage here is taken from an essay about his own working life in* The Annual of Bookmaking, *published by* The Colophon *in New York in 1938. That admirable quarterly, started by Elmer Adler (q.v.) ran, in its original series, from 1930 to 1935. It had the peculiarity that nearly every article in each issue was contributed and printed by a different firm, occasionally not even in the United States. Beilenson's firm, the Walpole Printing Office, produced over the years twelve of the articles, and he also compiled 'A Listing of Types and Papers' for* The Colophon Index *volume of 1935. Perhaps Beilenson's most important literary work was the impressive chapter on 'Printing in the Nineteenth Century' in the third volume of* The Dolphin, A History of the Printed Book, *in 1938. He also wrote the biography of F. W. Goudy from which we have already quoted, and edited the Journal of the American Institute of Graphic Arts from 1947 to 1950. When he died, aged only fifty-six, his many friends joined to make a Typophile Chap Book,* The Life and Times of Peter Beilenson, *published in 1964, which contains a check list of more than 400 books for which he had been responsible from 1928 to 1962.*

THE WALPOLE PRINTING OFFICE

The Peter Pauper name was first used in the Spring of 1928. I had been working at the Rudge plant in Mount Vernon since the Summer of 1926, except for a leave of absence the following Summer when I had set type for Mr Goudy in Marlborough. Then in the Spring of 1927 I ambitiously left Mount Vernon to serve as a layout man in a misguided advertising agency in New York. I was fired at the end of my first week. With nothing to do but re-establish my pride, I set and printed a little book with the type and on the small hand-lever press I had previously installed in the family cellar in Larchmont.

This book was *With Petrarch*, Synge's translation of a few of Petrarch's sonnets. Like most limited editions of 1928 it was an immediate sell-out. There were only 100 copies, and Byrne Hackett took ten and re-ordered ten, while Harry Stone bought all the balance after a few other small sales.

For an imprint to put on the book I set up the words 'Peter Pauper Press' because they expressed how I felt about life at the moment, and the name stuck. Laymen and female booksellers thought it cute, and I had always been a sucker for alliterations myself. Although most of my waking hours since 1928 have been spent in trying (not usually with success) to outmode the appropriateness of the name, it has frequently served to remind us not to be too solemn, vain, inflated or grandiose.

Not only did Byrne Hackett buy the first Peter Pauper book generously, but he persuaded Edwin Arlington Robinson to consent to a reprint of *The Torrent and the Night Before*, which I was commissioned to print. Following the *Torrent*, and another Summer with Mr Goudy at Marlborough, the second book with the Peter Pauper imprint appeared, in the Fall of 1928. This contained a couple of Hood's comic ballads and again Harry Stone bought all the unsold copies. But Peter Pauper Publications remained intermittent affairs. My work at Mr Cary's newly-established Press of the Woolly Whale prevented any new ones until the middle of 1929. Random House distributed these, and their success, or at any rate the success of Bennett Cerf's and Donald Klopfer's interest and salesmanship as applied to them, was most gratifying.

The Fall of 1929 marked the first appearance, in *A Letter of Dr Franklin to the Academy at Brussels*, of the imprint 'At the Sign of the Blue-Behinded Ape', which we have occasionally used for things too odoriferous or unrespectable for Peter Pauper.

The Fall of 1929 is however far more important to us than as the date of the first use of that elegant imprint. On November 1st, a few days after the first market crash, Ned Thompson and I opened the doors of the Walpole Printing Office. This partnership continued until 1932; when Ned started his Hawthorn House in Windham, Connecticut.

Ned was a Rudge alumnus too. So was Walter Emerson, a young pressman who insisted he ought to come with us, and who I now insist must never leave. We had rented a five-room New Rochelle apartment over an empty store, and hoisted into it my small press and my type, some type of Ned's, a John Thompson press bought from Rudge, and the other usual requisites of a small printing office.

We chose the name of Horace Walpole because that old eccentric had operated the first English private press of importance; because the eighteenth century still looked good to us as a model in 1929; and because we thought the whole name suggested a gentlemanly establishment whose proprietors might well wear powdered wigs and silk breeches.

In actual practice we wore inky aprons.

Our landlord soon found that he couldn't rent his store downstairs with our presses rumbling on the first floor above, and paid us to get out. So we moved in 1930 to the rear of a high old garage, in the front of which a new Sears Roebuck store had just been opened. Inside this ugly shell we kept the spirit of Horace Walpole free from blight or mildew during the damp years between 1930 and 1935. (In 1935 we moved to a small white building in the Fleetwood section of Mount Vernon, where, with considerably increased equipment, we work today.)

I say 'we' although to my regret Ned Thompson decided in 1932 he would like to live in Connecticut and run his own printing office there. Our partnership was therefore dissolved; but my wife took his place as a sort of common-law partner whose share in the business is understood by everyone, although her name has never been entered in the official book of the County Clerk.

It didn't take me long to learn that an intelligent wife is the perfect partner. She has tastes that are fresh and worldly – sure cure for the monastic typographer; she can't abide typographic shibboleths – only way to develop new styles; she fights without hesitation and forgets without rancour – the perfect disposition for a partner; and best of all (if she is really intelligent) she always gives in to you at the end – or lets you think so. Anyway, Edna had good ideas about bindings, and in general thought about books from the dressmaker's viewpoint (let us say) rather than from my typographer's viewpoint. The combination of the two was better than either one alone.

Our composite philosophy of fine printing – if so solemn a phrase can be given to an attitude we seldom try to put into words – is that it should be fun, not duty. Printing is our job; and like any job you are tied down to, it easily gets boring. But fine printing is better if it doesn't get boring, and our recipe to avoid boredom would seem to be somewhat as follows:

First, set the text of your book in a good, readable type, in a reasonable length of line – thus satisfying the visual requirements at the outset. Second, lie awake at night thinking up interesting decorative, illustrative and style effects. Third, start putting your decorative ideas into type, or start discussions with your artist, only to find that your partner has decided on something entirely different. Fourth, search for the right paper in all sample books, and beleaguer all paper merchants – in vain. Fifth, with restraint explain to your partner that her plans for this particular binding are not only horrid in themselves, but utterly inappropriate to the rest of the book. Sixth, decide that your partner's binding ideas are not so bad after all. seventh, let stew for a week, at which time an unhackneyed book will emerge – or start again.

Peter Beilenson (1905–1962), *The Annual of Book-making*, The Colophon, New York, 1938.

T.M. CLELAND *was a great decorative artist who at one time tried to become an actor: the connection between acting and book-illustrating crops up time and again. In his early days Cleland was involved in amateur theatricals as designer, stage manager and actor, but he only once took on the artistic direction of an entire professional production, Rafael Sabatini's Scaramouche in New York in 1922. Its failure perhaps turned him back to drawing.*

For many years his main work was the design of advertising literature, by its nature ephemeral. His consummate skill in this field is fortunately recorded in The Decorative Work of T. M. Cleland, a book over which Elmer Adler laboured for four years to produce, with some illustrations reproduced in up to twelve printings (Pynson Printers, New York, 1929).

At the age of 24 Cleland became art director of McClure's Magazine; in the late 1920s he art-directed Fortune Magazine; and in 1930 he designed and illustrated The Decameron for the Limited Editions Club of New York, to be followed by four further titles for them: Tristram Shandy, 1935; Jonathan Wild, 1943; Essays of Montaigne, 1948; and Tom Jones, 1950.

The book about Cleland's early work already mentioned was reviewed by D. B. Updike in The Fleuron, vol. 7. The first three illustrations in the book are, as it happens, three title-pages Cleland designed for the Merrymount Press in 1904 and 1913. Updike makes an interesting point: 'The work that I admire so much is open, however, to one criticism. It has been cleverly said that Cleland is first of all an actor... Just as an actor sees the dramatic possibilities in the part he is to play, so Cleland sees the decorative possibilities in the particular school of decoration in which he is, like an actor, for the moment 'cast'. He seizes, therefore, the most outstanding characteristics of the style that he has chosen to work in, and to make them 'carry across the footlights' he slightly exaggerates them. The result is usually charming... We are tempted to inquire what Cleland could do when, working in no particular 'manner', he approaches things or Nature directly...'. A good question; but in my opinion it needs no answer, because most of Cleland's work in whatever style is so outstanding that it is no longer pastiche but creative in its own right.

Cleland designed only one typeface, Westminster Old Style or Della Robbia (a roman with very small serifs) (American Type Founders, 1903) but he also designed swash variants for ATF Garamond and a range of decorative borders and ornaments, perhaps the least original of all his design output, shown in the American Typefounders 24-page booklet Cleland Ornaments and Borders, c.1926.

There has been no biography of Cleland, but a talk given by Max Stein (the Limited Edition Club's long-time Production Director) to Gallery 303 in New York and printed in Heritage of the Graphic Arts, New York, 1972, gives a useful personal account of the man, with a striking Philippe Halsman photographic portrait.

Cleland, we learn, was an expert craftsman in wood and metal, and a gourmet who established a restaurant on lower Fifth Avenue and ran it for a considerable time. He was an inveterate enemy of many facets of modern life which he did not always understand, including 'modern art'; but his graphic work remains, and there has been no work quite like it since.

MY MISSION IS TO SUPPRESS TYPOGRAPHY

I refuse to bore you or myself by enumerating all the tiresome stock-in-trade eccentricities of the typographic expert in search of something new – the epileptic fits he throws to attract attention to himself at the expense of the words he is printing. You see enough of them every day to know what I mean. Nearly every magazine and newspaper page, not to mention a good many books, present the same revolting spectacle – the order of the day, it seems, is disorder.

And speaking of magazines, it has fallen to my lot from time to time in the past thiry-five years to design and redesign a number of periodicals of one kind and another. Such jobs require really very little actual work – it's by endless argument and conference that they can wear you to the bone. My simple purpose with these things has always been to bring any measure of order the case will permit out of the disorder in which I generally find it. My mission, if I have any, is to suppress typography, not to encourage it – to put it in its place and make it behave like a decently trained servant. I find magazines rolling in the gutter covered with the accumulated mud of years of dissipation. I pick them up and brush them off, give them a cup of black coffee and a new suit of clothes and start them off on respectable typographic careers. But like other missionaries, more often than not, I find them a year or so later, back in the same gutter, drunk and disorderly and remorselessly happy about it.

T M Cleland (1880–1964), from 'Harsh Words', an address delivered at the 18th annual Fifty Books of the Year exhibition of the American Institute of Graphic Arts in 1940. Quoted by Max Stein in his talk on Cleland printed in *Heritage of the Graphic Arts*. Bowker, New York, 1972.

T M Cleland, chapter initial for an automobile catalogue, 1916–1919.

FRED ANTHOENSEN *was a fine New England printer. The excerpt chosen here is an outstanding statement of a good printer's ideals.*

Anthoensen was by birth a Dane. He arrived in Portland, Maine, with his parents, when aged two, and remained there for the rest of his life. At the age of nineteen he joined the Southworth Printing Company as a composing-room apprentice: in 1917 he was appointed the firm's Managing Director. He set about turning the firm into the sort of book-printing house he wanted it to be. What it became can be seen in his book Types and Bookmaking (from which our excerpt is taken) which he published in 1943. Under his direction the firm became the Southworth-Anthoensen Press and later the Anthoensen Press. The book contains his own account of the press and his aims, a bibliographical catalogue by Ruth A. Chaplin, and specimens of the Press's work and its types and borders. Anthoensen's insistence on meticulous proofreading and perfection in every detail of manufacture, and in making the design appropriate to the book itself and at a price the customer could afford to pay, made the Anthoensen Press one of the best book-printing firms in the USA.

Anthoensen produced five titles for the Limited Editions Club, actually amounting to eighteen volumes. The two single volumes were designed by Anthoensen, the others were designed and illustrated by W. A. Dwiggins, of which the first was Balzac's Droll Stories in three volumes, 1932. Of this work George Macy wrote 'If there is a series of heavens to which books may go, I think each copy of this book will eventually be assigned to the topmost of these heavens. It represents, to me, the complete successful consummation of the arts of the book.' He might have said the same of Rabelais' Gargantua & Pantagruel, 1936, also designed and illustrated by Dwiggins, in five volumes. Each volume has a spine label with a drawing in colour which either reads as an attractive picture by itself, or as part of a continuous picture when the five volumes are in their correct order on the shelf. It is a masterpiece of amusing design.

Plutarch's Lives, 1941, in eight volumes making 3,538 pages, was the third Dwiggins title, an extraordinary achievement of book-making.

See Types and Book-making by Fred Anthoensen, Portland, Maine, 1943; Fred Anthoensen. A Lecture, by Walter Muir Whitehill, given at the Composing Room, New York City, 23 February 1966; and 'The Anthoensen Press', by Ruth A. Chaplin, Print, vol VIII, no 5.

THE SOUTHWORTH-ANTHOENSEN PRESS

More than sixty-eight years ago the Southworth-Anthoensen Press had its beginning in the private press of the Rev. Francis Southworth, which he established to print a religous paper and tracts for distribution among seafaring men in the port of Portland, Maine. It was about the year of 1875 that the first small press and a few founts of type were purchased. With this equipment his four sons learned to print his publications. After a time outside work was taken in and a printing business became established. This was the era in printing history when the use of twisted rules in imitation of lithographic effects was much in vogue, and taste in printing called for a different type for each display line. Printing in the early 1890s was in a sorry state, and it was not until younger men (who had been stirred by the revival in printing begun by William Morris, and made their influence felt) joined the organisation, that a fresher outlook was fostered.

In 1901 I joined the press as a compositor. Mr D. B. Updike and Bruce Rogers were working in Boston and Cambridge, well on the road to distinguished careers. It was through the specimens of their work shown in The Printing Art, that handsome and scholarly printing journal without a peer, before or since, under the editorship of Henry Lewis Johnson, that I became interested in fine printing. At that time it was the best source of study for the apprentice who had but few dollars to spare for books. It was to this journal, too, that I owe so much in determining and shaping my own career.

My development continued until 1917, when I was admitted to the firm as managing director. I then had an opportunity to put into practice ideas I had been thinking about. Like Baskerville, 'I formed to myself ideas of greater accuracy... ;' to endeavour to produce books and other kinds of printing according to what I conceived to be their true use and purpose. Before this adventure in printing could be exercised, new materials had to be collected and an organisation perfected. As I look back, many disapointments met me on the way, to be overcome, and a fresh start made.

As might be expected the types in the cases were unsuited for fine printing. These were replaced by a bare half-dozen types chosen chiefly for their historic origin, which were seemingly beyond criticism for beauty and utility. The principal faces relied upon for the majority of the work were Caslon, Scotch Roman and Garamond. Our composing machines were also equipped with similar faces. In later years my search for original material resulted in the addition of a number of seventeenth- and eighteenth-century types from European foundries, the matrices for which were still in existence. A collection of old typographic borders and printers' 'flowers', among the best available, were obtained. In this manner there were gradually built up exceptional resources of material which today stands unique among printing establishments.

Nor is any department of a press of greater importance than its proof-room. Accuracy, then, was my principal aim, because no matter how well a piece of work is designed and printed, unless the proof-reading has been thorough and critical, the purpose for which it has been printed is defeated. Many authors are somewhat careless in grammar, spelling, punctuation, and besides are inconsistent in minor details, even though they thoroughly know the subject on which they write. Such manuscripts need editorial scrutiny to iron out inconsistencies before type-setting is begun.

That proof-reading has been a highly complicated matter with any press having pretentions to scholarly work, is shown by an interesting letter from Baskerville to Robert Dodsley on 16 January 1754, in which he suggests to the publisher a scheme for preparing correct texts: ''Tis this. Two people must be concerned; the one must name every letter, capital, point, reference, accent, etc., that is, in English, must spell every part of every word distinctly, and note down every difference in a book prefaced on purpose. Pray oblige me in making the experiment with Mr James Dodsley in four or five lines of any two editions of an author, and you'll be convinced that it's scarcely possible for the least difference, even of a point, to escape notice. I would recommend and practice the same method in an English author, who most people imagine themselves capable of correcting. Here's another great advantage to me in this humble scheme: at the same time that a proof sheet is correcting, I shall find out the least imperfection in any of the types that has escaped the founder's notice. I have received great encomium on my Specimen from Scotland.' In this letter we see the serious consideration that Baskerville gave to the printing of correct texts, which does not differ greatly in method, today, in well-established presses.

Occasionally we are told to print a book exactly 'like copy', which does not always turn out very well. In 1925 for instance, we were asked by Alfred A. Knopf of New York to make a reprint of an English edition of *The London Perambulator*, by James Bone, with instructions to follow the English style and spelling. When the book was published a letter was received from Mr Louis N. Feipel, then editor of the publications of the Brooklyn Public Library, listing about forty 'typographical' errors. Mr Feipel, it seemed, had a hobby of noting and listing errors when reading books, and, sending them to the printer or publisher to their confusion. Simply following copy, even if it is 'English usage', is not a safe rule to follow. The proof-room staff, therefore, must possess a great variety of information, or the ability to locate it in reference books, when work of a critical or scholarly nature is undertaken.

As will be seen, a reorganisation of all departments of the Press was a preliminary step to fit it for the kind of work I wanted to do...

...The study of types and their employment by such masters as Baskerville, Bulmer and Bensley, has always been a dominant interest with me. While Bulmer is generally named as the first typographer in English printing in the eighteenth century, I prefer to place Baskerville first, as a matter of justice. Baskerville has had a greater influence on today's printing than most of us are aware of. His types, distinguished by an extended roman and narrow italic, are a significant innovation in design, and when he introduced them, he gave birth to a new form of printing, the 'modern' style. The *Virgil*, his first book, came out in 1757, and this was the first extensive use of his types* though he seems to have been experimenting since 1750. In letter design he increased the contrast between the fine lines and stems, imparting a delicacy and refinement that was a noteworthy achievement. Since Baskerville was a writing master he was probably influenced by calligraphic models in the use of continuous curves. His design is, therefore, characterised by a fluent line, as employed by the eighteenth-century writing masters. In the italic there is nothing of that cramped character seen in the italics of other foundries of his time. Their obliqueness is less pronounced, and a whole page printed with Baskerville's italic is not wearisome. 'In the italic letters,' says Dibdin, 'whether capital or small, he stands unrivalled; such elegance, freedom, and perfect symmetry being in vain looked for among the specimens of Aldus and Colinæus.'

In his printing, Baskerville wished to obtain brilliant effects and did three things to bring this about. The first, of course, was to create his own type, as no existing type met his views, as he has revealed in his Preface to Milton's *Paradise Lost*, 1758: 'I formed to myself ideas of greater accuracy than had yet appeared and have endeavoured to produce a set of types according to what I conceive to be their true proportion.' Second, he made his ink intensely black, which in a great measure gave his books much of their fine effect. Finally, to still further heighten the effect of his printing, he borrowed the idea from his japanning trade of hot-pressing the sheets, to give the printed pages a smooth, calendared finish. This method brought to his printing the appearance of printing *on* the paper and not *into* it, as is evidenced in his handsome edition of Shaftesbury's *Characteristicks*. The title-page of this book, with its design by Simon Gribelin, has 'all the power and brilliance of copper plate,' and in this book, I believe, Baskerville comes closer to realising his views for the perfect book. 'The title-page, in Baskerville's estimation, was a part of his work which required in all cases the most painstaking care, and, as a result one cannot but give him the credit of designing a series of title-pages that have rarely, if ever, in point of beauty been excelled.'* He definitely departed from the custom of his day to crowd as much information as possible upon the title-pages, an innovation which gave him more space in which to arrange his lines in a concise and simple manner. This is well exemplified in the title-page of his *Virgil*, to which Reed, in his *English Letter Founderies*, gives high praise: 'The work will, in my opinion, bear a comparison, even to its advantage, with those subsequently executed by the first typographer of our age [Bulmer]. There is a clearness, a softness, and at the same

* *His first specimen sheet also appeared in 1757.*

* *Straus and Dent, John Baskerville, 1906.*

time a spirit, altogether harmonising in Baskerville's book.' Dr Johnson must have been impressed with Baskerville's edition of *Virgil* for he gave his copy to his old Oxford college. It has become a landmark in the history of typography.

All other details of his books were just as carefully worked out as were the title-pages. He used generous leading between the lines of type, avoiding the least suspicion of crowding his pages. He surrounded his type pages with margins that deserved the name. The words in capitals, both roman and italic, were nearly always letterspaced. He used no typographic decoration, except an occasional row of type ornaments. Two of these, numbers 1 and 2 shown in plate XIV of Straus and Dent, were the most frequently favoured. By simple methods, and suitable arrangement of type sizes, he obtained his splendid triumphs. In the words of Macaulay his books 'went forth to astonish all the librarians of Europe'.

Fred Anthoensen (1882–1969), *Types and Bookmaking*,
Portland, Maine, 1943.

THE

LIFE of ESOP.

CHAP. I.

Of the place of his birth.

IT happened to Homer, the prince of Grecian poets, that the place of his nativity was never certainly known; and it would be as difficult to afcertain the country which gave birth to Efop, fo much have ancient authors differed alfo upon this fubject. Some have thought him a [1] Lydian born in the city of Sardis, the capital of that kingdom; others have believed he drew his origin from the ifland of [2] Samos.

John Baskerville's *Select Fables of Esop...* for R. and J. Dodsley, 1761: The top of page iii, actual size.

JOHN DREYFUS *succeeded Stanley Morison as typographic adviser both to the Monotype Corporation, in 1954, and to Cambridge University Press (which he had joined as a learner just before the war) in 1959. He is a prolific and authoritative writer and lecturer on typographic history: among his most important published works are The work of Jan van Krimpen, Haarlem, 1952; 'William Morris: typographer' in William Morris and the Art of the Book, Pierpont Morgan Library, New York, 1976; A History of the Nonesuch Press, London, 1981; and A Typographical Masterpiece (Eric Gill's collaboration with Robert Gibbings in producing the Golden Cockerel edition of the Four Gospels in 1931), The Book Club of California, San Francisco, 1990, and London, Bain & Williams, 1993.*

The piece here reprinted comes from 'Mr Morison as "Typographer"', a well-illustrated article published in Signature, new series, no. 3, March 1947. Apart from being an important essay on typography in general, one of its features today is the date of publication: it appeared when typography was not at all the recognised profession that it has now become. It underlines the immense influence wielded by Morison when there were many fewer 'typographers' than there are now. To develop a 'house style' for a great business, right across all its printed matter, is today almost a commonplace: it was not so in 1947.

For a bibliography of Dreyfus's writings, see his Into Print, British Library, 1994.

MR MORISON AS TYPOGRAPHER

The consistent feature of all Morison's typography is that the elements of it rest upon an analysis of the nature of the text and the purpose of the printing. In so far as jobs fall into categories, there arises in his mind a rational solution to a recurring problem. A solution is a solution that is applicable in relevant and parallel situations. Special cases he handled imaginatively and sensitively, but always in subjection to a sense of consistency and logic. For example, he now rarely uses upper and lower case for titles of books. As an instance of his rationalism, it may be recalled that, in the matter of running headlines, he argues that these 'may be set in capitals of the text, in upper and lower case of the text, or in a combination of capitals. Full-sized capitals over-emphasise what is, after all, a repetitive page-feature inserted chiefly for the convenience of librarians and readers interested in the identification of leaves which have worked loose. If set in upper and lower case, the headline loses in levelness, so that it seems well to employ SMALL CAPITALS: these are best separated by hair-spaces, since the unrelieved rectangular structure and perpendicularity of capitals tend to defeat instantaneous recognition.' Thus a problem had been examined and a solution that was rational had been accepted. Only if there was reason to change the treatment of this feature in a particular case was the rule departed from. In Morison's mind all running headlines will be set in hair-spaced small capitals forever unless the forms of the letters are changed.

The principles of book-typography which Morison set forth in the final number of *The Fleuron* were not new. Rather they were the sum of his own and others' experience. He has never desired to be original. He himself wrote that he proposed 'to formulate some of the principles already known to book-printers which investigation confirms and which non-printers may like to consider for themselves'. The principles which he formulated are acceptable, not because they led to the production of typography which was 'original', looked 'nice' or even 'fine', but because Morison's arguments show them to be rational.

Morison's influence upon others is due to his power of analysis of the *raison d'être* of the work in question. It has enabled him to bring about large-scale typographical reforms; enabled him, for example, to persuade the Post Office to redesign the telegram forms. *The Times* adopted his recommendations for the restyling of their newspaper. The revision was unique in the history of newspapers, for it required the designing and cutting *ad hoc* of a range of text and heading founts and the substitution of roman for gothic titling on the front page. The effect upon book, magazine and newspaper typography in Europe and the USA has been notable, and is still in progress. The entire *corpus* of the new founts made for *The Times* aggregated 5,973 separate punches. The reader can appraise the work involved from examination of the inset facing page 20 [in this issue of *Signature*]. The weight of the mainstroke of 'The Times New Roman' compares with that of Pierre Didot's roman; its set is determined by the editorial requirements. The italic is inspired by that of F. A. Didot. The chief novelty, indeed the basic contribution here made to the art of newspaper typography, lies in the sharpness of the contrast in weight between the body type and the headlines. He used the opportunity to revise the whole of the matter used in Printing House Square: poster letters, notepaper headings, labels and tickets. More recently Morison has designed new titles for the *Daily Express*, the *Daily Herald*, the *Continental Daily Mail* and the *Financial Times*.

When, in the final number of *The Fleuron*, Morison contributed to the body of the issue his now famous 'First Principles of Typography', he referred to typography as 'that admittedly minor technicality of civilised life, i.e. the aesthetic arrangement of type'. It is, then, not surprising that fifteen years later he decided to curtail his typographical activities. He has, however, found time to revise a large number of forms for Cable & Wireless Ltd., and his latest achievement is the new edition of the Roman Breviary, begun at Cambridge, for the publishers Burns Oates & Washbourne Ltd. He still visits Cambridge and advises the Monotype Corporation.

Despite his other responsibilities, his influence on typography in general con-

tinues. He has reminded printers of their duties to authors and to themselves, and
has provided them with a variety of good types, and has shown how they should be
used. It is a service for which any member of the reading public who 'takes print
for granted' should be grateful. The typographer who may come across specimens
of his work, will find in them something to admire; if they will take the trouble to
use his own method, i.e. to analyse and discover the *raison d'être* of the composition, they will find the exercise rewarding.

Those who work with him observe that he does not claim to 'feel', but is
content to think, that a certain form is the most appropriate to impose upon a
given piece of 'copy', and he will produce his reasons for so thinking. It is a habit
that leads him to demand reasons from those who propose alternatives. He is, in
fact, not a little stubborn in the use and defence of the methods he has found by
experience to suit the work. He appears, also, to believe that the active and conscious application of the reasoning faculty to the problems of the printed page is
an element in that intellectual hygiene but for which the mind, or at least his mind,
might hesitate to put forth the effort to consider problems of a far higher order.
Hence Morison may be described as, to use once again the words of Moxon, 'such
a one, who by his own judgement, from solid reasoning within himself', has elected to regard 'Typographie' less as an opportunity for self-expression, as the word is
commonly understood, than as a means of self-discipline.

John Dreyfus (1918–), *Signature*, new series no. 3,
March 1947. The article, 'Mr Morison as
"Typographer" ', is prefaced by an editorial note:
'The Editor is indebted to Mr John Dreyfus of the
Cambridge University Press for compiling the follow-
ing article. Information obtained from interviews with
Mr Morison about his work and his opinions is
embodied in the text. The Editor also wishes to thank
Mr Walter Lewis, Mr Brooke Crutchley, and Mr F. G.
Nobbs.'

WHEN I was writing Modern Book Design for Faber & Faber, in 1949, I dared to write to Bernard Shaw asking him to tell me something about the design of his books, which, before 1900, were in some ways innovative, and to which I knew he had contributed. He generously replied in his own hand, in the words which follow.

Shaw had decided that if he produced and published his own books, he would make more money. So he had taught himself how to do so, and then taught his printers, R. & R. Clark in Edinburgh, and Grant Richards, the publisher he had chosen, to do what he wanted. Battle ensued, but Shaw won, and not only because he was the customer.

Shaw was not really a designer, but he had some taste and a lot of determination and common sense. He gave his books a house style which served him very well and which has never looked dated. It is interesting to notice that his title-pages – and those of a few other publishers before and just after 1900 – were not centred.

MY INTEREST IN TYPOGRAPHY
BEFORE THE KELMSCOTT PRESS

My acquaintance with Morris led me to look at the page of a book as a picture, and a book as an ornament. This led to a certain connoisseurship in types and typesetting. I chose old face Caslon as the best after Jensen. I discarded apostrophes wherever possible (dont, wont, cant, shant etc but not Ill, shell, hell for I'll, she'll, he'll) and banished mutton quads between sentences because they made 'rivers' of white in the black rectangle of print. I was particular about margins. When I visited Chantilly I turned over every page of the famous Psalter.

All this began with Morris and his collection of manuscripts. The Kelmscott Press came afterwards when I already knew what he was driving at.

For my Standard Edition I changed from Caslon to Plantin because the small type I had to use in Caslon was very troublesome to keep clean. I fought linotype and monotype for some time because it would not justify as well as handset could be made to do; but at last, as always happens, the machine outdid the hand, and got all the best types on it.

I think this is all you want to know

G.B.S 28/3/1949.

George Bernard Shaw (1856–1950), letter to Ruari McLean, 28 March 1949, courtesy National Library of Scotland.

Pleasant Jefferson Conkwright, *born in 1905 in Oklahoma, had by 1964 won more awards for book design than any other American designer. No fewer than 41 of his books were selected by the American Institute of Graphic Arts for their annual 'Fifty Best Books' exhibitions.*

He spent ten years at University of Oklahoma Press, and in 1939 took over the design and production of books at Princeton University Press, where he remained until his retirement in 1970. He died in 1986.

He insisted that the books he designed should be comfortable to hold and read, that they should lie flat when open on a table, and that the spines should be easily legible on a bookshelf. The authoritative passage on University Press book design reprinted here comes from Graphic Forms – the arts as related to the book, published in 1949 by Harvard University, for whose Belknap Press Conkwright also designed books.

He was a charming and modest friend who, when he visited England, went for long walks (with a pedometer) studying lettering on buildings and elsewhere with a cunning and scholarly eye.

UNIVERSITY PRESS BOOK DESIGN

For a long time university press books have been looked upon as somehow a different breed from other kinds of books. This is a wrong view. Most of them are sold in the same markets and bear the same booksellers' discounts and authors' royalty as other books. They will break when you open them too vigorously; they will soil and fade when you treat them too roughly; and they will bleed when you cut them too closely – the same as other books. I wish they were different from other books. I wish they could be printed more evenly, on better paper, with duller and blacker ink, bound with better material, and stamped with a leaf or ink that would endure for generations. But in spite of careful rearing, university press books have acquired most of the physical vices of other books.

University press titles are good and not-so-good, like those of other publishers. Some of them have an extremely high blood count; some are almost scandalously virile. Twenty years ago Christopher Morley wrote an introduction to a university press catalogue in which he said that it had long been a sadness of his that the general republic of readers should hear so little of the thrilling books being published by the learned print shops. He exclaimed, 'Why should the Professors have all the fun? Such books as Professor Tinker's edition of Boswell's letters is surely just as rowdy a book as *Trader Horn!*' He observed that it was 'no longer necessary for a university press to publish its work almost as surreptitiously as *The President's Daughter*, or Clara Tice's drawings for Pierre Louÿs. Since the public has always a huge appetite for being scandalised, it is only fair to say that the works of scholars and scientists are always much more engagingly candid than even the pinkest of tabloids.'

The Princeton University Press has recently published a book entitled *The Court Wits of the Restoration* which is pretty strong stuff – a scholarly companion volume to *Forever Amber*, with bibliography and notes. This press has considered republishing the Earl of Rochester's poems, too, but I think Peter Beilenson has beat us to that – I believe under the imprint of the Blue Behinded Ape. Real scholarship is never limited to prescribed subjects, and the main business of university presses is scholarship. More people are discovering all the time that scholarly searches for truth can be high adventure, and more exciting than fiction.

The function of university press books, as with all books, is to communicate the author's ideas. (This statement has become a platitude because it is so obviously true.) A book's fitness to purpose depends on how well the author's ideas are communicated. One way to check a book's fitness to purpose is to conduct a little opinion survey shortly after the book has been published. It's rarely profitable to ask the author's opinion about the fitness of his book for several months, because authors naturally have some parental blindness at the birth of each little bundle of manuscript. But when the book is grown, and has gone out into the world and sinned or gained glory, the author usually can and will more properly appraise the fitness of his book. This appraisal can be helpful to the designer, either in new editions of the same book or in new books of like nature.

This polling method should not be leaned on too heavily. But technical and scientific books, such as university presses concentrate on, should not be tackled by a designer or left unwatched after publication without some consultation with the author or some of his colleagues. Certain unusual sizes and shapes may make them fitter books, and such things as extraordinary margins may have an obviously useful purpose in books of this kind.

It is possible to design a good looking scientific book without consultation with any scientist, or without any knowledge of science. But the looks of the book, especially the parts that so attract us at first – binding design and title page – may be only skin deep. It is also probable that the scientist himself, with a small amount of plagiarism, could design a book that might have a homely mug outside, but would have a heart of gold inside. With more knowledge of the science, and the needs of the scientist, it's reasonable that the designer can lay out a more useful book.

If this is true for books of science, it is also true for books of art, or history. The more of the subject of the text a designer knows, the more likely he is to turn out a fit book. One idea of how to design a book is something like this: First, the designer reads the manuscript and masters it, which gets him into the spirit of the work;

then, after quiet meditation, his cerebrum begins to turn in harmony with the text, and after a spell of this up comes a graphic interpretation of the author's message, exactly in tune with it. This isn't always the way it works. Some years ago, at the University of Oklahoma, I was given a book to design. The title of it was *The Philosophy of Our Uncertainties*, with an explanatory subtitle 'The Uncertainty of Our Philosophies'. After wrestling with it for days I thought, but not very positively, that I had finally comprehended a couple of sentences. Just how do you go about designing a book you don't understand? The way I did it was to fool with some ornaments, which is about the worst thing I could have done. The result was a series of round and square interlacing units, badly done, and signifying nothing. The best thing to do in such a situation is to go down a well-travelled road in broad daylight, and whistle.

University press books are generally meant to be works of more than ephemeral value. Some of them are advertised as 'definitive' – a much-used word also employed by other publishers. A 'definitive' work on any subject means: This is it; everything is here said about this subject that needs to be said. And the implication is that everything is said that will ever need to be said. Scholarly books of this kind, that are referred to frequently, need to be made more sturdily, and need certain basic fitnesses that novels, or books of more temporary interest, do not need.

One basic fitness scholarly books should have is an ability to lie open flat, when on a scholar's table, on his lap, or wherever he may have pushed it to one side on his workbench. It's disrupting to him, and highly annoying, to be forced to mark his place with an old paperweight or his spectacle case. Another basic fitness, I think, is that all sides be trimmed flush; it's much easier to riffle the pages to the required text. In an untrimmed book the pages go by in lumps of four or eight at a time.

The binding should be sturdy, and the title on the spine stamped durably. This is a hard thing to accomplish these days. In the Princeton University library there is an open shelf containing a wide selection of the most popular current books. This shelf, and all shelves like it that are extensively used, are sad things for any conscientious book-builder to behold. Broken hinges, faded stampings – some so bad as to be wholly unreadable. Some books with as few as five or six lendings are almost complete wrecks. A few, somewhat more sturdily constructed, after as many as twenty lendings are pretty bloody, but still doing business. The worst possible cloth to use on scholarly books is light coloured unfinished cloth. My observation is that dark, smooth cloth, stamped with genuine gold, is the best binding material. But it will pay any designer, I believe, to study carefully the open shelves in university and public libraries.

There has been a lot said and written about type faces and their fitness to certain purposes. Within certain small limits I think some type faces can suggest or be more in harmony with the spirit of the text than other faces. Some faces look poetic, and some look very prosy indeed. Some look like go-getters, and some look indolent. Some do suggest the past, and some are obviously callow youths. But this sort of conjuring of moods and periods with type can easily be pushed to the point of nonsense.

Some types, especially the square-serif and the sans-serif varieties, are so disconcerting to the eyes of a scholar that they should never be used for the text in books designed for him. Others have distinct, but less obvious personalities; some of these are aristocrats with long and honourable lineage – such as a few of the Caslons. Some have aristocratic names but have questionable origins – such as the machine-set Bodonis. There are other personality faces available on all type-setting machines that have quality in their own right, like Centaur, Caledonia, and Weiss, to mention but one from each of the composition machine companies. These personality faces can be used in printing scholarly books to advantage, and perhaps with some subtlety, in communicating the author's ideas.

There is another group of types, lacking personality but still used in an enormous amount of printing in this country, especially in books of reference – dictionaries, encyclopedias, anthologies, science books, and the like. These are the numbered types: Modern No. 1, 4, 8,[1] and so on, and Old Style No. 1, 3, 7,[2] and so on. Included in these no-personality types is Century, which is still used extensively. I think in most cases one of the personality types would be just as suitable for these reference books, and would provide a slight relish to those who are able to distinguish the difference. But the Old Styles and moderns have communicated an incalculable amount of knowledge in their lifetime, and have a vast potency of life in them yet.

1. Probably American Monotype faces.
2. Certainly American Linotype faces.

What is more important for the scholar than personality type is clear, readable type. Scholars as a lot are uncomplaining fellows; they have endured much and have learned to focus their eyes (sometimes through triple lenses) on smaller type than they should be forced to do. As a charitable principle, it is good, I think, to relieve the eyes of scholars wherever possible.

P. J. Conkwright (1905–1986), 'University Press Book Design', from *Graphic Forms: the arts as related to the book*, Harvard University Press, 1949.

THE FOLLOWING *passage is taken from the Introduction to* On designing and
devising type, *commissioned from van Krimpen by Paul Bennett for* The Typophiles *in
New York, published in 1957. It is a quirky, self-revealing and self-critical account of the gene-
sis and creation of his own type-faces, of which the best-known are Lutetia, Romanée (chris-
tened, incidentally, 'during a good dinner at a then well-known English country inn' at which
two bottles of Vosne-Romanée were enjoyed), Van Dyck, and Romulus.*

*Van Krimpen was born in Gouda, near Rotterdam, the son of a corn merchant. He was sent
to the Academy of Art at The Hague at the age of sixteen, where apart from drawing and painting he became especially interested in poetry and printing: Edward Johnston's* Writing &
Illuminating, & Lettering, *in Anna Simons' translation, and* The Imprint *(which began in
1913) became strong influences. He took up designing books and lettering professionally. In
1923, when he was thirty-one, he was invited to join the firm of Enschedé to look after what at
that time they were least strong in, design, and remained there virtually for the rest of his life.*

*The best introduction to van Krimpen's work, with illustrations superbly printed by
Enschedé, is John Dreyfus's* The Work of Jan van Krimpen, *a record in honour of his sixti-
eth birthday, Haarlem, 1952. The best expression of van Krimpen's own views is perhaps in
his* A Letter to Philip Hofer on certain problems connected with the mechanical cutting
of punches, *Harvard College Library and David Godine, Boston, 1972. It contains a facsimile
reproduction of the 39-page calligraphic letter (in which the famous argument with his friend
Stanley Morison about the mechanical cutting of punches is fully aired) and an invaluable
introduction and commentary by John Dreyfus. Walter Tracy's* Letters of Credit, *Gordon
Fraser/David Godine, 1986, contains a thoughtful and authoritative evaluation of van
Krimpen's importance as a type designer.*

ON DESIGNING AND DEVISING TYPE

Lettering as, so to say, a school for designing type has still another advantage. The
man who practises it will, whether he be told so or not, learn to understand that
'letters are things and not pictures of things'; or he will be no good even in lettering. He may, at the same time, make the arbitrary signs of the alphabet so much his
own that under his hand the subtle personal variations develop unconsciously.
This, of course, is the right thing: if they are conscious and premeditated they must
needs be worthless. Of any type-face come into being along these lines there
should be said, as Mr Stanley Morison does in a letter to me of a certain fount
sponsored by him, 'How far successful it is in type is not for us to say'. By which he
obviously means that posterity will judge and that its success will or will not be
proved by its survival as it stands or as an influence.

I do not know of many – perhaps I should rather say of any – designs for a typeface the initiative for the making of which was taken by the designer without his having the certainty, or at least a fair possibility, that his design would be produced; which seem to contain a promise of being successful in the way Mr Morison is thinking of. As a rule they are by young, too young, men who have neither submitted to discipline nor mastered sufficient knowledge of the craft of typefounding and its intricacies whichever of its nowadays manifold ways one may have in mind. As a consequence they will, if and when carried out, result in a compromise that is neither satisfactory to the designer nor to the producer.

All the foregoing is the philosophy of thirty-five years later. Its conclusion is that now, and apart from an answer to the question whether there is any promise of success in my own endeavours and performances – which it is not for us to give – I should be and am glad that I never attempted to design a type-face that was not commissioned and that I was not asked to make one before I was thirty years of age.

What I found I had learned before I started on my own was that, generally speaking, with the English and Americans there was a tendency rather too slavishly to follow historical examples excellent though many of these examples may have been. And that the Germans assumed too great a freedom in a field not naturally their own – theirs being Gothic and its several derivatives – having, at the same time, the presumption that they could and would teach the world at large what Roman type ought to be. The whole of which (with the Germans I mean) resulted in a lot of deplorable, and not seldom detestable, founts which, unfortunately, had a considerable temporary success in England and the United States in particular, and in particular in printing for publicity, and so gave German typefounding an infusion of life blood that must have been quite welcome in its war against the composing machines of every kind.

When, in 1923, I started on my first type design Mr Stanley Morison, whose dissertations on typographical dogma I had avidly followed from their very beginning in The Imprint, had (though rigorously opposed to an all too direct influence of calligraphy on type and most of all to calligraphic characteristics in it) not yet come to deny that type has anything to do with calligraphy, as he has done from the final issue of The Fleuron onwards, to maintain that type does and should derive from sculptured script. I had grown old enough to be aware, with or without Mr Morison's lessons, that type and calligraphy are two essentially different things and that calligraphic influence in type should, as I put it in that same final issue of The Fleuron, be no more than an underlying force. Shall I be able ever to convince him that sculptured script, inscriptions and the like, derive from some form of calligraphy and that, therefore, neither calligraphy nor sculpturing nor engraving should be disregarded when we think of type? I almost doubt it. For in the same letter I have already quoted from, and which is of a quite recent date, he writes in a way that seems to prove that he still sees the spooks alive which he, by his own mind and hand, has killed many years ago.

He says: 'When I, for better or worse, became interested in what is now called typography, the prevailing doctrine was firmly set, not by the typographers (for the simple reason that there were none) but by the calligraphers (of whom there were many), and these calligraphers were learned as well as experts. They dominated the situation in this country and, to a considerable extent in Germany, upon which country Britain depended for a good deal of its "display" material. It was a world dominated by [here he mentions three well-known calligraphers] on the one hand and [here is another well-known name] and the private presses on the other.

'It is possible that where you and I differ, is in the relative assessment we give to the crafts, calligraphy and engraving. I have been at great pains to maintain the engraving craft in the service of typography; to graft from the old tree of the hand-engraver upon the young sapling of the machine punch-cutter. This, you will say, is the wrong way to graft. If the hand punch-cutters had been numerous enough to organise themselves so as to take command of the machine I doubt very much whether you or I would have much to debate; the difficulties would have been solved, and engravers would have used the machine in accordance with their own traditional capacity. As it was, the machine fell into the hands of engineers who knew nothing about letter design fifty years ago...'.

And further on: 'I hold, however, that, in the last thirty years or so, due to the calligraphical doctrine I mentioned earlier, typography has been made to bear the weight of all sorts of calligraphical experiments, many of which went far to break down the true (as I hold them to be) standards of type-cutting. Thus came in a flood of pseudo-calligraphic designs.'

Our discussion went about the correct, or at least more desirable, way of using the punch-cutting machine. Whether I agree with Mr Morison on what he says about it – which, in fact, I do not: I say indeed that his is a wrong way to graft and that it would have yielded quite as little good results as the machine fallen into the hands of engineers – is of no importance here: I have just quoted him so extensive-ly to show how, in my opinion, he is throwing away the child with the bath-water. I can not here expatiate further on these points; perhaps later on, when saying a few words about the several type-faces I am responsible for, there may be an opportu-nity to revert to some of them.

I will not end this short report of my, as I have already said recent, difference with Mr Morison, and therewith this introduction, without quoting his last lines bearing on the matter and which seem to be perfectly conciliatory. Seem to be; since he leaves out my real point about calligraphy and so enables me fully to agree with him as far as he and it go.

These last lines run: 'Do you, or do you not, stand with me in recognising the fact that roman type from the end of the fifteenth century down to the twentieth century, was a casting from a mould made for the purpose of embodying a matrix from a hand-engraved punch? Secondly, do you stand with me in believing that four hundred years of such engraving creates in the image printed from these castings a second nature which is so strong as to be unchangeable? Thirdly, do you stand with me in believing that the imitation of the work of the hand-calligrapher by the hand-engraver is open to the same objection that you bring to [a name]'s pathetic self-satisfaction with his imitation of [another name] – with all warts? If you and I agree upon these three points then we can agree upon everything.'

I hope so but, my point of calligraphy as an underlying force being left out, I can, alas, not be certain.

Jan van Krimpen (1892–1958), *On designing and devising type*, New York; The Typophiles, 1957.

ABCDEFGHIJKLMNOPQ_RSTUVWXYZ
abcdefghijklmnopqrstuvwxyz
1234567890

ABCDEFGHIJKLMNOPQRSTUVWXY
abcdefghijklmnopqrstuvwxyz   Z&
1234567890

ABCDEFGHIJKLMNOPQRSTUVWXYZ
abcdefghijklmnopqrstuvwxyz
1234567890

Showings of, from the top, Romanée, Romulus and Van Dijck.

S EM HARTZ *wrote the following article for a keepsake to be given to those who attended a lecture by John Dreyfus on Jan van Krimpen in the 'Heritage of the Graphic Arts' series at Gallery 303 in New York on 14 October 1965. It is an astute piece of observation by one who knew his subject intimately, although he was never van Krimpen's pupil.*

Hartz, born in Leyden in 1912, was the son of a Dutch painter and musician mother. He was apprenticed as an engraver to the great stamp and banknote printing firm of Enschedé in Haarlem, and became the firm's Art Director after van Krimpen's death in 1958. Hartz has designed and engraved over 300 postage stamps and many banknotes, engraved portraits of the Dutch royal family, provided lettering for many buildings in Holland, and designed three distinguished type faces, Emergo, Juliana, and Molé Foliate. He is also the author of The Elseviers and their Contemporaries, 1955: *his knowledge of both written and colloquial English (and also French and German) is remarkable.*

Selected illustrations of his work, and nine articles about him (two in English), are published in S. L. Hartz in de grafische wereld, Rijksmuseum Meermanno-Westreenianum, 's-Gravenhage, 1969.

ON ASSESSING THE EARLY WORK OF JAN VAN KRIMPEN

On assessing the early work by Jan van Krimpen one is struck by the seemingly Germanic influence apparent in design and letterform. It is only after one realises that, at the moment van Krimpen became interested in them, German printing and lettering manifested the teachings of Johnston and Gill, that this influence is seen to be more English than Germanic.

Anna Simons taught lettering, as a stand-in for her teacher Johnston, in a State-promoted course for art teachers at Dusseldorf. Count Kessler commissioned Johnston, Gill, and Noel Rooke to do lettering and wood engravings for his Cranach Presse and for Insel Verlag, the great publishing house he was connected with. Johnston even designed a type for Kessler.

Mason and Emery Walker wrote articles and supervised influential German printing. Even Johnston's classic treatise *Writing & Illuminating, & Lettering* was read by van Krimpen in Anna Simons' translation. At that time the Germans were as assiduous in the buying of talent as the Americans are now.

All this activity started as early as 1904 or 1905 and culminated in the Graphic Art Exhibition of 1914 at Leipzig; Newdigate said that he seemed to see, in the German Pavilions, 'the hand of Johnston on every stall and on every wall'. Young van Krimpen avidly studied all there was to be seen.

Meanwhile a significant thing had happened in Holland. De Roos had designed a new and original typeface, produced by the Amsterdam Typefoundry. The type was an instant success and is in use to the present day. Van Krimpen used this Hollandische Mediaeval up to the 1920s when he and his friends were influenced by the renaissance of Caslon in England. Then for several years he used Caslon almost exclusively.

Jean François van Royen paved the way for van Krimpen's later development, when he suggested that some of the ancient typefaces owned by the Enschedé's should be used for the Zilverdistel publications. This first contact by van Krimpen with the Enschedé firm became a lifelong companionship, the incidents of which are excellently described in Dreyfus's book on van Krimpen.

In the meantime his own lettering lost much of the 'drawn' character so evident in De Roos' work.

The Lutetia face was the culmination of this slow development towards the printing type that was bound to come. To the mind of the present writer the first cutting of Lutetia after van Krimpen's drawings, but without his personal supervision during the making of the punches, is more successful than the later version. The punchcutter, in his unhampered rendering of the designer's drawings, seems to have interpreted rather than followed them, producing a happy looking typeface. The designer, however, insisted on a recutting of the type and although it certainly is flawless in its final form it has a slightly stilted look which is absent from the first version. On the other hand the symbiosis between van Krimpen and his punchcutter Radisch proved to be beneficial to both.

Van Krimpen's designs became more and more finished leaving nothing to the punchcutter's initiative, the daily contact between the designer and punchcutter grew to perfect understanding, and the designer thought more and more, as it were, 'in steel', learning to appreciate the delicate adjustments the good punchcutter makes almost without realising what he or his tools do to the design.

The almost funny mistake of trying to design a roman to an existing seventeenth-century italic by Van Dijck shows how little chance the artist has to step out of his own time. Instead of a successful resurrection, like many of the well-known book faces in everday use now, Romanée, intended to be a copy of an old type, became a wholly independent design. It shows once more how personality, if any, shows in the handiwork even if the perpetrator wants to suppress it.

The two decades that passed between the designing of the roman and the italic made for a discrepancy. United they fall, apart they stand as fine designs. In Spectrum the solution was found. Roman and Italic are in perfect harmony, though the present writer thinks of Romanée as the finest roman van Krimpen designed.

Jan van Krimpen's work as a typographer is well known in Britain. Not so well known, perhaps, in that country are the books he did for American and French publishers. A double title of a book done for George Macy's Heritage Press in New York are included in the inset.

The few examples illustrated can do little to give the reader an idea of the development of the complex nature of van Krimpen's mental make-up, for a subtitle for an article on van Krimpen could well be: 'From Angry Young Man to Angry Old Man'. This anger can be easily explained if one takes into consideration how circumstances in the trade developed during his lifetime.

De Roos and van Krimpen came to the front in the battle against the gradual decline and loss of taste in typography at the turn of the century, of which the younger typographers of this epoch have but a very faint idea. It is worth while to inspect the best books made at the time of which some of our old publishing firms have kept quite a collection; it makes one realise how far even these attempts at perfection are below the level of our run-of-the-mill productions today.

The tragedy of De Roos and van Krimpen is that after the Second World War – perhaps in the nostalgic atmosphere of a shrinking empire – England set the fashion in admiring and making pastiches of Victorian tastelessness. This fashion was taken over in a humourless and watered-down form in the Netherlands. Thus both De Roos and van Krimpen lived to see the things they had fought against, each with his own weapons, held up as models of virtue.

De Roos has special artistic abilities which gave him the opportunity to retire into his own world where he worked as happily as an old gardener in a walled-in vineyard. But the steadfast character of van Krimpen, coupled with his focalised talent, made it impossible for him to accept with wise resignation things he despised. He would always retaliate if he had the feeling that book typography was harmed in any way. For he was – and this is often forgotten by those who opposed him – a specialist with all the inhibitions of specialisation.

No typography outside the typography of the book existed for him, and all the busy doings of advertising, sales-promotion and the like, he abhorred, like the people and jargon connected with them. Unforgiving he stood in the breach for what he thought to be right. Lonely because of his unrelenting criticism of situations and persons, harsh and unforgiving, knowing that his realm was isolated.

No doubt the young van Krimpen was formed by the circle of young poets and literary critics to one of whom he was related by marriage. His mind whetted by their brilliance, his enormous powers of perception and absorption stood him in good stead. His thirst for knowledge and keen judgement in matters of taste stayed with him to the end like the capacity to enjoy the other good things of life.

The distinction of van Krimpen's work is best seen among specimens of the same character. A portrait by Hilliard or Oliver is not seen to advantage in the company of Van Goghs and Rouaults.

The epicurean and the sybarite in van Krimpen are mirrored in his typography. The mathematician's order and elegant precision are manifested in his type designs. There are countless examples of types used in a better way by others than by the designers themselves. But nobody has, as yet, used his types to better purpose than van Krimpen himself. This is not surprising after all, because, notwithstanding the fact that van Krimpen was a great propagandist of 'invisible' typography, his type designs are so very much his own, so personal that they are seen at their best when they are used by their creator. He was a designer for designers, as there are painters for painters, admired by their brother artists but less known among the interested public.

It is hardly possible for a contemporary to judge the greatness of one man compared with those that surround him. Those considered gods in their time are later forgotten, and the really great loom slowly from the murk of time to take their place. Van Krimpen's true eminence will be judged by future generations. To those who can only look back a little way he seems an important figure, not only because of the example he set, but also because of his relentless persecution of everything slipshod or illogical.

Van Krimpen died with sword and whip in hand, proud and lonely in his own world.

> Sem Hartz (1912–), from A Keepsake presented at a lecture on Jan van Krimpen in the series 'Heritage of The Graphic Arts' delivered by John Dreyfus in New York at Gallery 303 on 14 October 1965, printed and presented by Joh. Enschedé en Zonen, Holland.

Device for Enschedé by Sem Hartz.

Paul Rand *was born in Brooklyn, New York, in 1914. He studied at the Pratt Institute, Parsons School of Design, The Art Students League and under George Grosz, the great and savage German illustrator who emigrated to the USA in 1933. By 1936, Rand was Art Director of Esquire and Apparel Arts. He went on to become one of America's outstanding designers, with an extraordinary lightness and gaiety of touch, never boring, and an amazing fertility of invention. Perhaps his most famous designs were for IBM and Westinghouse: he also designed many memorable magazine covers and book-jackets, especially for Knopf. For illustrations of his work, see Paul Rand. His Work from 1946 to 1958 (Knopf, New York, 1959) and A Designer's Art, (Yale University Press, 1985), from which the two pieces quoted here are taken.*

The first piece is part of a lecture given in New York in 1959. It is a discerning appreciation of just how much American design at that time owed to the modern movement in Europe, in particular to Jan Tschichold.

THE GOOD OLD 'NEUE TYPOGRAFIE'

In 1959 in a paper titled *Typography USA*, the Type Director's Club announced: 'At last a new form...an entirely new concept in typography has been realised, a typography that is purely American. This new typography, the product of contemporary science, industry, art, and technology, has become recognised internationally as the "New American Typography"!'

In the light of what has happened and what is happening in this field in America, it is very difficult for me to understand this claim. This is not to say that the statement is deliberately misleading, but merely that I, personally, am unaware that anything of the sort is occurring.

The writer goes on to ask: 'What is the new form?' My response: I don't know. And to the next question: 'What does it look like?' I can only say that the best of it looks like typography that could have come from Germany, Switzerland, England, Holland or France. Briefly, it is an offspring of the International Style, which means not only a blending of the ideas of different peoples but an interaction of the different arts – painting, architecture and poetry: the poetry of Mallarmé, the ideograms of Apollinaire, the collages of Picasso and Braque, the montages of Heartfield and Schwitters, the paintings of Doesburg and Léger, the architecture of Oud and Le Corbusier.

To deny the fact that American typography is basically a continuation of, sometimes a retrogradation from, and sometimes an improvement upon the 'new typography' which was nurtured on the continent of Europe, is to ignore the revolutionary impact of Cubism, Dadaism, and all the other 'isms' of the early twentieth century. It is also to overlook the influence of movements such as *de Stijl*, the ideas of the Bauhaus, and the contributions of those who changed the face of traditional typography.

There is little question but that such a thing as American illustration or even American automobile or refrigerator design exists. Whatever their merits, they are American, not Americanised. On the other hand, I believe the New American Typography can more accurately be called the New Americanised European Typography, given its origins.

This is not to say that individual American designers have not made valuable contributions to typographic design, but these contributions have been mainly variations of basic European principles. Nor do I mean to deny the fact that an American designer such as Morris Benton, in redesigning such typefaces as Garamond and Bodoni, has done significant work. In this connection, however, it is my understanding that while the redesign of typefaces is vitally important, the typeface is only one ingredient in the overall design complex. It provides only the what and not the how. Furthermore, it is somewhat ironic to note the very generous use of European typefaces in the New American Typography. How many printed pieces use Venus, Standard or Didot, not to mention the classical designs – Garamond, Caslon, Baskerville, Bodoni, Bembo – all of European origin?

It is difficult for me to think of any single book on modern American typography that would, for example, equal the Swiss publication *Typographische Monatsblätter*, let alone such classics as Tschichold's *Die neue Typographie*, *Typographische Gestaltung*, or even his later, more conventional *Designing Books*. In 1929 Douglas C. McMurtrie wrote *Modern Typography and Layout*, a book which contained some excellent illustrative material as well as some scholarly text. The make-up of this book, however, was in the modernistic style – a rather questionable example of typography, American or otherwise.

No fair-minded person. American or European, can deny the influence of the American designers Goudy, De Vinne, Bruce Rogers, and Dwiggins on both American and European typography. However, when we compare the enormous impact on modern typography of just one European designer – Jan Tschichold* – there is little doubt that the influence of the aforementioned designers has been far more limited.

This is still true today, even though Tschichold later switched to traditional typography.

Before we are able to evaluate the New American Typography, we must necessarily place it in its historical context – a rather difficult undertaking for designers, people engaged in doing rather than philosophising. I believe that at the present time we are too close to the trees to evaluate the situation. No doubt in time we can hope to produce a more indigenous kind of typography, one which satisfies our basic needs through original form solutions, rather than one which is obsessed with a style. I am afraid that at the present time it is impossible for me to answer the question, 'What is this new form?'.

Good typography, American or otherwise, is not a question of nationality but of sensitivity to form and purpose. In the 1920s, when Tschichold wrote his revolutionary book on modern typography, he did not call it German, Swiss or French, he called it simply – Die neue Typographie.

Paul Rand (1914–), *A Designer's Art*, Yale University
Press, New Haven, 1985; from a lecture given in 1959.

THE GRID SYSTEM

Like the architect's plan, the grid system employed by the graphic designer provides for an orderly and harmonious distribution of miscellaneous graphic material. It is a system of proportions based on a module, the standard of which is derived from the material itself. It is a discipline imposed by the designer.

Unlike the Modulor, it is not a fixed system based on a specific concept of proportion, but one which must be custom-made for each problem. Creating the grid calls for the ability to classify and organise a variety of material with sufficient foresight to allow for flexibility in handling content that may, for one reason or another, be altered. The grid must define the areas of operation and provide for different techniques, pictures, text, space between text and pictures, columns of text, page numbers, picture captions, headings, and other miscellaneous items.

Here is the grid designed for this book. Devising such a grid involves two creative acts: developing the pattern that is suitable for the given material and arranging this material within the pattern. In a sense, the creative ability required for the former is no less than that for the latter, because the making of the grid necessitates analysing simultaneously all the elements involved. But once it has evolved, the designer is free to play to his heart's content: with pictures, type, paper, ink and colour, and with texture, scale, size, and contrast.

The grid, then, is the discipline that frees one from the time-consuming burden of making certain decisions (dimensions, proportions) without which fruitful and creative work is extremely difficult. One can move directly to those aspects of the problem in which individual expression, novel ideas, and freedom of choice are essential.

The grid system has as many detractors as it has adherents. Its detractors generally misunderstand its use or its potential – and that it is merely a tool. It has been condemned as stifling, rigid and cold. But this confuses the product with the process. The grid does not automatically ensure an exciting solution. The designer must still exercise all the experience at his command: discretion, timing, and a sense of drama and sequence. In brief, the intelligent designer will recognise that the grid can help him achieve harmony and order, but also that it may be abandoned when and if necessary. To function successfully, the grid system, like all workable systems, must be interpreted as freely as necessary. It is this very freedom which adds richness and a note of surprise to what might otherwise be potentially lifeless.

Paul Rand, *A Designer's Art*, Yale University Press, 1985.

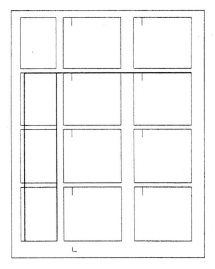

THESE EXCERPTS *from a talk given by William Golden to the Type Directors Club of New York in April 1959 (the year of his death) make a very important point: 'that the designer could also think...the "layout man" was becoming an editor'.*

This applies perhaps above all to magazine design. It has been said that the right way to design a magazine is for the designer to become also the editor. It is often forgotten that magazine design consists of a great deal more than just finding a typographic dress for a collection of words – and possibly pictures – put together by an editor. Certainly, design starts when the first planning of the magazine and its contents is undertaken.

William Golden was a remarkable man. Humbly born on the Lower East Side of Manhattan as the youngest in a family of twelve children, he became in 1940 the Art Director of CBS (the Columbia Broadcasting System). While there, he was responsible for some of the most original designs ever used in the communications industry, including the famous CBS 'eye' trademark (see illustration) designed primarily for television. The pupil was an iris diaphragm shutter which clicked open and shut, revealing whatever text was needed, inside the circle.

After Golden's early death, his wife Cipe Pineles edited and designed The visual craft of William Golden *(Braziller, New York, 1962). It is arguably one of the best books about a designer ever made. It contains articles by, among others, Will Burtin, Ben Shahn, and Feliks Topolski, and a photograph portrait of Golden which corroborates Topolski's almost lyrical description of his friend: 'Unbelievably, his handsomeness embraced his spirit'.*

IT IS A VERY COMPLICATED JOB TO PRODUCE SOMETHING SIMPLE

What is right about current typography is so apparent when you see it that it requires no explanation. What is wrong is a little more complex.

It is not as difficult to define what is wrong as it is to find how we got there.

I have my own notion of how we got where we are, and though I have neither the competence nor the ambition to be a typographic historian, this is roughly how it looks from one viewpoint.

Some thirty years ago the rebellious advertising and editorial designer in America was engaged in a conspiracy to bring order, clarity and directness to the printed page. He fought against the picture of the factory, the company logotype, and the small picture of the package that invariably accompanied it. He protested that the copy was too long, and that he was obliged to set it so small that no one would read it. He argued that the normal ad contained too many elements. (He even invented the 'busy' page in some effort to accommodate himself to it.) He insisted that this effort to say so many things at once was self-defeating and could only result in communicating nothing to the reader.

He was essentially picture-minded, and only reluctantly realised that he had to learn something about type. It was and still is a damned nuisance, but when he realised how thoroughly its mechanical and thoughtless application could destroy communication of an idea, he had to learn to control it – to design with it.

More and more typography was designed on a layout pad rather than in metal. Perhaps the greatest change in American typography was caused by this simple act – the transfer of the design function of the printer to the graphic designer.

The designer was able to bring a whole new background and a new set of influences to the printed page. He could 'draw' a page. There was more flexibility in the use of a pencil than in the manipulation of a metal form. It became a new medium for the designer.

Under the twin impact of the functionalism of the Bauhaus and the practical demands of American business, the designer was beginning to learn to use the combination of word and image to communicate more effectively.

Under the influence of the modern painters, he became aware (perhaps too aware) of the textual qualities and colour values of type as an element of design.

And surely a dominating influence on American typography in the prewar years was exerted by the journalists.

Newspapers and magazines were the primary media of mass communication. The skilful development of the use of headline and picture was a far more prevalent influence than the European poster. The newspaper taught us speed in communication. Everyone knew instinctively what the journalist had reduced to a formula: that if you read a headline, a picture, and the first three paragraphs of any story you would know all the essential facts.

The magazine communicated at a more leisurely pace and could be more provocative since it addressed a more selective audience. Because the magazine dealt more in concepts than in news it was far more imaginative. There was more opportunity here, to design within the framework of the two-page spread. But still, the device that bore the main burden of interesting the reader, was the 'terrific headline' and the 'wonderful picture'.

Perhaps it was the growth of radio, a rival medium, that hastened a new effort on the part of the magazine.

Certainly the new technical developments in photography increased the range of its reportage.

But what gave it a new direction and style was not so purely American. I think it was men like Agha and Brodovitch. These importations from Europe set a pace that not only changed the face of the magazine and consequently advertising design, but they changed the status of the designer. They did this by the simple process of demonstrating that the designer could also think.

The 'layout man' was becoming an editor. He was no longer that clever, talented fellow in the back room who made a writer's copy more attractive by arranging words and pictures on the printed page in some ingenious way. He could now read and understand the text. He could even have an opinion about it. He might even be able to demonstrate that he could communicate its content better and with more interest than the writer. He could even startle the editor by suggesting content. It wasn't long before he began to design the page before it was written, and writers began to write to a character count to fit the layout.

Whatever successes this revolution achieved were accomplished by demonstration – by individual designers proving to their clients and employers (by solving their problems) the validity of their point of view and the value of their talents. It was accomplished without a single design conference in New York or in Colorado or anywhere else in America.

William Golden (1911–1959), talk given to The Type Directors Club of New York, 18 April 1959, reprinted in *The visual craft of William Golden*, ed. Cipe Pineles Golden, Kurt Weihs, and Robert Strunsky, published by George Braziller, New York, 1962.

The CBS eye designed by Golden for television, 1951.

Tʜɪs ᴇxᴛʀᴀᴄᴛ *comes from Hofer's introduction to* The Artist and the Book 1860-1960 in Western Europe and the United States, *published by the Museum of Fine Arts, Boston, and Harvard College Library, in 1961. The book accompanied an important exhibition assembled by Hofer at the Museum of Fine Arts in 1961. The subject of both exhibition and book was not 'book illustration' but books containing original graphic work, often called livres de peintres — books whose essence lay in the images or pictures they contained, not the words.*

The Artist and the Book, with Hofer's text, had its illustrations superbly reproduced by the Meriden Gravure Company's 300-line screen offset-lithography. It is also perhaps unique in having a screen laid across the type to make it look lighter. At the proof stage, the designer found that the typeface chosen was too heavy in relation to the illustrations, and since to reset would have been prohibitively expensive, the printer, Harold Hugo, Director of Meriden Gravure Company, achieved the desired effect with a screen which is not perceived by the naked eye.

Philip Hofer was the editor of Baroque Book Illustration, 1951, the first important book printed by Meriden using 300-line screen, showing a quality in the reproduction of engravings never previously achieved.

Hofer was also the moving spirit behind two other magnificent works printed by Meriden: Parts I and II of Harvard College Library Department of Printing and Graphic Arts Catalogue of Books and Manuscripts: French 16th Century Books, 1964, and Italian 16th Century Books, 1974, each in two large volumes and each compiled, under Hofer's eye, by the late Ruth Mortimer. The title-page of every book catalogued is reproduced.

Philip Hofer was essentially a wealthy book collector. His obituary in The Times on 22 November 1984 points out that his expertise in the study of the links between drawings and prints, and the collections he made of book decoration, layout and illustration, built up, from 1933 onwards, 'such a monument to the art of the book as he and no other could have conceived'.

For forty years his base was the Printing and Graphic Arts Department at Harvard University, which he had initiated and of which he was Curator. He was a generous man to those who shared his interests, even if they were competitors. His own collections were bequeathed to the Fogg Art Museum and the Houghton Library in Cambridge, Mass.

THE ARTIST AND THE BOOK

This exhibition is to show, primarily, what major artists of Western Europe and the United States have contributed in book form during the last hundred and, especially, the last sixty 'explosive' years. The absence of well known names will indicate that some important European and American artists passed the medium by. Among these Cézanne, van Gogh, Monet, and Seurat — to take the French artists as an example. But those French masters who did concern themselves were far more numerous: Daumier, Courbet, Manet, Toulouse-Lautrec, Bonnard, Vuillard, Redon, Rodin, and nearly all the later 'School of Paris', beginning with Derain, Dufy, Picasso, Braque, Rouault, and Matisse. As a result, the French have recently awarded books by these artists a special name or classification: *les livres de peintres*. The phrase has also come to mean books that contain *original* graphic work by the masters in question. Books by sculptors of equal eminence are included in this category – hence the Museum of Modern Art's 1936 title – but *not* books by that special classification of artists who are primarily engaged in illustration.

For this reason it was decided that the word 'illustrators' used in the 1936 exhibition would be misleading in this one. And for another reason too. The painters and sculptors of wide reputation have not always been willing to illustrate, in the literal sense, the work of an author selected by the publisher. They have rather chosen, especially in recent years, to make varied and daring abstract designs, or to express new graphic ideas of their own involving complicated techniques and surface textures to which the publisher has been hard put, sometimes, to attach a relevant literary accompaniment. Thus today there are many remarkable 'modern books' that are not 'illustrated', but 'created' or decorated, and many that are hardly books at all except in their format. One need not applaud these developments, but one must recognise them. Ideally, the illustrated book should be a harmonious combination of textual and pictorial elements, each significant, and each of relatively equal importance. This is the classical tradition, and it is still the one which publishers normally support.

To use the book form more flexibly, however, can be justified on several grounds. First, because it enables both the artist and the publisher to reach a wider clientele. Second, because the book, properly bound and shelved, is one of the most durable of all art forms, being resistant to rough handling, fire, water, breakage – indeed to almost all the normal hazards. Third, since lithographs, woodcuts, engravings, and other graphic processes are usually printed in quantity and relatively cheaply, the public can be offered the artist's original work at a much lower price than his paintings or drawings which are unique. And, finally, now that the artist is well paid for his work – as professional illustrators have usually not been – a rapidly growing number of the most talented painters and sculptors have become attracted to the arts of the book. This quite startling recent evolution is particularly evident on the continent of Europe which has, as usual, followed the lead given by France. It is not yet apparent in the Anglo-Saxon world of Great Britain and America, where a prejudice against 'book illustration', long held to be a minor art form, has been strongly entrenched. In 1960, in continental Europe, by contrast, collectors were seeking the *Tauromaquia* of Pepe Illo illustrated with twenty-six etchings by Picasso before publication at a price of more than two thousand dollars a copy! Soon after, it reached four thousand.

Another main purpose of this exhibition, therefore, is to demonstrate to the English-speaking world that during the last century *the book has, in fact, become a major vehicle of artistic expression*: that it is one in which the artist is not necessarily secondary to the author, but is often and rightly his equal. Indeed, in some cases, illustration is the major substantive factor in the book that finally appears. This is especially true in France, which possesses not only great artists, but also great technicians. Finally, the illustrated book usually offers the purchaser two values at once: an artist's designs and a text in words – a combined pictorial and literary expression of man's best creative talent. Inexpensive books with reproductive illustrations will also do this – but only at a loss of irreplaceable artistic values. The layman may be content with photomechanical prints. The connoisseur never is except for reference purposes.

At the end of the fifteenth century, a single artist in Germany, Albrecht Dürer, revolutionised the attitude of the Central European artists to the arts of the book, by printing and boldly signing fifteen large woodcuts illustrating the *Apocalypse*, with his initials, 'A.D.'. Thereafter, many other Germanic masters did likewise till the tradition died out in the eighteenth century. In France, the Netherlands, and Italy, by contrast, no such tradition prevailed, although slowly in these countries the more important artists were drawn to the book form for such reasons as are given at the beginning of this introduction. Then, at the end of the nineteenth century an imaginative Paris publisher, Ambroise Vollard, gave the French artists the patronage, the freedom, and commissions which had been wanting. Thereafter, despite two world wars and every kind of economic difficulty in France, the *livres de peintres* became so popular that even the enormous cost of present-day *quality* production has not slowed a movement which it is not an exaggeration to call an explosion as well as a revolution.

Of course, Vollard's initiative was timely or it would never have succeeded so quickly and brilliantly. Moreover, he spent a fortune accumulated in picture dealing on educating the public, in producing books which took years to prepare, and in exacting the highest standards of workmanship and material. Had he noted the magnificent folio *Sonnets et Eaux-fortes* to which many leading French artists contributed in 1868 at the behest of the Paris publisher Alphonse Lemerre? If not, he certainly was aware that an increasing number of French nineteenth-century painters were experimenting with the book form despite the fact that nearly all their efforts had ended in financial failure. The great problem was to open the intelligent bookbuyers' eyes and pocketbooks. By offering them the new concept of the *livres de peintres*, outstanding names, and sound values, Vollard succeeded before his death in 1939 in changing completely the prevailing taste of the leading collectors. And this exhibition will attest, by the number of entries due to Vollard, and to certain other great publishers, such as Kahnweiler in Paris, and Paul and Bruno Cassirer in Berlin, what a debt artists and the public owe to them for the startling developments of the past six decades, in which there has occurred such an outpouring of great illustrated books on the continent of Europe.

Philip Hofer (1898–1984), from introduction to *The Artist and The Book 1860–1960 in Western Europe and the United States*, Museum of Fine Arts, Boston, and Harvard College Library, 1961.

ODE XLVII

Sur les vieillards.

J'aime à voir les danses joyeuses des jeunes et des vieux. Un vieillard qui danse est vieux par les cheveux, mais il est jeune par l'esprit.

63

Lithograph by Derain (reduced) in *Odes Anacréontiques*, Cercle Lyonais du Livre, 1953, illustrated in *The Artist & the Book 1860 – 1960*.

'PRINTERS AND DESIGNERS' is the text of a paper read to the Double Crown Club in London on 3 December 1963. It is one of the best statements ever made about what ought to be the relationship between designers and people who use designers, and what they owe to each other to function properly – in brief, what design is all about. It was written in the early days of the revolution in printing technology which still, thirty years later, perplexes us. Spencer's statement that 'Today most high quality printing is produced in relatively large printing offices' is, as he forecast, no longer true: word-processing, typesetting, reproduction of illustrations, plate-making, etc., are all more and more being handled by small firms or individuals. Also to be noted is Spencer's emphasis of the point that the purpose of the printed word is not so much to be read as to communicate, which is different.

The second passage, also published before 1970, is from the introduction to Spencer's book Pioneers of Modern Typography, Lund Humphries, 1969 (revised edition Lund Humphries, London / MIT Press, Cambridge, Mass. 1982).

Spencer pioneered 'modern' typography, in the Tschicholdean sense, in England after 1945. He was an early freelance designer for publishers and industrial firms; he edited a brilliant and innovative periodical Typographica, which ran to 32 issues between 1949 and 1967; he became design adviser to the printers, Lund Humphries in Bradford, Yorkshire, who in the 1930s were the first people in Britain to give design commissions – and an exhibition in London of his work – to Jan Tschichold. Spencer's Design in Business Printing was published in 1952; he taught at the Central School of Arts and Crafts from 1949 to 1955, where several of his pupils later became internationally famous graphic designers, among them Colin Forbes, Alan Fletcher, Ken Garland, and Derek Birdsall; and from 1966 he was on the staff of the Royal College of Art, London, becoming Professor of Graphic Arts until his retirement in 1984.

Photography has always been an important part of Spencer's creative life. In 1961 he drove from Marble Arch to London Airport (a distance of about 20 miles) photographing every road sign, and published a selection of these in twelve pages of Typographica (new series) 4, demonstrating a ludicrous 'jumbled jungle of words'. The issue certainly played a part in the subsequent creation of Britain's national road signs system. Spencer on any aspect of lettering or typographic design and legibility has something important to say.

PRINTERS AND DESIGNERS

It is a well-worn platitude that the purpose of the printed word is to be read. This is a gross understatement. The purpose of all printing, whether of words or of pictures, is to communicate – ideas, information, instructions or emotions. The printed message should not be merely read but understood. Often its purpose is to spark off ideas or activities.

Society will, in the long run, use printing only for those tasks which printing can fulfil more effectively, reliably and economically than other competing mediums of communication.

The present decade is a fascinating and exciting period in printing and publishing. A wide range of technical developments is waiting to be exploited by imaginative printers, designers and authors and bold publishers willing to adopt energetic (and not necessarily conventional) methods of selling and distributing their products. In a century so packed with important developments in science and technology and man's political ideas and social outlook, the book as a tool of civilisation has an invaluable function to perform. If all the achievements of scientists, scholars and technologists in this century are not suddenly to collapse like a house of cards, specialists in one field must somehow keep in touch with the thoughts and aims and achievements of other men working in others. Television, films, radio all have an important part to play in answering this challenge. But the book still has unique advantages: it is passive; it is permanent; it is portable. The owner of a book can take what it has to offer wherever and whenever he wishes – and at his own pace. He can consult several books on the same subject at the same time, and so try to arrive at a balanced personal judgement. No other method of communication offers all these advantages.

And what is true of the book is equally true of many other kinds of printing. But while it is true that for many purposes the printed word has advantages over other existing techniques of communication, it does not automatically follow that the printing industry, as it is at present organised, can rely upon a rosy and assured future. Many important developments in the past ten or twenty years have been in the field of 'office printing'. Like the scribes of the fifteenth century, any of today's professional printers take a rather lofty view of such developments. But some of the techniques of office printing offer considerable advantages of speed, convenience, and cost over conventional printing methods. The end product may not be of the same quality as 'proper' printing, but then conventional printing is itself a poor substitute for calligraphy. And just as conventional printing gradually evolved its own aesthetic standards so too will the newer techniques of reproduction.

There are therefore today several alternatives to conventional printing as a means of communication. Printing, if it is to be effective and is to compete with other media, has got to be good. And good in this sense means not just technically well-printed but well-designed. And well-designed means properly planned to do its job – clearly laid out, certainly, but also printed on the materials and by the process and to the standard appropriate to its particular purpose and function. Extravagantly produced ephemera may, technically, be good printing but it is not good design.

There is, of course, no such thing as 'undesigned' printing. No matter how brief the message (or how bad the end result) all printing is designed by somebody – the client, the printer's representative, the order clerk, the works manager, the composing room overseer, the keyboard operator, the compositor at the case. Indeed, quite often they all take a hand in shaping the final result. Somebody has to decide the format, the width of margins, what typeface to set the words in, the size and position of illustrations, the colour of ink and kind of paper, the method of binding. Consciously or unconciously considerations of taste, fashion, tradition, convention, convenience, efficiency and expediency determine the final result.

When printing was a far less complex activity than it is today, printing offices were small and compact and all these decisions were made by the master printer who personally discussed each job with his customer and personally instructed the members of his 'team' (and often carried out part of the work himself). The master craftsman's standards were higher and, generally, his personal skills were greater than those of his employees.

Today most high-quality printing is produced in relatively large printing offices. At his most effective, today's master printer is a business man with a shrewd understanding of economic trends, able to weather takeover bids and all the demands and machinations of twentieth-century commerce and to negotiate with staff and trade unions. He creates opportunities for good work and printed results in which he and his staff can take pride.

I have said that the purpose of all printing is to communicate. Printing does this most effectively when it is consciously planned and arranged by someone qualified by his training and experience to attempt to equate the demands of author, reader and producer. This, today, is the function of the professional designer.

The properly trained professional designer has a clear understanding of the techniques of modern printing. His task is to lay out and arrange a piece of printing so that it will serve its purpose effectively and with reasonable economy. His specifications and instructions must be clear and precise, and it is his responsibility to ensure that he retains adequate control over his work during the course of production.

It is sometimes suggested that the designer should not concern himself with the process of reproduction. This I believe is rank nonsense. Are building materials and construction techniques no concern of architects?

The competent graphic designer today is not just a man who decorates the surface of a sheet of paper. The paper, the printing technique, the method of binding – these are all things that vitally affect the function, the appearance and the cost of any piece of print and as such they are all part of the designer's responsibility.

How, then, is the professional designer to fulfil his responsibilities and to per-form his task efficiently? As a free-lance or in direct association with a printing firm? To obtain – or, more often, to extract – a clear brief the designer must nor-mally deal direct with the client. An intermediary will invariably, perhaps inevitably, change the emphasis of the client's instructions – vaguely expressed preferences, for example, generally become absolute conditions – and many pertinent questions are left unasked. Most clients provide a crude specification rather than a proper brief. What the designer wants from the client is a clear statement of the purpose of any projected piece of print – is it intended to persuade or inform, to sell a prod-uct or instruct the buyer? Who will read it – rich or poor, highly educated or semi-literate – and under what conditions – at home, in the office, or travelling from one to the other, indoors or outdoors? These are all factors which ought to influence the format and size of type, the kind of paper and colours used. And the client ought to decide in consultation with the designer the appropriate budget for the job. (One man's shoestring is longer than another's. And the sky as a limit has an unhappy habit of drawing much closer after the preliminary design has been pre-pared!).

If the client has confidence in his designer – and if he has not he ought at once to choose another – he should try to give him a full and honest brief concerning the purpose of any piece of print, and sensibly discuss both the budget and the pro-gramme for producing it. He should avoid making arbitrary decisions regarding size, number of pages, colour and other details which are properly matters for the designer to decide. The client should select a designer whose taste and judgement he respects and he should not seek to impose upon his designer his own tastes and prejudice in matters of colour, type or other elements of design. (An intelligent, experienced designer will of course respect an established house style and not lightly depart from rational standardisations of size or colour which the client may already have introduced).

These, then, are all reasons why the designer must deal direct with the client. This direct relationship, which is something the freelance designer normally enjoys, is denied to the majority of employed designers, including many of those who work for printers. This is unfortunate, because it seriously reduces the contri-bution the designer is able to make, encourages careless 'hack' work and generally leads to frustration on the part of the designer, and dissatisfaction on the part of the client. All this suggests that it is as a freelance that the designer can operate most efficiently and with proper authority.

Yet there are also strong arguments why the designer should work in close day-to-day touch with a printing firm.

What complicates the printing process is the fact that although printing employs many of the techniques of mass production each job is unique. (Stamps and packaging and banknote printing are obvious exceptions). Only through an intimate knowledge of a firm's technical facilities and the individual abilities of those it employs is it possible for a designer in printing fully to exploit its resources.

But the designer can only really make an effective and worthwhile contribution within a printing firm if he has adequate authority.

This means his advice must be sought and allowed to influence a wide range of policy decisions. He must generally have direct access to clients and be actively supported by sales representatives who have at least as clear an understanding of the firm's design policy as they do of its printing standards and technical resources. And of course the designer's authority must be understood and respected in the works. A printing firm cannot evolve a sound design policy – or even, today, hope to offer an adequate design service – on the basis of an occasional bright idea thrown out by some obscure backroom boy hidden from clients and the light of day and fed only on *Graphis* and *Design* magazines.

Very few printing firms do, in fact, provide the fertile ground essential to a consistently high standard of design.

The growth of offset litho and gravure, and of photocomposition and other ways of producing text matter in an acceptable form for photographing on to the plates, will, I believe, lead during the next twenty years to great changes in the organisation of the printing industry in this country.

For reasons both of economy and expediency, the great majority of printing firms will gradually relinquish all control over the preparation of the printing forme or artwork. They will concentrate on standards of press work and reproduction and service but they will not be in any way responsible for the layout or initial preparation of what they print. But the effect of this movement away from the traditional pattern of the industry will be, I think, to confirm the position and the structure of the relatively small number of firms, of medium size, who successfully provide an integrated design and printing service.

In short I think the future pattern is likely to be this:

Most printing design will be planned by professional designers in private practice. Most printers will print but not design or take any part in the initial preparation of what they print. But a limited number of firms in which design and production have been properly co-ordinated will continue to offer clients a 'package deal'.

These firms will inevitably specialise, in the type of work they produce, to a far greater extent than is usual at present.

In those printing firms in the future which offer such a service the designer will play a vital role in the shaping of policy.

It is therefore, I suggest, quite clear that in future, whether he acts in private practice or as a principal of a printing office, the designer is going to be faced not only with opportunities but also with considerable responsibilities. But is the design profession in fact equipped to meet these responsibilities? And, especially, is design education in this country geared to the probable future demands of society and industry? Increasingly during the past twenty years, graphic and industrial design and typography have passed into hands that have been formally trained to serve the requirements of the profession and to produce work of a high standard of technical competence. But far too many art and design schools have been content simply to turn out skilful performers in an accepted idiom rather than men able to think out solutions in a logical and creative way.

Unfortunately, there are I believe close and uncomfortable parallels between late nineteenth-century typography and the situation in graphic design today.

Until the middle of the nineteenth century typographical experiments were largely confined to variations of the type design, but the invention of the platen machine led, about 1870, to a new kind of printing known as 'Artistic Printing'. This style made considerable use of coloured inks and of elaborate ornament and decoration (often quite unrelated to the subject matter of the text), and incidentally brought about the first real departure from the centred layout of the book printer. Artistic Printing, at its best, encouraged high standards of craftsmanship and considerable technical ingenuity. But, especially in the diluted form of its commercial application, it was skill misapplied so far as the true purpose of printing is concerned.

It was not long before most printers had utterly lost all notion of true printing tradition. They had squandered their creative inheritance and were either imprisoned in a web of sterile convention or involved in an orgy of technical gimmickry without any discernible regard for the printed word as a means of communication. Not surprisingly quite soon they lost the respect of both the public in general and of their customers in particular. Aesthetically bankrupt and confused, the printing industry was quite incapable of picking up, or even of recognising, the frayed ends of its severed traditions. It was ready to relinquish (though not without resentment) control of design to 'amateurs' such as William Morris and those who followed in his wake.

The flippant and irresponsible use of important technical innovations debased late nineteenth-century printing. The printing industry lost sight of its true function and allowed its compositors to manipulate words for their own and their colleagues' amusement without regard to the value of the results as communication. In the end, the word was rescued from all this gimcrackery by painters, writers, architects and others who came to printing from outside the industry and, who, during the first half of this century, gradually eliminated vulgar affectation and restored to printing both logic and discipline.

Today we are in the throes of another technical revolution in printing. Metal is gradually being eliminated from composition. Released from its discipline the designer is free to place his lines of type at angles, and he can curve, cut or split display lines and juxtapose one line of type closely against another, or he can, if he wishes, superimpose one word upon another. This freedom from mechanical restriction provides the designer with wonderful opportunities for producing imaginative and sympathetic visual solutions and of conveying the author's message with great precision. But equally the designer can, if he chooses, use this new opportunity – as the late nineteenth-century compositors used theirs – not for better communication, but merely for superficial pattern making.

Unhappily, there are clear indications that both in the graphic and product design fields far too many designers are today working for the approbation of their colleagues rather than in an honest attempt to solve specific design problems to the best of their ability. They are motivated by fashion rather than conviction and they are rapidly undermining the basis and principles of twentieth-century design. Inspired by personal uncertainty, some of them are trying to turn the design process into a kind of professional mystique enclosed in a rigid yet ever-contracting circle which excludes all true creative activity. But the designer needs to have a heart as well as a head and his head should contain more than just a pair of eyes. Just as I do not believe the honest designer can or should, or ever wants to, shed sound traditions nor do I think he ought ever willingly to embrace sterile or artificial conventions – not even newly created ones.

The design profession is today faced with a challenge to its integrity. There are at present, I suggest, too many 'designer's designers' at work with the result that the public is in many cases being starved of the sound and aesthetically satisfying products to which it is entitled. This is a condition which can ultimately be cured only by design education of adequate breadth and vitality.

It is of course the principal aim of the new diploma courses which recently began in selected art schools in Britain to ensure that designers should in future be educated and not merely trained.

It is to be hoped that the men who emerge from these courses during the late 1960s will be well equipped to tackle many of the vital and responsible tasks which will then face the printing industry and the design profession.

The future of the printing industry will depend ultimately upon how responsibly designers face up to their task. While printing serves society as an efficient means of communication it will survive. If it ceases to fulfil this function more effectively than other mediums of communication then it will wither.

Because it had no adequate alternative means of communication, late nineteenth-century society was I think more tolerant of its printers' frivolity than late twentieth-century society is likely to be.

Herbert Spencer (1925–), a paper read to the Double
Crown Club in London, 3 December 1963.

PIONEERS OF MODERN TYPOGRAPHY

Many early examples of modern typography are manifestos and other publications issued by the designers themselves, but in Holland in the mid-1920s two men especially were responsible for applying to commercial advertising the principles of de Stijl and of Constructivism: Piet Zwart and Paul Schuitema. They did so without making concessions, and Zwart's press advertisements for NKF and Schuitema's designs for Berkel are among the most vigorous and penetrating early examples of the new typography. Zwart and Schuitema devised both the message and the technique used to convey that message. They utilised the types they found in the printer's cases, but they liberated them from their horizontal straitjacket. When they used photographs or photomontage, as they often did, they did so not as an embellishment, but in order to make the message immediate and international.

In Germany, in October 1925, modern typography was introduced to a wide audience of practical printers for the first time through the publication of a special issue of the printing trade journal, *Typographische Mitteilungen*. Written by Jan Tschichold, who was then 23, this publication established Tschichold as an ardent and persuasive advocate of asymmetrical typography. In his practical work during the late 'twenties and early 'thirties, using the machine-composition series of typefaces that were then becoming available, Tschichold demonstrated the subtlety, the precision, and the elegance of which modern typography is capable. But in the articles and books which he wrote during this period, Tschichold attempted to formulate a narrow definition of modern typography. The simple rules-of-thumb which he then proffered were quickly grasped by compositors and printers and, at first, Tschichold's dogmatic assertion of his ideas served to quicken the pace at which asymmetric typography was adopted by the German printing industry. However, in relation to the emerging techniques of reproduction and new needs and opportunities in publishing and in advertising, Tschichold's attempt to codify modern typography in this way was neither necessary nor relevant. It was an endeavour which controlled the spirit of modern typography and one which, if it had succeeded, would have done much to vitiate it and to diminish its essential vitality and flexibility.

The fundamental difference between traditional, centred typography and modern typography is that the one is passive and the other is active, though not necessarily aggressive. Asymmetry and contrast provide the basis of modern typography.

At the beginning of this century most printing was still done by letterpress from metal type. The Futurists, however, as we have seen, had successfully thrust off the horizontal discipline which the invention of printing from movable types had imposed upon the page. Many years in advance of the development of methods of phototypesetting and the invention of dry transfer lettering they had produced compositions which were fundamentally non-linear in conception and which, even with today's resources, can hardly be surpassed as demonstrations of typographical freedom and flexibility. As writers and artists, they had looked at the page with the eyes of the recipient rather than, as the printer had done, with those of the producer. In their determination to achieve printed images that were dynamic, the Futurists had presented their printers with extraordinary demands, and they had persuaded, cajoled or bullied their compositors into remarkable feats of ingenuity in the manipulation of typographical material.

In his *Manifesto of Futurism* Marinetti had proclaimed the importance of contrast. In the early works of the Futurists, and also in those of the Dadaists, contrast was achieved through the combination of a wide – and, sometimes, a wild – variety of types that were markedly different in weight and size as well as design. The departure from symmetry and horizontality imbued these compositions with a sense of movement and vitality, but it was the Constructivists and de Stijl who explored the spatial opportunities of asymmetrical design and who first clearly indicated how tension, impact, drama, and excitement, on the one hand, and clarity and eloquence, on the other, could be introduced into the printed page through the free but sensitive distribution of space and the interplay of type and paper. The work of the Constructivists and de Stijl also showed how colour could be employed as a fundamental design element rather than as a mere embellishment added as an afterthought.

The early typographical works of Lissitzky, Schwitters, van Doesburg and Zwart are animated by the imaginative use of contrast in the utilisation of space, by the dramatic distribution of black and white, and by the skilful exploitation of colour. Their pages vibrate from the impact of powerful and sometimes surprising typographical juxtapositions. With care and discrimination they selected from the wood and metal types they found in their printer's cases those letters that were sympathetic to their conceptions. When the letter-shapes they required were not readily available they did not hesitate to construct them out of metal rules and ornaments and other odds and ends ferreted out of forgotten corners of the composing room. The choice of typefaces in these early works was, however, subjective and quite uninhibited by the theories that were later to assume such importance at the Dessau Bauhaus, and to determine the design of much printing produced in Germany during the late 'twenties and early 'thirties.

After 1925, Herbert Bayer, at the Bauhaus, and Jan Tschichold, at the Munich School, both energetically encouraged the use of sanserif types and both designed geometrically-constructed sanserif alphabets. Sanserif types reflected the notion of 'beauty in utility', which had become the pivot of Bauhaus experiments, and they also permitted more subtle typographical contrasts of visual weight. Bayer argued strongly in favour of a single alphabet – 'why should we write and print with two alphabets? We do not speak a capital A and a small a' – and after the move to Dessau the Bauhaus began to abandon the use of capital letters in its publications. Both Tschichold and Schwitters experimented with phonetic alphabets.

The debates about typefaces, about serifs, and other typographical minutiae which, during the late 'twenties and subsequently, have often surrounded modern typography, have sometimes obscured its fundamental characteristics and the advantages, in terms of visual fluency and clarity, which flow from the imaginative use of contrast and asymmetry. This book records some of the achievements of those pioneers of modern typography who, in a period of war and revolution and of political and economic instability, with slender resources but fierce determination and unwavering dedication, created a new and richer visual vocabulary.

Herbert Spencer, *Pioneers of Modern Typography*, Lund Humphries, London, 1969 (rev. edn Lund Humphries, London / MIT Press, Cambridge, Mass. 1982)

THE TWO passages here reprinted are taken from a lecture given in 1966 on the occasion of the opening of the new Graphic Arts Collection in the Library of Yale University. The booklet in which the lecture was printed is itself remarkable: set in Giovanni Mardersteig's Dante type, and printed in Verona, its illustrations are in collotype and offset printed by the Meriden Gravure Company in Connecticut. Leonard Baskin's text is an erudite mini-history of the illustrated book.

To Colour Thought's frontispiece reproduces a colour plate from William Blake's A Small Book of Designs, printed in Lambeth, 1795-6; Blake is one of Baskin's heroes and probably started his involvement in printing. When an undergraduate at Yale in 1942, Baskin set and printed his own poems. Later, he founded the Gehenna Press, first as a private press and then undertaking commercial commissions. A check list of its output appeared in the American periodical Printing and Graphic Arts in June 1959.

Baskin, as well as being a serious designer and printer of books, is also a world-famous sculptor, an engraver and printmaker, a scholar and writer – a total artist. A fine example of two of his skills – drawing, and designing – can be seen in Caprices & Grotesques, printed at the Gehenna Press in 1965.

In 1962 an exhibition of his work, including sculpture, drawings, prints, and books, was held at Bowdoin College, Brunswick, Maine: the catalogue affords a memorable panorama of Baskin's vision. See also Leonard Baskin: The Graphic Work 1950-1970, with an introduction by Dale Roylance, published by the Far Gallery, New York, 1970, designed by Baskin and printed by Meriden and Stinehour, with a photograph of the artist by Jonathan Unger.

TO COLOUR THOUGHT

I have this afternoon to consider the business of the Graphic Arts within the University; by Graphic Arts I mean printed books, with or without pictures, which are deemed worthy to be housed within the University's libraries regardless of their textual matter. I do not include manuscripts because I know very little about them.

It is difficult to articulate the obvious. Books of great physical beauty are their own raison d'être and require no apologia to warrant their admittance into this venerable and magnificent library. But since it has been something of a tradition at Yale, if not deliberately to scorn the book as physical entity, to display no quick delirium to acquire such books, the recent founding of a collection of printing and graphic arts in Yale University Library serves as an occasion for remarks in celebration of this belated but welcome recognition of a great university's duty to cherish and husband books for the excellence and wonder of their making.

It is my intention to categorise and briefly discuss some of the cardinal qualities which such a collection would contribute to the scholarly and aesthetic life of the university. I should like to begin by remarking on the oft-remarked similarity of the book as object to architecture as object. Both architecture and the book serve a marked and necessary function. Architecture provides shelter; the book transmits thought. Within the notion of shelter are held such wildly disparate forms as tents and palaces. Beyond the basic needs of shelter, architecture has contrived buildings to encompass great assemblies, coliseums, cathedrals, music halls and theatres, and giant warehouses and houses of work, such as this very building with its huge study halls and endless serried ranks of books. The book parallels architecture's prodigality in shape and function. The terrain, from the nastily printed pamphlet (which can carry the tower of genius) to those elephantine granaries, encyclopedias and dictionaries, encompasses a hundred-fold of books. Humans have never seen fit to leave well enough alone, but have been compelled to decorate, beautify, and embellish their artifacts small and large. Primitive people were driven to cover their most mundane utensils wth systems of ornament, intricate patterns and traceries. So too, humans in vertical societies were hardly content to simply house themselves and their family but needed to concoct a bewilderment of designs in structure and in decoration to make life more livable – to lend grace and add felicity to the quotidian humdrum. The artificers of the book from the inception were hardly content to baldly set forth the thought of humans but strove to transmit thought with harmony, art and grace. At times the makers of books charged every space with a turmoil of decoration; at others, composed the pages with classic severity, eschewing any trace of ornament. Endless effort has spent itself in this enterprise. Alas, there has been no end in the making of scrubby and scruffy printing, particularly now when almost naught is issued from human hands alone and those hands have not reined the machine, just as there are endless nasty buildings scarring the earth and blasting the sight. As we study architecture in its extrafunctional sense, so must we consider the book in its existence beyond its manifest purpose, and the history of the book is as various, as interesting and as enriching as the history of architecture.

The graphic book has made contributions to knowledge in a variety of ways. Several of the natural sciences owe their critical transition to exact sciences to the pretty picture books. Dioscorides, who lived in the first century AD, compiled a vast materia medica which for nearly 1700 years was the principal source for students of botany and the art of healing. Dioscorides made quite specific drawings of plants and herbs that mainly comprise the body of his work, but as these drawings were copied through the centuries, travelling from one scriptorium to another, the plants lost semblance of specificity and knowledge was stillborn. What was required was a means of correctly drawing and printing those drawings so that multiple impressions could disseminate exact knowledge. Such a device was found in the woodcut, and in the early middle sixteenth century the cutting of wood blocks was so highly developed that when Otto Brunfels issued his great *Herbarum icones* in 1532 with woodcuts by Hans Weiditz, the cuts set forth for the first time in immutable, persistent exactitude the likeness of each plant. A scholar in Friesland, say, would know that fennel, lady's-mantle and henbane had particular configurations and could not be confused with any other plant. The science of botany had its beginning in this book. The Weiditz woodcuts are superb works.

Almost at the same time, though a few years later, Leonhard Fuchs published a mighty herbal. The flower fuchsia was named for him. The woodcuts in Fuchs' herbal are if anything more beautiful than those of Weiditz, but are nowhere near so exact. For the first and almost last time the Fuchs' herbal bears on its last leaf portraits of the three artists who are responsible for the illustrations: Heinrich Füllmauer who drew the plants; Albrecht Meyer who transferred them to the block; and Rudolf Speckle who cut the blocks. Woodcutting had by now assumed the status of a trade, the practitioners of which were termed *die Formschneider*...

...Books of typographic and graphic interest constitute so great and diverse a body that this already wearisome talk would never cease if I were to attempt a delineation of all its limbs; but only a posy's worth of printer's flowers is left. Walpole, Boswell, Johnson, Garrick, Goldsmith, are all very well but doesn't it weight our delight in 'Little Miss Muffet sat on a tuffet' to know that her father was Thomas Moffett whose *Insectorvm...theatrvm*, 1634, was the first English insect book. Or that when the Thames froze in 1638 an entire London town moved onto the surface of the river for revelry, small printing presses were set up which printed broadsides of the miraculous freeze, and imprinted for a small fee the name of the buyer in red, much like having one's name in a hero's role in the headline of one of the mock newspapers purchasable at Coney Island and Times Square? When Melville reviewed Fenimore Cooper's *The Red Rover*, he dealt exclusively with that book's binding; and when Whitman was setting *Leaves of Grass* he struck out several lines to improve the page – physically – for more seemly margins. Franklin, that most presumed practical of men, took great care to print handsomely. *Cato Major* and his Passy passports are composed and printed with delicacy and strength. The structure of poetry is related to typography. In *The Arte of English Poesie*, London, 1589, Richard Puttenham shows a page of geometric shapes to serve as models for poets and says: '[Verse in geometrical form] is somewhat hard to perform, because of the restraint of the figure from which ye may not digresse. At the beginning they will seem nothing pleasant...but time and usage will make them acceptable enough, as it doth in all other new guises, be it for wearing of apparell or otherwise.'

Before the majority of the design students are sucked into the barren and vicious worlds of advertising and industry, let them hold, feel and see the monuments of great typography. They and their work will be ennobled in the experiencing of Jenson and Ratdolt, Aldus and Thomas Anshelm of Pforzheim, the most original printer who turned the fifteenth century. Nor should they be deprived of the stellar iciness of Bodoni or Cobden-Sanderson; luckily Yale possesses many books printed by these masters and others such as Bulmer, McCreery, and the Whittinghams. Morris and Ricketts, who revived printing, Pissarro and St John Hornby who continued the work, Meynell and his Nonesuch Press and a host of other presses and printers, quicken and inspirit fatigued sensibilities and instruct deeply and wisely.

Much great work of art exists only in books. To name but a handful, the woodcuts of the Bellini School in the Aldine *Hypnerotomachia Poliphili*, and the Parma *Ovid*. The works of Holbein in *The Dance of Death*, Bible woodcuts, and Lucas Cranach, Hans Baldung Grien, Dürer, and many more German artists. Blake. Rembrandt made at least five etchings as book illustrations. The bulk of Romein de Hooghe's work is in books. Callot etched two emblem books. Rubens made many title pages for Plantin and designs for *fête* books, and the list could be expanded almost endlessly down through Menzel, Redon, Picasso, to younger living artists. Collecting these books is the only means of preserving these works of art.

Architectural books are among the most glorious books. Perhaps Leonardo did draw the woodcuts in the Como Vitruvius of 1521, and what a host of wondrous books follow from Perret to Androucet Du Cerceau to Frank Lloyd Wright. And illustrated books on perspective, ornament, medicine, natural history, funeral customs, hats (Rubens used such a book by Vogtherr), the history of shoes, flowers, chess and games, playing cards, in a word all that occupies human beings has been present in books with pictures.

The memory of Carl Purington Rollins, for so many years Printer to the University and Typographer to the Yale University Press, could in no better way be served than in the general cognizance of form's role in enhancing content. Obtrusive typography is bad typography, but when a great text is composed with dignity, intelligence and probity, printed with that just measure of strength and pleasingly bound, the thought in that book lifts off to us more sweetly and more deeply. May I conclude with the familiar lines from Massey:

> *That we by tracing magic lines are taught*
> *How to embody, and to colour thought.*

Leonard Baskin (1922–), *To Colour Thought*, New Haven, Conn., USA, 1967. Text of a lecture given at Yale University Library, 9 May 1966. The text here printed incorporates some corrections by the author.

RUDOLPH RUZICKA *was born in Bohemia (Czechoslovakia) and brought to Chicago by his parents in the early 1890s, unable to speak a word of English. From this beginning he became a figure in American graphic art of whom Philip Hofer wrote in 1935 (at the opening of the Ruzicka Exhibition of the American Institute of Graphic Arts): 'Ruzicka, the artist and craftsman, is only a fraction of Ruzicka, the Scholar, the Humanist, and the Man'.*

He was a superb wood engraver, in black and white and in colour, a designer of three book typefaces for Linotype (Fairfield, Fairfield Medium, and Primer); a fine typographic designer, and an author: his little book Thomas Bewick, Engraver (for the Typophiles, 1943), is one of the best short works on Bewick ever written.

In 1968 (when Ruzicka was 85) he drew ten alphabets 'with random quotations', for his friend Edward C. Lathem, Dartmouth College's Librarian, which were finely printed by the Meriden Gravure Company for the Friends of the Dartmouth Library. We show two of the alphabets, in reduced size, after Ruzicka's note.

See also The Newberry Library Bulletin, vol. VI, no. 9, August 1978, for 'Rudolph Ruzicka, artist and craftsman', an extended essay by Philip Hofer.

STUDIES IN TYPE DESIGN

The temptation to clothe the twenty-six leaden soldiers in new array is irresistible. This is the only apology offered for suggesting still further additions to the seemingly infinite variety of existing typefaces.

A perceptive critic will see at once the eclectic character of some of these studies in the ancient forms and can readily point out their stylistic anomalies.More serious would be the technical problems involved in translating the designs into type: the mechanical problems of fitting and of kerns, vital in metal though perhaps immaterial in the rapidly developing photoelectronic processes. For one concerned with legibility, there would remain the task of relating stem, hairline, counter and serif to each other and to the weight of the larger mass – it is a far cry from design to typeface. But it is a pleasure to watch and hopefully march in the parade.

Note: Two of the pages in Ruzicka's lettering (originally in size 350 x 280mm, in two colours) are here reproduced. The first is from Paul Valéry, 'La Feuille Blanche', written for La Feuille Blanche, Moulin Richard-de-Bas, France, translated by Professor Ramon Guthrie, Dartmouth College. The second is from Walt Whitman, Leaves of Grass, 'A Font of Type'.

Rudolph Ruzicka (1883–1978), Studies in Type Design:
Alphabets with Random Quotations, Dartmouth College,
New Hampshire, 1968.

The truth is that every sheet of blank paper by its very emptiness affirms that nothing is as beautiful as what does not exist. In the magic mirror of its white expanse the soul beholds the setting where signs and lines will bring forth miracles. This presence of absence both spurs on and, at the same time, paralyzes the pen's commitment. There is in all beauty an absolute that forbids our touching it—it sends forth something sacred that gives pause and strikes the man about to act with doubt and awe.

Aa Bb Cc Dd Ee Ffff Gg Hh Ii Jj
Kk Ll Mm Nn Oo Pp Quq Rr Ss
& Tt Uu Vv Ww Xx Yy Zz : 1966

Studies in Type Design by R. Ruzicka ©1968 by Trustees of Dartmouth College

Paul Valéry, La Feuille Blanche, (reduced). Transl. Prof. Ramon Guthrie, Dartmouth College.

Thislatent mine—these unlaunch'd voices—passionate powers,

Wrath, argument, or praise, or comic leer, or prayer devout,

(Not nonpareil, brevier, bourgeois, long primer merely,)

These ocean waves arousable to fury and to death,

Or sooth'd to ease and sheeny sun and sleep,

Within the pallid slivers slumbering.

& a b c d e f g h i j k l m n o p
q r s t u v w x y z ⁊ 1967

Studies in Type Design by R. Ruzicka ©1968 by Trustees of Dartmouth College

Walt Whitman, Leaves of Grass, 'A Font of Type' (reduced).

N<small>O</small> DEFINITIVE 'History of Printing' has ever been written, nor is likely to be: the subject is too vast. One of the most interesting of the selective histories is Michael Twyman's Printing 1770–1970: an illustrated history of its development and uses in England, 1970. He concentrates on periodical, jobbing and ephemeral printing, rather than on books, since these areas are more closely related to the social life of the country. They also reflect how graphic design gradually gained in importance until it became a recognised profession in the present century.

The extract chosen for this work comes from the first chapter, 'The information explosion'. The book's well-illustrated text is followed by 130 pages entirely of illustrations, taken largely from the Printed Ephemera Collection made by Dr John Johnson and now in the Bodleian Library.

Michael Twyman is Professor of Typography and Graphic Art in the University of Reading. He is the author of John Soulby, printer, Ulverston, 1966, and Lithography 1800–1850, Oxford University Press, 1970, another important contribution to that total history of printing which will probably never appear from one author or in one volume.

INFLUENCE OF PRINTING ON THE ENVIRONMENT IN THE NINETEENTH CENTURY

Something of the influence of printing on the environment in the nineteenth century can be gleaned from studying contemporary prints, paintings, and photographs of London, many of which show posters displayed on every available piece of wall. Billposting was one of the new trades of the nineteenth century, and illustrations of the billposter in sets of London characters or books of trades usually show him respectably setting about his work. In fact, the billposter's job was really rather a disreputable one, and he often worked surreptitiously at night so as to be able to disfigure a private wall or paste over a competitor's advertisement. Sampson describes the billposter as 'a nuisance of the most intolerable kind', and records that his peak period of activity was early on Sunday mornings, when he would aim to be early enough to avoid detection, but not so early as to run the risk of having his work disfigured by rival billposters.

Sandwichmen have been another familiar part of the London scene since before the middle of the nineteenth century. They first made their mark when two hundred of them paraded the streets of London to announce the first number of the Illustrated London News which appeared in May 1842. Another standard method of advertising was to employ men to thrust bills into the hands of passers-by at street corners, railway stations, and other vantage points. William Smith, the enterprising manager of the New Adelphi Theatre, records in a little book on advertising a walk he made through London during the week of the Cattle Show in 1861 when he accepted everything he was offered and collected 250 bills, books, and pamphlets. Smith was a precursor of the market researchers of our own day, and he estimated that if only half the people following the same route had taken half of what they were offered the number of items distributed during nine hours on that day would have amounted to 2,300,000. In the following year during two hours spent at the Smithfield Cattle Show, he was given 104 items of printing; and as he was just one of 50,000 visitors that day, he estimated, on the same basis of half the number taking half the bills, that some 1,300,000 items must have been distributed in the course of the one day.

Michael Twyman (1934–), *Printing 1770–1970*, Eyre & Spottiswoode, London, 1970.

Sandwichmen advertising the first number of the *Illustrated London News*, 1842. Part of a wood-engraving from the *Illustrated London News*, 14 May 1842 (reduced).

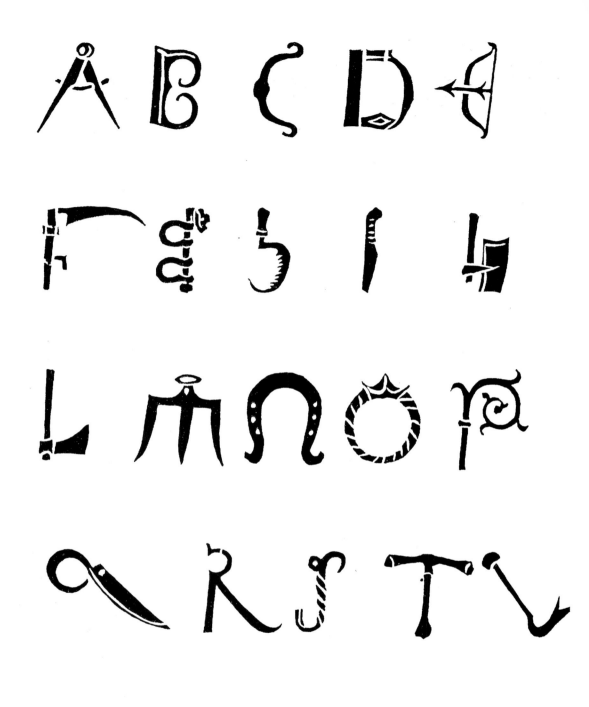

An alphabet published in
1523, reproduced in
Massin's *La lettre et l'image*,
1993 (reduced).

T HE WORDS which follow are taken from the English first edition of Massin's Letter and Image (translated by Caroline Hillier and Vivienne Menkes). They are included not so much for their own importance but to call attention to a great visual anthology of graphic art, republished in 1993 in a larger page size and in full colour. La lettre et l'image is an exact description. The images range from Chinese and other oriental and medieval calligraphy to an extraordinary collection of contemporary jeux d'esprits and illustrations involving letters. We show on facing page an alphabet of tools which might have been drawn today, but we find it was published in Venice in 1523. It is a book not only of importance to typographers, but of the widest human interest.

Massin, for twenty years art director of the Paris publisher Gallimard, is also well known as author, journalist, and publisher.

THE UNIVERSAL LANGUAGE OF MANKIND

The image is the universal language of mankind. It made its appearance on the vaults of prehistoric caves long before men thought of erecting temples or tombs. Thousands of years separate it from writing, the abstract projection of thought....

The image annihilates time and space. It is read instantaneously, and presents an immediate impression of the world....

New York's great artery, Broadway – and its epicentre, Times Square – have the greatest typographical density in the world....

Newspapers, shops, prospectuses, tracts, posters, prescriptions, mail, telegrams, books, dictionaries, year books, theses, instructions for use, maps, personal column ads, 'lonely heart' columns. Teleprinters, comic strips, tokens, tickets, and bank notes, ornamental menus, windows of bookshops and estate agents. And all the neon lights which run, the words which blink, the letters which climb up signs or tumble down them. Publicity vans, walking publicity, sandwich-men, and paper carriers which walk along in step with their owners....

And all the 'danger' notices, or 'fragile', 'wet paint', 'emergency exit', 'police', 'wait', 'cross', 'no parking', 'Sunday Parade', 'no entry', not to mention all these eye-level prepositions: 'in', 'out', 'up', 'down', 'pull', 'push'....

The sense of sight is nearly ten times more sensitive than the other senses; from the twenty-six letters of the alphabet, the number of possible combinations is 620,448,401,733,239,439,360,000. Or, as Cocteau said, 'The greatest literary masterpiece is no more than an alphabet in disorder'.

Massin (1925–), *Letter and Image*, Studio Vista, London, 1970. New edition, *La lettre et l'image*, Gallimard, Paris, 1993.

MILTON GLASER *was born in New York City in 1930 and graduated from the Cooper Union School of Art and Architecture. With Seymour Chwast (q.v.) and Ed Sorel he founded Push Pin Studios in 1954. Glaser at its beginning was its creator and prime mover; by 1970 it had twenty members.*

The passages that follow give some insight into Glaser's mind. They are from the introduction to Milton Glaser: Graphic Design, *The Overlook Press, Woodstock, New York, 1973, a fascinating volume with over 200 pages illustrating his work in colour. In the hand, eyes and imagination of Milton Glaser, design in the United States became something larger than it had ever been before.*

A CONVERSATION ABOUT DESIGN

Peter Mayer questions Milton Glaser:

Is there a difference between design and art?

Several, but they are not as obvious as one might suspect. In some areas the objectives of art and design are harmonious and congruent. Confusion often arises in those instances when the disciplines and objectives are separate. In design, there is a given body of information that must be conveyed if the audience is to experience the information. That objective is primary in most design activities. On the other hand, the essential function of art is to change or intensify one's perception of reality.

Through most of history perception and information existed simultaneously in works of art. The stained glass windows at Chartres tell the story of the stations of the cross to a nonliterate public...and great artists were used to that end. As society developed the information and the art function diverged, and distinctions were made between high art and communicating information to increasing numbers of people. High art, of course, is supposed to have the more elevating characteristics.

When you are asked to help 'sell' a product, do you see yourself as going beyond the public's consciousness of the product, changing the people's perceptions, in other words?

Perhaps the answer can be found by indirection: the reason new forms usually don't emerge from the design activity – as they do in what we'll call the art activity – is that design in many ways is a vernacular language. Design-related work assumes that the audience addressed has an *a priori* understanding of the vocabulary. The essential heart of most art activity is the self-expressive potentiality that the form offers, enlarging therefore the possibilities for the invention of new modes of perception for both the artist and the audience. Meaningful works address us in a way that alters our perception of our reality. Walking past a forest it is possible to say,

'That looks like a Cézanne', the implication being that Cézanne has altered our visual perception of forests. Design works differently. It conveys information based on the audience's previous understanding. Because design deals with familiar forms, much of it depends on the cliché. In fact, the study of cliché as a mode of expression is fundamental to an understanding of design. Clichés are symbols or devices that have lost their power and magic; yet they persist because of some kind of essential truth. Clichés are fundamental sources of information, debased sources waiting to receive new energy. In design, as in so many other things – from human relationships to logotypes – frequent contact often produces immunity to the experience. Two things can help here; an attempt to maintain an innocent vision and the capacity to respond to internal and external changes.

Do you feel that there is a moral aspect to your work, or perhaps to graphic design in general?

I think that attempts to deal with the relationship between art and morality are very complex.

Perhaps I'm alluding to a designer's responsibility to the society, if he has one.

One can see the complexity in the difficulties some designers who work for ad agencies are experiencing now. The sense is growing that much work produced by advertising agencies may be harmful to the community addressed.

Does that concern you?

Intensely. But I feel that anyone involved in communications comes up against the problem...and always has. Now we're beginning to realise that all aspects of communication, whatever the form, have extraordinary implications to the community receiving the information. And so we can't afford not to pay much attention to the quality of information that is distributed. In fact, we know that a comic strip may have a more profound effect on its community than a work of Picasso. For that reason alone, a critical examination of banal graphic phenomena is a worthy investigation indeed. Recent critical attention paid to comic strips and posters supports that idea. In other words, it's important to have a critical view of these artifacts because they are so terribly significant in establishing the mythology and the ethos of a people.

Because one can clearly see in your work a continuing interest in the historical sources of the communication of ideas, as well as the persistence of forms, I wonder if there was something in your student years at Cooper Union, or in Italy, that led to your interest in style and tradition.

At Cooper Union, like most students, I studied the fundamentals and was fortunately exposed to a world of many stylistic alternatives. At Bologna, studying with Giorgio Morandi, I encountered a classical past and met a great man.

Why do you work in so many styles?

Psychically I know it has a lot to do with boredom, with my inability to sustain interest in one form or to be committed to one form of expression for any length of time. At one point in my life I realised that anything I did long enough to master was no longer useful to me. I've always felt that I could explore many phenomena, that, in fact, the whole visual history of the world was my resource. But I really can't say how my interest in many styles developed. Perhaps out of weakness. Perhaps there was an incapacity to deal with certain kinds of problems or to solve them in one idiom. You could say that self-expressive activities have their source as much in a person's inability to deal with certain kinds of problems as in anything else. So I can't really say why my own interest has always been in essentially breaking down the expectation of what design should be. One of the things I decided early on was that as a designer I didn't have to be committed to either design, typography, or illustration, that I could, in fact, design a store or make a toy. When I entered the field there was a very rigid distinction between the designer and the illustrator, in terms of function. There were very few designers who illustrated and very few illustrators who had any idea of how to design. My desire to exercise as much control over my own work as I could usually kept me away from situations in which I would have to entrust my illustration to someone else's notion of design. George Salter, a teacher of mine at Cooper Union, was a major influence. He was an excellent calligrapher and also an illustrator. I feel that his work always had that unity and conviction that emerges from dealing with the total surface. But you can only exercise that broad control if your understanding of technique, culture, and history are broad. Obviously everything that you've ever seen in your life has the potential to be integrated into your work, but it's hard to take advantage of that fact.

★ ★ ★

Do the new media and technology, in your opinion, have an important effect on the designer and his work?

Let me make a generality about how a designer or an artist works at his best level. The best work emerges from the observation of phenomena that exist independently of each other. What the designer intuits is the linkage, singular or plural. He sees a way to unify separate occurrences and create a gestalt, an experience in which this new unity provides a new insight. It doesn't really matter, in a sense, what the subject matter is...or the means to convey it.... What is essential is the perception of the linkages between phenomena. So whatever it is, whether it's time and space or heat or light or you and me...the critical act is to understand the linkages and to bring phenomena that have never been unified into some kind of unity. That's what design is about and that's what art is about, and it doesn't really matter what the media considerations are.

Milton Glaser (1930–), *Milton Glaser: Graphic Design*,
The Overlook Press, New York, 1973.

Symbol designed by
Milton Glaser for the
Ambler Music Festival,
1967. Reduced.
Original is in full colour.

Ambler Music Festival / Institute of Temple University

THE FOLLOWING TEXT, *about Eric Gill's letter forms and types, comes from one of the most elegant books on typographic matters to be published since 1950.*

Harling had made his name, both as typographer and writer, before 1939, when the Second World War intervened. In 1936 he wrote, for Printing magazine, the earliest serious article on Jan Tschichold to be published in English; in November of the same year the first number of a new periodical, Typography, appeared, and established Harling, its editor and designer, as an important new force in British design, along with James Shand, its iconoclastic printer and publisher. One of Harling's strengths was that he could write as well as he could design. The designer who can write his own words is at a considerable advantage

The large wood letters enlivening Typography's covers, in strong colours, were probably derived from the covers of the French Arts et Métiers graphiques designed by Cassandre some years earlier. The letters themselves were Victorian: Harling was an early connoisseur of the Victorian period, and before 1939 had written two books, Home – a Victorian Vignette and The London Miscellany, drawing largely on Victorian images.

From the mid 1930s Harling was advising the typefounders Stephenson Blake, for whom he designed a range of leaflets and advertising, and also three display typefaces, Playbill (1938), Tea Chest, and Chisel (1939). In 1946 came Alphabet and Image, another innovative periodical from Harling and Shand, which after eight issues became Image and ran for another eight issues before succumbing in 1952. Harling also filled in his day by art directing a London advertising agency, advising several book publishers and The Financial Times, and, for two years after Morison's death, The Times, writing novels for Chatto & Windus, helping to design The Sunday Times from 1945 to 1985, and editing House and Garden. Which shows that typography need never be a boring profession.

NOTES ON ERIC GILL AND PERPETUA

The following notes on Eric Gill's letter-forms and type designs derive from two pieces published in *Alphabet & Image*, an occasional quarterly, which James Shand of the Shenval Press and myself started in the early post-war years when it was possible for two youngish men (one preferably a printer) to start such a magazine on a shoestring, give or take an eyelet.

The pieces were written, primarily, because Gill's Felicity and Joanna Italic seemed to me two of the joys of twentieth-century type design, and, partly, because, as a typographical student, I had been fortunate enough to attend some of Gill's latterday lectures at the Central School.

Years after the lectures I visited him at Pigotts, the pleasantly familial commune which he set up near Disraeli's old home at Hughenden in Buckinghamshire, and where he started, with Réné Hague, his own printing shop.

Gill did owe a great deal to others. Although Gill Sans is nominally attributed to Gill (and according to legend, derived from a fascia board he had designed for Douglas Cleverdon's bookshop in Bristol), he owed, in company with all other modern type designers, a considerable debt to his technical advisers and collaborators, particularly to those in the drawing-office and, above all, to the punch-cutters. A comparison of Gill's original designs with the revisions made by the Monotype technicians gives some indication of the help that Gill received. As originally projected, Gill's sans serif would certainly not have held its own in company with either Futura or Erbar. Or, for that matter with Johnston's. But he had the wit to learn quickly from those who could advise him in this new technology, and in its final form Gill Sans proved superior to all others available to printers and typographers who might be interested in having a sans serif type that was not a dehumanised, wholly mechanistic alphabet.

In a sense, of course, all the post-war sans serifs derived from Johnston's teaching and influence, but a comparison of designs by Johnston, Erbar, Renner and Gill shows that Gill's is the most reasonable and readable of those letter-forms, set far apart from the T-square precision of the German types and the occasional fussiness of Johnston's alphabet.

Perpetua

Perpetua is never dull and its beauties always rediscoverable. The alphabet is undoubtedly seen in its most majestic form in the 72-point Titling, but is also handsome when upper and lower case are used in some brief injunction or declamatory passage in the 18-point or 14-point size. The firm and authoritative structure of each letter-form is then clearly seen. Such subtleties as the curve of the final downward stroke of the upper-case R; the balanced M; the able grouping of the ungainly components of W; the balance of solid and void in G, are taken care of in masterly fashion. Then consider the lower-case: the involved yet simple a; the masterly arrangement of the opposed bowls on g (the most wayward letter-form in the English language); the felicitous tail to the y, giving necessary weight to the descender so that it should not intrude into the alphabet by its very lightness; the pleasing curves to m and n. Apart from Jubilee, none of Gill's later typographic designs departed radically from the essential structure of the letter-forms in Perpetua. The same paradox of decorative austerity is apparent, even in his sans serif design.

By a mischance, the italic, which is now so widely used, is less pleasing than the earlier version, a true sloped roman named Felicity, amongst the most agreeably decorative yet readable of all sloped forms. Unfortunately this exquisite type has

been displaced by the more mundane Perpetua Italic. A few printing houses have
Felicity, but even in those, the use of the type is restricted and thus scarcely known.
The story of Felicity is doubtless no more than a lesser tragedy in one of the lesser
studies of mankind, but sad enough all the same.

Robert Harling (1910–), *The Letter Forms and Type
Designs of Eric Gill*, Eva Svensson, The Westerham Press,
1976.

Aa Bb Cc Dd Ee Ff Gg Hh
Ii Jj Kk Ll Mm Nn Oo Pp
Qq Rr Ss Tt Uu Vv Ww
Xx Yy Zz 1234567890

A showing of Perpetua (reduced) from *The Letter Forms and Type Designs of Eric Gill.*
Perpetua is also the typeface used in the illustration on p. 78.

JOHN LEWIS *is one of those typographers who are also essentially artists – as can be deduced from the following passage extracted from his Typography: design and practice, 1978.*

Having been a medical student, a medical illustrator, and during the Second World War a camouflage officer, he joined the printing firm of W. S. Cowell in Ipswich in 1946. Cowells were technically advanced, but knew nothing about design. The first job Lewis was given, as 'studio manager', was to produce a type book aimed at publishers of illustrated books. A year later, A handbook of printing types, *written, edited, and designed by Lewis, appeared and immediately put Cowells in the forefront of printer-designers. It was, and still is, one of the best books of its kind, with illustrations by Henry Moore, John Piper, Blair Hughes-Stanton, John Nash, Barnett Freedman, Edward Bawden, and Graham Sutherland. It was followed in 1956 by* A Handbook of Type and Illustration, *which was even more profusely illustrated by living artists, mostly working in the Royal College of Art, London, where Lewis was now in charge of typography. This handbook is not only a beautiful book itself, but an invaluable guide to the making and reproduction of illustrations for books.*

Among books written by John Lewis, his Printed Ephemera, *1962, a survey of mainly English and American jobbing printing, makes an important and highly entertaining contribution to the history of graphic design.*

John Lewis's autobiography Such Things Happen, *1994, contains a list of his publications.*

PAINTERS AND TYPOGRAPHY

The first revolution in the staid art of book design came from the painter Whistler. The part played in the development of typographic design by artists who were primarily painters or sculptors or even architects has never been fully acknowledged. They are a mixed gathering ranging from James McNeill Whistler to Peter Behrens and from Wyndham Lewis to Max Bill. It was in the 1870s that Whistler turned his attention to the design of his exhibition invitations and catalogues. His typographic layouts were remarkable for his use of white space, with type set in narrow measures. His margins were sometimes punctuated with shoulder notes decorated with variations of his Butterfly symbol. His chapter openings and title-pages were set in text-sized capitals asymmetrically arranged, his copy was most carefully placed on the page.

In 1878 Whistler published the first of his booklets *Whistler v. Ruskin Art and Art Critics.* It was bound in simple, limp brown paper covers, printed in black. He used this style of binding for everything he published from then on, though for more substantial works such as *The Gentle Art of Making Enemies* which was published in

1890, the books were quarter bound with paper covered boards and yellow cloth backs, blocked in dark brown.

Whilst *The Gentle Art* was in production, Whistler and his publisher Heinemann would foregather at the Savoy for a belated breakfast. And there, on a deserted balcony overlooking the river Thames, they would discuss every little production detail. Whistler would sometimes spend hours positioning a single Butterfly.

* The Life of James McNeill Whistler E. R. & J. Pennell. Wm Heinemann, London and J. B. Lippincott and Company, Philadelphia, 1908.

Mr and Mrs Pennell in their biography* of Whistler describe how whilst *The Gentle Art* was being set: 'Whistler was constantly at the Ballantyne Press where the book was printed. He chose the type, he spaced the text, he placed the Butterflies, each of which he designed especially to convey a special meaning.... He designed the title-page: a design contrary to all established rules but with the charm, the balance, the harmony, the touch of personality he gave to everything.... The cover was now in the inevitable brown, with a yellow back.'

The Gentle Art is much more than a typographic frolic. It is a beautifully designed book. Though Whistler was primarily a painter, he used words with the respect of someone who rejoiced in their use. He was the first modern typographer to show that typography is primarily a matter of placing words so that their sense becomes clearer, more pointed and more precise.

Technically, Whistler's typography is interesting for the way he made use of such rather indifferent typefaces as his commercial printers carried, and overcame their equally indifferent presswork. This was quite contrary to the views of William Morris and most of the succeeding private press printers, who were often obsessively concerned with type design and the materials on which they printed.

The manner in which Whistler made great play with white space and the way his copy was placed on the page with such precision was not to be seen again until the New Typography had reached its apogee in the years after the Second World War. Whistler's consistent use of text size letters for his chapter openings is yet another factor that the post-Bauhaus typographers used.

No two men were less alike in their likes and dislikes and in their way of life than James McNeill Whistler and William Morris. Yet they had at least two things in common. One was a penetrating eye for detail; the other that they both wrote. That being so, it is not surprising that for a while both of them became interested in typography and particularly in the design of their own books. Yet no books could be less alike in their appearance than *The Gentle Art of Making Enemies* and the Kelmscott *Chaucer*.

Whistler...brought a new approach to the design of books. Morris brought new standards to how books were printed.

John Lewis (1912–), *Typography: design and practice*, Barrie & Jenkins, London, 1978.

T HE PASSAGE *that follows is taken from a printer's autobiography which gives an excellent account of the development of book design in the USA and Europe from 1925 to 1975. Joseph Blumenthal was intended to follow in his father's footsteps and become a 'captain of industry. Alas, I never became more than a corporal.' At the age of twenty-six he decided that he would prefer a life 'somewhere in the world of the book', and wrote a letter to every publisher in New York for a job. He was lucky: he got one answer, and one job.*

By 1926 he had begun to learn, from scratch, what good printing was about, had found a partner, and set up his own Spiral Press in New York. As he writes in Typographic Years: 'The Spiral Press thrived in its modest way from the beginning. It was my belief in 1926, since strengthened by time, that the market for fine printing is not limited except as it is limited by the capacity to produce it.' A bold belief, but one which Blumenthal justified. To many people of distinction he was their printer of choice. Virtually all of poet Robert Frost's first editions were products of the Spiral Press, as was the first printing of the United Nations charter. The Press became a leading influence for good design in American printing and Blumenthal himself a much respected authority – not only as a designer of books and the typeface Emerson but as an author: see his Art of the Printed Book, Pierpont Morgan Library, New York, 1973; The Printed Book in America, David R. Godine, Boston, 1977; and Typographic Years, Frederic C. Beil, New York, 1982.

PRINTING EDUCATION

After two years with a hand press on a hill top, the way back to the sidewalks of New York was made easier by a proposal in 1933 from the New School for Social Research that I give a course on book design and production – an addition to their already active arts and crafts groups. Rather than lectures and blackboard instruction, I offered to bring a hand press and organise a workshop course where students could set and print their own pages, There would be two sessions each week at night, two-and-a-half hours each. Thus I became a teacher, one more small and temporary source in the scattered education available to people who wanted direct exposure to the craft. An interesting group of mature students signed up. They all wanted 'to get their hands on type'. In addition to the expected production people from publishing houses, there were editors, librarians, book illustrators, a bookseller, and a manufacturer of household lamps. Each student was required to plan and design and produce a project with a title page and a few text pages incorporating the bare bones of bookmaking. The completed pieces, which showed considerable imagination, were acquired by the New York Public Library, whose Curator of Rare Books was a member of the class.

Joseph Blumenthal (1897–1990), *Typographic Years,*
Frederic C. Beil, New York, 1982.

HERMANN ZAPF *is, first, a great calligrapher; secondly, he is a great type designer. He became known to the world of book design when Feder und Stichel (Pen and Graver) was published in Frankfurt in 1950. It consisted of twenty-five alphabets in historic styles of letter, which Zapf had drawn between 1939 and 1941. They had so impressed August Rosenberger, the master punch-cutter at the Stempel type foundry, that he cut them in lead. They were then printed with great care on Italian hand-made paper. Jan Tschichold told Paul Standard that no book produced in the past hundred years could show a comparable perfection of printing. The book was reprinted in 1952 equally finely, but in a larger edition, on Fabriano paper, with a preface by Standard and his translation into English of Zapf's historical essay at the back.*

Of Zapf's many typefaces, among the best known are Palatino (1950), Sistina Titling (1951), Melior (1952), Saphir (1952), Optima (1958), ITC Zapf Book (1976), and ITC Zapf International (1977).

See Hermann Zapf, About Alphabets. Some marginal notes on type design, The Typophiles, New York, 1960; Hermann Zapf, calligrapher, type designer and typographer, Stempel Foundry, Frankfurt am Main, 1960; Hermann Zapf, Manuale Typographicum, Museum Books, New York, 1968; and ABC-XYZapf, Fünfzig Jahre Alphabet Design, edited by Knut Erichson and John Dreyfus, Bund Deutscher Buchkünstler, Offenbach, and Wynkyn de Worde Society, London, 1989.

IS CREATIVE ART IN DESIGN REALLY NEEDED IN THIS DAY OF ELECTRONICS?

Designers have fewer limitations in designing alphabets for the new systems of today. Digital composition and the use of the laser beam mean that designs need to be tailored especially to these electronic devices. Designers must find out what is possible within the new systems or at least within a specific machine.

A lot of mathematics and technical knowledge are involved in our work today. I would not call us artists any more. I think 'alphabet designer' is more accurate, and our comrade is no longer the punchcutter but the electronics engineer. If the technician learns that he doesn't have to work with a crazy artist, and the designer learns a little about electronics, they will make an ideal team. It is still teamwork as it was in the good old days of metal type.

A type designer faces a big problem today, however. I am not speaking about the protection of typefaces but about poor copying of drawings everywhere, which may make the designer sad for the rest of his life. He sees his children; his alphabets manipulated beyond his wildest imagination. Fantastic equipment with specially prepared lenses can stretch, hit, bend, and distort our letters in every direction.

These modifications may be excused when they provide additional composition effects, especially for display purposes, and if it is not overdone. For example, some digital machines can produce small caps and small caps italics. This is an important addition compared to metal composition of the past. Typographic creativity can be expanded with these modifications as long as it is controlled by people with knowledge and taste.

THE LETTERS of the alphabet are two-dimensional objects; the space around and between them, and inside them, is an essential factor in their identity. Even when the

THE LETTERS of the alphabet are two-dimensional objects; the space around and between them, and inside them, is an essential factor in their identity. Even when the

This sample shows the reduced readability of a text with an extreme narrow intercharacter spacing in comparison with normal spacing between the letters. (Typeface: Optima Medium).

Here is another serious problem of today: many new photocomposing machines have the ability to reduce the intercharacter spacing, the fitting as we used to call this. In addition to normal spacing, the distances between the characters can be manipulated further to tight, extra tight, or even to extremely tight. In these instances the characters are not separated; they touch each other, kiss each other, and sometimes they overlap each other. One term for this funny game is 'sexy spacing'. But as always it is mostly overdone. Too narrow intercharacter spacing reduces readability. One of the basic principles of typography – unchanged for 500 years – was summed up perfectly by Cobden-Sanderson: 'The whole duty of typography, as of calligraphy, is to communicate to the imagination, without loss by the way, the thought or image intended to be communicated by the author'.

It is much easier to play with your machine or with your video display terminal (VDT) compared to metal composition, which was much more controlled. Working with metal type you saw what you did at once, and you could correct your mistakes or you could try alternate solutions directly with the type in front of you. On your VDT, however, you don't see (at least not yet, unfortunately) how good or awful 'sexy spacing' looks, how the kerned characters fit or if a simple line in all caps is properly spaced.

Hermann Zapf (1918–), *Hermann Zapf & his design philosophy*, Society of Typographic Arts, Chicago, 1987 from 'The designer in the world of Metafont', Stanford University, Dept of Computer Science, Stanford University, California. A lecture, 10 February 1983.

THE FOLLOWING *passage, written as long ago as 1984, indicates what intelligent printers already saw as threatening – or revolutionising – their landscapes.*

Roderick Stinehour founded the Stinehour Press in a wood in Vermont in 1950. Under his guidance it became internationally prominent for its typesetting and fine printing. In 1953 it began publishing Printing & Graphic Arts, *edited by Rollo Silver, Ray Nash and Rocky Stinehour, a distinguished journal later edited only by Nash, which ran for ten years. The Stinehour Press became closely associated with the Meriden Gravure Company, who pioneered 300-line offset printing; in 1977 the two firms amalgamated and Meriden's plant was eventually moved to Vermont.*

Stinehour is now a Fellow in the Book Arts at Dartmouth College, New Hampshire, and director of the Book Arts Workshop there.

See The Stinehour Press, *a bibliographical checklist of the first thirty years, Meriden-Stinehour Press, Lunenburg, Vermont, 1988.*

COMPUTERS AND PRINTING

For over 2,000 years the tools of thought have changed little in essence; basically it has been ink, paper, and the means of applying one to the other. But the computer will surely give intellectual activity a new shape. The question is, what shape will emerge? And what form for the printed word? There are now more than five million computers in the United States, and for some time the amount of computing power has been doubling every two years. The average computer user now has access to information that would fill the Library of Congress and can control as much computing power as a large university computing center. Will this reduce the need for books, or make it unnecessary to print and distribute books in the ways of the past?

There are laser printing units using xerography that can print a complete book from the digitised type page stored in disk memory banks. Such a custom book printer can churn out pages, verso and recto, at the rate of a leaf every second. A complete book of 124 pages would be ready for binding in sixty-two seconds. It takes little imagination to envision a bookstore of a decade hence filled with 'sample' volumes only. One would need only to pick a title and the book would be printed and bound on the spot. Such a bookstore could readily keep on hand three or four times the number of titles now stocked at a fraction of present costs, since there would be no shipping charges, no overstock or understock problems, and no returns.

Recently the Library of Congress has been working with publishers on a pilot project to test the use of optical discs for the storage and dissemination of journals and periodicals. The material would be copied onto twelve-inch discs that can hold up to 20,000 pages on a side. A reading machine would enable the user to read the material on the disc and give a command to the machine to print out the material on a connected high-speed printer.

What does this technology have to do with books as we now know them? There are many predictions abroad today about the shape of things to come in a computer age that is just emerging in the first flush of a new day. Books are obviously only one means of disseminating information and cogitative writing in the midst of an increasing plethora of electronic options. Even the Congress of the United States seeks guidance. A recent Congressional resolution has asked for a study to explore the influence of the computer and video technologies on books, reading, and the printed word. An advisory committee, meeting at the Library of Congress, was told by Sen. Charles Mathias, Jr, to 'set no limits to your vision for perhaps the future of the book is not as solid as it might appear'. The committee is exploring four specific questions: What difference does it make that the forms and functions of books are changing? How do technology and literacy affect each other? Who is responsible for stimulating reading and the reading habit? How is publishing facing the challenges of new technologies?

The results of this study will be issued in, have you guessed it, a BOOK, entitled *The Book in the Future*, to be presented by Librarian of Congress Daniel J. Boorstin to the Congress no later than December 1, 1984. Perhaps that is when we shall all learn what the outlook will be for this seemingly endangered species, or at least the official outlook.

Meanwhile, we who are gathered here today have the greatest vested interest in the book of the future as well as of the past: scholars, students, librarians, booksellers, publishers, and printers.

Henry Stevens of Vermont, the nineteenth-century bookseller, once said, 'Books are both our luxuries and our daily bread. They have become to our lives and happiness prime necessities.' I have pondered this saying often – 'Books are both our luxuries and our daily bread'. It has become a kind of motto, one that I believe is most apt for a printer... Books embody all the humanising arts that make thought tangible and give form to ideas, so that mind can touch mind over vast distances and through the ages of time itself.

Roderick Stinehour (1925–), excerpt from 'Books and Technology: A Printer's View', reprinted from the *Proceedings of the American Antiquarian Society*, vol. 94, Part 1, April 1984.

S EYMOUR CHWAST *was born in New York City in 1931 and graduated from the Cooper Union School of Art and Architecture. In 1954 he joined Milton Glaser (q.v.) and Ed Sorel to found Push Pin Studios. They soon became (and still are) the most lively, multifarious and amazing design group in the world, honoured in 1970 by an exhibition in the Louvre. Their prolific invention and light-hearted attitude to graphic design can be seen in the Push Pin Graphic, a periodical irregular in size, content and appearance, which for some time Chwast edited and to which he was often the main contributor.*

Chwast's work is communication, for both editorial and advertising purposes, but he is not primarily a typographer. He uses typography in a traditional way to make straightforward statements which the job requires; but his visual impact is achieved by wildly inventive illustration.

See The Push Pin Style, Palo Alto, California, 1970 (in which three typefaces designed by Chwast are illustrated) and Seymour Chwast, The Left-Handed Illustrator, Polygon Editions, Basle, Switzerland, 1985.

A DESIGNER WHO ILLUSTRATES

Steven Heller interviews Seymour Chwast:

Are you a designer who illustrates or an illustrator who designs? I am a designer who illustrates. I observe the formal principles of design (proportion, harmony, dynamics, symmetry, line, mass, texture) while I am manipulating elements to suit my purposes. The way I articulate the solution is most often with an illustration (which is most often the client's expectation).

How do you approach your drawing? I often battle with the paper. While I could never work with a crow quill, a Speedball pen or Rapidograph enables me to bear down on the paper. My drawing is weak. But I am not as interested in that as I am in making a graphic idea work. That's why I'm less concerned with *finish*. The concept has always been most important, and therefore I look for the style most appropriate to express the idea. Surface, neatness, rendering, and craft are things that interest me less.

With typography, are you more conservative than with illustration? I play with type since it is a design element, but I respect its rules. The rules of drawing and basic design are also supreme, but they can be stretched and expanded. Choice of type style is an aesthetic judgement. Observing an exquisite typeface beautifully displayed is a sublime experience. But what we have is the widest range of ugly faces and a willingness on the part of designers to use them. I have a fantasy in which I become Type Czar of the World and eradicate all the bad ones.

My sense of typography is rooted in tradition, so it tends to be conservative. For instance, typographic letter forms were originally designed to fit the limitations of the metal. I disavow ligatures and tend to print my type in black. Understanding the rules means knowing what you can't do. I generally don't illustrate with typography, but rather use it to integrate with, or counterbalance the image. That's why I don't use freehand lettering, which competes with the image. Sometimes my type may be elegant to go along with a very inelegant drawing.

Seymour Chwast (1931–), *The Left-Handed Designer*, edited by Steven Heller. Polygon Editions, Basle, Switzerland, 1985.

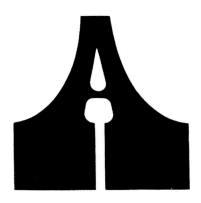

A letter 'looking like a drop of ink' designed by Chwast for the label of an ink-bottle, later developed into an alphabet.

The Push Pin Studio logo, designed by Chwast with Reynold Ruffins and Milton Glaser.

T HE DISSECTION *of the differences between 'legibility' and 'readability' in the follow-*
ing passage is one of the first things that must be learned by anyone interested in typogra-
phy. It is taken from Walter Tracy's Letters of Credit, subtitled 'A view of type design'. A few
items from the first chapter, on 'The vocabulary of type', follow: the whole book is, in this field,
essential and highly enjoyable reading.

Tracy was apprenticed as a compositor in the great printing house of William Clowes in
1928. This was followed by varied experience in printing and design until in 1947 he joined
the small publishing firm of Art & Technics, where he came under the influence of James Shand,
and, in his own words, 'felt his mind expanding'. Shand had for some time been in close contact
with the Linotype Company of Great Britain, and before 1939 had started for them a typo-
graphical periodical, Linotype Matrix. He now asked Tracy to write and design it, which
Tracy did with great credit for some ten years. In 1948 Tracy joined the Linotype Company
full-time as manager of typeface development, and he remained there for thirty years. His work
concerned newspaper text faces: he designed Jubilee, Telegraph Modern, and, for The Times,
Times-Europa, to replace Stanley Morison's Times. He also designed two important classified
advertisement faces, Adsans and Maximus. For all this work, Tracy was elected to the distinc-
tion of Royal Designer for Industry, which seems to contradict his own modest claim to be 'a
better critic than performer'.

See W. Tracy, Letters of Credit, Gordon Fraser, London/David Godine, Boston, 1986, and
The typographic scene, Gordon Fraser, London, 1988.

LEGIBILITY AND READABILITY

There are two aspects of a type which are fundamental to its effectiveness. Because
the common meaning of 'legible' is 'readable' there are those – even some people
professionally involved in typography – who think that the term 'legibility' is all
that is needed in any discussion on the effectiveness of types. But legibility and
readability are separate, though connected, aspects of type. Properly understood,
and used in the meanings appropriate to the subject, the two terms can help to
describe the character and function of type more precisely than legibility alone.

Legibility, says the dictionary, mindful of the Latin root of the word, means the
quality of being easy to read. In typography we need to draw the definition a little
closer; we want the word to mean the quality of being decipherable and recognisable – so that we can say, for example, that the lowercase h in a particular old style
italic is not really legible in small sizes because its in-turned leg makes it look like
the letter b; or a figure 3 in a classified advertisement type is too similar to the 8. So
legibility is the term to use when discussing the clarity of single characters. It is a
matter for concern in text sizes, and especially in such special cases as directories,

where the type is quite small. In display sizes legibility ceases to be a serious matter; a character which causes uncertainty at 8 point will be plain enough at 24 point.

Readability is a different thing. The dictionary may say that it, too, means easy to read. In typography we can give the word a localised meaning, thus: if the columns of a newspaper or magazine or pages of a book can be read for many minutes at a time without strain or difficulty, then we can say the type has good readability. The term describes the quality of visual comfort – an important requirement in the comprehension of long stretches of text but, paradoxically, not so important in such things as telephone directories or air-line time-tables, where the reader is not reading continuously but searching for a single item of information.

Legibility, then, refers to perception, and the measure of it is the speed at which a character can be recognised; if the reader hesitates at it the character is badly designed. Readability refers to comprehension, and the measure of that is the length of time that a reader can give to a stretch of text without strain. The difference in the two aspects of visual effectiveness is illustrated by the familiar argument on the suitability of sans-serif types for text setting. The characters in a particular sans-serif face may be perfectly legible in themselves, but no one would think of setting a popular novel in it because its readability is low. (Those typographers who specify a sans-serif for the text columns of a magazine may be running the risk of creating discomfort in the reader – to the ultimate benefit of a rival journal.)

Legibility and readability are the functional aspects of a type design. But there is more to a typeface than the functional. A type designed for newspaper text may prove equal to, say, Bembo in a carefully conducted readability test; but it would not be chosen for the composition of a book. This is only partly because the newspaper text type was designed for high-speed production methods which do not allow for much finesse. A stronger reason is that in the editorial columns of newspapers we prefer the text and headlines to be set in plain matter-of-fact-types, and in books we want faces of refinement and distinction. Set a novel in a newspaper type and the effect will be so uninviting that the success of the work will be jeopardised. Set a newspaper in a book type and we will not take it seriously. (There was once a newspaper which used Caledonia for its text. That excellent book type helped the paper to gain awards for good design but, ironically, contributed to its early demise.) So as well as the functional aspects of type designs there is the aesthetic aspect; and it is the proper balancing of the functional and the aesthetic which we look for in the work of the type designer, just as we do in other fields of product design.

THE VOCABULARY OF TYPE

Font (in Britain it is so pronounced, but spelt *fount*) is a type founder's term of quantity: the total number of letters and other items needed for a particular purpose, capitals, lowercase, numerals, punctuation marks, ligatures, monetary signs, and so on. The font needed for the composition of a telephone directory, with its several kinds of numerals, is different from the font needed for the setting of a novel. Font is not another word for typeface or design, as some writers have thought – Stanley Morison, for one.

The strip of negative film on which the characters are arranged in some photocomposition machines is called a font. The term is also used for the sets of digitised characters in more recent systems. Because of the international marketing of such systems the four-letter spelling of the word (which was the original form, according to an editor's note in Moxon's *Mechanick Exercises*, second edition 1962) is becoming familiar in Britain and Europe. It is used in this book.

Gothic. Traditionally, the word has been used for two quite different sorts of letter: the pen-made letter sometimes called 'black-letter' or 'Fraktur', and the sans-serif form. In this book gothic means only the first sort, as in the review of Rudolf Koch's types.

Roman is a term of several meanings. It can mean upright as distinct from italic. It can mean normal weight as compared with bold weight. And it can refer to a ser-iffed face as distinct from sans-serif. The sense in which 'roman' is to be understood is usually clear from the context; but is sometimes necessary to be explicit and to say, for instance, 'bold roman' if that is what is intended.

Walter Tracy (1914–), *Letters of Credit*, Gordon Fraser, London, 1986.

THE FOLLOWING *piece forms the Introduction to the second edition of* Twentieth Century Type Designers, 1995. *If the question 'Do we need so many new types?' was relevant when the first edition was published in 1987, it is even more so today, when new faces, often only minute variants of existing ones, proliferate at a bewildering speed. However, the real need for a new face, or the improvement of an old one, because of new printing requirements, is well shown in the illustrations of American telephone directory columns of 1938 and 1978 accompanying Sebastian Carter's text. The book is an excellent guide to its subject, particularly for its illustrations of typefaces and the faces of the designers themselves.*

Sebastian Carter, the son of Will Carter, works with his father in the Rampant Lions Press in Cambridge. He is no relation of the type designer Matthew Carter, also in this anthology.

DO WE NEED SO MANY NEW TYPES?

The skeleton shapes of the letters of our alphabet change hardly at all. Why then do skilled designers devote so much time, sometimes their whole lives, to drawing different versions of the outlines?

This simplified formulation of a basic question about type design, with which I began the first edition of this book, was criticised by one reviewer, Robert Bringhurst, the Canadian poet and typographer, writing in *Fine Print*. 'Some designers do, of course, draw outlines,' he wrote, 'but those who make substantive contributions to the tradition do something else: they create letters precisely by rethinking their skeleton shapes, by reinventing them, muscle and bone, from the inside out. To ask why they do so is much like asking why, since all trees have branches and leaves, God chose to make more than one species.'

This is eloquently put, but I did not intend my question to be taken quite so literally. In recreating letterforms the type designer inevitably modifies the proportions of the basic shapes, but within very conservative limits. To do so more than this offends readers, and to do so much more makes letters illegible.

In his *Essay on typography* (1931) Eric Gill illustrated a celebrated, if exaggerated, contrast between acceptable letter forms (the left-hand letters of each row) and what he called 'fancy madness'. He regarded the second D as permissible if extreme condensation is required, but the rest as beyond the pale.

Gill was a muscle and bone man if ever there was one, yet in practice the skeleton shapes of his letters were markedly constant. The characteristic Gill R with its curvaceous tail was discernible in its essentials in all his roman types, yet he drew and redrew the profiles in many different ways.

The reasons for this are manifold, and illustrate the responses of most designers to type design. The simplest is that he was asked to: he was approached by a manufacturing company, Monotype, with commissions for a roman type, Perpetua, and a sans-serif, Gill Sans. Subsequently he designed faces for other customers, and one, Joanna, for his own use, though Monotype later took it over. The variety of forms was the result of the different styles of type he was producing, the dislike creative people feel for repeating themselves, and the desire of customers for something different.

Yet while they are unmistakeably Gill's creations, they are equally unmistakeably in a long tradition of type design. Typefaces in daily use are shaped by a complex blend of historical influences and personal preferences. In the classic romans, even when stored in a Postscript file, there are traces of the manufacturing techniques used to make their ancestors, the punchcutter's file, the scribe's pen, even the stone carver's chisel. These have been transmuted through centuries of slow development in the conventional ideas about the ideal shapes of letters. The changes made by individual designers are limited by the need to respect both these inherited conventions and readers' dislike of change. As Stanley Morison wrote in *First principles of typography* (1930), 'Type design moves at the pace of the most conservative reader. The good type designer therefore realises that, for a new fount to be successful, it has to be so good that only very few recognise its novelty. If readers do not notice the consummate reticence and rare discipline of a new type, it is probably a good letter. But if my friends think that the tail of my lower-case r or the lip of my lower-case e is rather jolly, you may know that the fount would have been better had neither been made.'

Offending readers with distortions of the basic proportions of letters, or even attracting their notice with minor eccentricities of detail, creates a resistance not only to the type but to the message of which the type should be the faithful messenger. This is a negation of its purpose. Many writers on the subject have emphasised the theoretical 'invisibility' of type. The best-known analogy is the one made by Beatrice Warde with a crystal goblet, through which the wine – the text – can be seen without distortion. But goblets, though translucent, are not invisible, and indeed can be studied independently of their contents. Students of type can never again read a text without being conscious of the face in which it is set. It becomes all the more important that the type should be good.

It is always a source of surprise to people fresh to the study of type design that minute differences, which one might think were barely visible to the naked eye, are so important. This is because when you are reading, although you are aware of surrounding lines, all your attention is focused on a short string of words, and the letters are perceived as larger than they actually are. Tiny irritating details are magnified by repetition. In the words of Chauncey Griffith, the typographical spirit behind Mergenthaler Linotype for many years, 'Few people can distinguish what a difference of a fraction of a thousandth an inch can make in [a type's] appearance. But the individual piece of type is like a thread. A single thread might be dyed crimson, scarlet or pink and the human eye would find the difference hard or impossible to detect. But once that thread is woven into cloth, the colour is very apparent. so type must be judged after it is woven into the texture of a paragraph or a page.'

When we contemplate any branch of design history, we tend to waver between conflicting responses. On the one hand we wonder at the amount of effort expended in the sophisticated manipulation of basic shapes, and on the other we welcome the results. We see highly simplified classics of design – a chair by Marcel Breuer, a fork by Arne Jacobsen, or Paul Renner's Futura typeface – and we wonder why anything else is required. But then we experience a natural revulsion, and embrace variety, experiment and amusement, even if it sometimes leads to kitsch. After a while we swing back again to purity. In everyone but a few single-minded zealots there reside both the puritan and the pluralist.

We should welcome typographic variety as the natural consequence of human creativity. Rudolf Koch, the great German calligrapher and type designer, wrote: 'The making of letters in every form is for me the purest and greatest pleasure, and at many stages of my life it was to me what a song is to the singer, a picture to the painter, a shout to the elated, or a sigh to the oppressed – it was and is for me the most happy and perfect expression of my life'. By no means all the designers mentioned in this book operated at this level of creative ecstasy, but all were driven by a love of letters and a burning desire to refine the common stock of printing types.

Much type design has been undertaken by less flamboyant characters, usually working for the drawing offices of type manufacturers. Their task has been to adapt existing designs for the demands of new typesetting methods, to expand master designs into families, or to give the necessary technical guidance to new designs on their way to completion. People such as Sol Hess of the American Lanston Monotype Company, Morris Benton of American Type Founders, Fritz Steltzer of English Monotype, and their staffs, are the largely unsung heroes and heroines of the business. Even with the recent introduction of computer software to aid this kind of work, the work still has to be done. The quality of what they do is intended to be undetected by the untrained eye, and that is its merit.

Sebastian Carter (1941–), *Twentieth Century Type Designers*, 2nd edn, Lund Humphries, London / W. W. Norton, New York, 1995.

A FTER DISTINGUISHED SERVICE *as a bomber pilot in the Royal Air Force from 1940 to 1946, George Mackie spent his working life in Scotland, mostly in Aberdeen, where he taught in Gray's School of Art: for twenty-five years he was Head of the Department of Design and Crafts. He has given as much time to painting, in watercolour and oils, as to graphic design.*

While in Aberdeen he also, for thirty years, designed books for Edinburgh University Press. His collaboration with Archie Turnbull, the Secretary of the Press, is the subject of the following passage taken from an article in Matrix 8. Mackie also for some years designed and illustrated guides for the properties of the National Trust for Scotland. In all his work, Mackie combines skilful and inventive typography with his own original lettering and drawing, often in colour. He was deservedly awarded the honour of Royal Designer for Industry in 1973.

Fifty books designed by Mackie for Edinburgh University are catalogued in An Exhibition of Books, to honour ARCHIE TURNBULL...and GEORGE MACKIE, *Edinburgh, 1987. See also* Books, mostly scholarly, and some Ephemera, designed by George Mackie. *An exhibition at the National Library of Scotland, Edinburgh from 21 March to 2 June and from 15 September to 31 October 1991 at the Dartmouth College Library, Hanover, New Hampshire.*

DESIGNING FOR AN ENLIGHTENED PUBLISHER

My self-education progressed by trial and error, and most importantly by coming across, or searching out, from a half-millennium of printing, all sorts of books.

I discovered, for I had never heard of it, a copy of *The Nonesuch Century*, in Rota's bookshop in Vigo Street, and bought it, gritting my financial teeth. I saw it as a series of object lessons, and a beautiful object in itself. Lucky Meynell, working in the 1920s, with the typographic renaissance crackling all around him, and the finest book printers in the kingdom all anxious to do his bidding, even unto thirty-seven different varieties of title-page for one book. Turnbull [Publisher to Edinburgh University Press] occasionally allowed me a second revise. Which explains in part the exactness of the layouts which I did in those early years. All very well for Bernard Roberts, then a master printer in his own shop, to look down his nose at designers' layouts. He had no more need of them than Updike who, as Robbins (then printer to Yale University Press) once told John Dreyfus, couldn't even sharpen a pencil, let alone use one to work out an accurate specification. For me, working in Aberdeen for an Edinburgh publisher who used a variety of print-ers across the country, layouts were the means whereby he got to know what I was proposing; and the means whereby he and I got from the printer exactly, or almost exactly, what we wanted, with no expensive changes of mind. I was discovering

Ruskin about this time, and I used to have an occasional qualm because I was treating the comp as an unthinking and unfeeling artisan, and not as a sentient and creative individual. I consoled myself with the thought that Ruskin had little appreciation of books as physical objects. Besides, the faster the comp completed the job, the larger his eventual bonus.

The exactness of my layouts also represents a *solution* which I finally achieved, sometimes after many attempts. Without showing type as accurately as possible, I found myself unable to judge whether the problem *was* solved, and whether it would look right in printer's ink. I make no attempt to represent in pencil the blackness of ink. The layout is a kind of printed page seen through an overlay of tracing paper. Display typography, as in a title-page, shares some problems with pictorial composition. All elements have to be content with their relative importance and position within the rectangle; and these are of course decided not by optical whim but by intellectual judgement. But any design worth its salt is the consequence of feeling as well as thought. Typography has its own abstract, non-alphabetic quality whose aesthetic demands can only be met by a response which is visceral. The result should be a rational structure invested by a largely undefinable identity. The structure will represent some kind of gravitational field with the major elements compelling the lesser parts willingly to accept their inferior scale and positionings. All words thereby have their own clarity and degree of importance.

Mixing metaphors further, the announcements on the title-page can be thought of as frozen speech, with the tone of voice and strength of utterance determined by choice of type, size and position. White paper creates the rhythm of varying lengths of pause. Alas, many title-pages today, from publishers once respected for good manners in things typographic, shout and importune the reader like commonplace placards. A book is never more than an arm's length away. I agree with Morison's dictum (whether he said it or not) that two sizes up from text size is enlargement enough for all purposes.

George Mackie (1920–), 'Designing for an
Enlightened Publisher', *Matrix* 8, Winter, 1988.

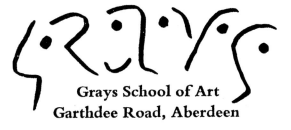

Grays School of Art
Garthdee Road, Aberdeen

ADRIAN FRUTIGER *was born and educated in Switzerland, but has spent his work-*
ing life in France: Charles Peignot invited him to work in Paris for his great typefounding
firm of Deberny & Peignot in 1952.

The passage here quoted is from Section 3 of the Introduction to Frutiger's book Signs and
Symbols, their Design and Meaning, 1989, an English translation of Der Mensch und
seine Zeichen, 1978. It is a fully illustrated examination of the graphic representations of
human thought: a remarkable work of the greatest significance to all designers.

Frutiger is perhaps best known as the designer of the typeface Univers, 'the most rational and
basic of the post-war sanserifs' (Sebastian Carter, Twentieth century type designers, 1987).
Among the most 'universal' typefaces in the Western world today, it is available in 21 different
weights and widths, to which Frutiger gave identifying numbers to avoid cumbersome descrip-
tive titles like 'Ultra Bold Expanded'.

Frutiger has designed numerous other typefaces and also industrial lettering systems and
alphabets, e.g. for The Paris Métro, Charles de Gaulle airport, Electricité de France, and Gaz de
France. He is the author of Schrift/écriture/lettering, Zurich, 1951. For a well-illustrated
English introduction to his work see a 24-page booklet Graphismes by Frutiger, printed by
Curwen Press and published by Monotype in 1964; see also an excellent 76-page paperback,
Adrian Frutiger, son œuvre typographique et ses écrits, Maison du Livre, Villeurbanne,
1994.

LIGHT AND SHADOW – BLACK AND WHITE

We live in an age when there are many ways of converting what is thought into visible form. Throughout this book we are concerned only with a two-dimensional
expression in the conventional sense of graphic drawing and communication, simply by placing one-coloured ink on white paper. All other means of communication
(audio-visual, cinematic, etc.) have been deliberately excluded. The object of the
exercise is to concentrate on the essence of pure drawing and to limit ourselves to
that.

The white surface of the paper is taken to be 'empty', an inactive surface, despite
the visible structures that are present. With the first appearance of a dot, a line, the
empty surface is activated. A part, if only a small part, of the surface is thereby covered. With this procedure, the emptiness becomes white, or light, providing a contrast to the appearance of black. Light is recognisable only in comparison with
shadow. The actual procedure in drawing or writing is basically not the addition of
black but the removal of light. The sculptor's work also consists essentially of taking something away from the block of stone and in this manner forming it: the
final sculpture is what remains of the material.

Seen in this way, signs acquire a completely different value with regard to their capacity to communicate. All the comments that follow are supported by this duality of 'light and shadow', 'black and white'.

Adrian Frutiger (1928–), from Introduction ('Three Themes') to *Signs and Symbols, Their Design and Meaning*, transl. Andrew Bluhm, Studio Editions, London, 1989.

THIS PASSAGE *is taken from an article on the design and printing of Library and Exhibition catalogues – a subject, too often neglected, which requires expert advice for the reason that such publications are often underfunded, required in a hurry, and left to a non-typographer to produce. Yet what kind of publication should be more carefully and artistically produced than the catalogue of a fine book collection? At the very beginning of his paper Greer Allen quotes that vital piece of printing wisdom 'Fast schedule, high quality and low price: each affects the other. The client can specify any two, but never all three!'*

The whole paper deserves close attention from librarians at all levels.

Greer Allen himself started printing and designing at the age of eight. The bulk of his professional years were spent as printer to two universities. In 1947 Yale's printer, Carl Rollins, pointed him toward the University of Chicago, where he designed virtually all of its press's titles during the 1950s and directed its printing department in the 1960s. He returned to Yale in 1971 to become Yale University Printer, establish its printing service and to teach in the School of Art's graphic design programme and in Columbia University's Rare Book School, now at the University of Virginia. In 1984 he abandoned the administrator's life for one of full-time graphic design, and numbers among his clients the art museums and libraries of Yale and Harvard, the Metropolitan Museum of Art, the Art Institute of Chicago and the Newberry Library, Philadelphia Museum of Art, and the Colonial Williamsburg Foundation.

LIBRARY EXHIBITION CATALOGUES

In John Gay's *The What D'Ye Call It* we find the squire instructing a troupe of roving actors:

> And is the play as I order'd it, both a tragedy and a comedy? I would have it a pastoral too: and if you could make it a farce, so much the better – and what if you crown'd all with a spice of your opera? you know my neighbours never saw a play before; and d'ye see, I would shew them all sorts of plays under one.

It is immaterial whether the squire's play was a success. One thing is sure: the failure to conceive and project the clear central purpose for the catalogue has plunged as many into mediocrity as have inept design and substandard printing.

The importance of clarity of purpose can be understood in the comparison of two catalogues on American bookbindings. The catalogue of the Maser collection, for all its valuable information and rich colour illustrations, flits uncertainly betweeen homage to the donor and serious bibliographic exposition. In the Papantonio collection catalogue, however, goals have been prioritised so that a natural and commanding flow of purpose is evident. The man, his role – quickly covered by preliminary text – flow naturally into the substance of the book. The purpose becomes clear immediately. The Foreword's first line states the reason for the exhibition; the Introduction answers the question, 'Why *these* books?' and briefly details their relationship.

Now, although the catalogue accompanies and records the exhibit and – one might hope – captures some of its immediacy, the catalogue clearly cannot *be* the exhibition nor should it try. Once the exhibit has been dismantled, the catalogue commences its lone, long life as a book, free of those volumes neatly labelled in glass cases, free of the geography of the exhibition hall which has determined a narrative sequence and largely how many books could be shown. Naked it stands before the reader who might never have seen (nor cared to see) the exhibition. No doubt, Donald Gallup had this in mind when he declared that an exhibition catalogue becomes valuable only in so far as it contains references to material beyond the exhibition or collection, extending the catalogue's scope enough to make it a useful tool in its subject field.

Once the catalogue's purpose has been clearly articulated and understood among its creators, the *design* – that is, the *way* in which text and illustrations are presented – can be used to support that purpose. The design will be successful when the type is inviting and easy to read, when the illustrations are within reach of the references, when everything the designer has introduced helps to clarify what is meant and there is nothing superfluous to lead the reader to do a double-take or ask, 'What's this supposed to mean?'

In developing a catalogue, Mies van der Rohe's 'Less is more!' speaks with a fresh force. What a temptation it is for the designer (whether library staff or hired professional) to start with the text and illustrations and take flight from there – rivalling the words and eclipsing the pictures with devices so fresh, different and smashing that the main thrust of the book is smothered by the manner in which it is presented. Also, it is important to beware of graphic solutions which have been constructed (or must be defended) by an intricate rationale of verbiage. 'Mmmm, yes, now I see what you're trying to do,' must never pass for a nod of approval. The best exhibition catalogues have started and finished with text and pictures – pure, simple and to the purpose.

Greer Allen (1924–), 'The Design and Printing of Library Exhibition Catalogues', *Rare Books & Manuscripts Librarianship*, vol. 5, No. 2, 1990.

MATTHEW CARTER, *the son of Harry Carter (q.v.), as a young man learned punch-cutting and hand engraving at the printing-house of Enschedé in Holland. He is now one of the world's leading experts in computerised type design.*

From 1980 to 1984 he was Typographical Adviser to Her Majesty's Stationery Office in London, and was elected a Royal Designer for Industry in 1982. He is now a Principal of Carter & Cone Type Inc. in Cambridge, Mass., a company that designs, manufactures and sells new typefaces in industry-standard formats. Among his best-known faces are ITC Galliard (a classical book face), Bell Centennial (for setting the US telephone directories), Bitstream Charter, Mantinia, and Sophia.

Two useful recent articles on Carter's work are: 'Matthew Carter' by Erik Spiekermann in Eye, *no. 11, vol. 3, 1993, and 'Mantinia and Sophia', typeface review by Robert Bringhurst in* Print *XLVIII:II, March/April 1994.*

'Now we have mutable type' is part of a talk given to the Royal Society of Arts in London in 1990, explaining to a lay audience some of the facts of life for a modern type designer.

NOW WE HAVE MUTABLE TYPE

If you design typefaces, like Galliard, and they survive in the world ten or a dozen years, you get some feedback, indeed you depend upon that feedback to learn from seeing your work in use. If you're lucky, sometimes the use is good. When it's good, that is the most rewarding part of this job, the sense of remote collaboration with another designer (most likely unknown) who has pulled together the type, and the other raw materials, into something finished.

Some nice things turn up in the mail, but others are sent out of pure sadism. This slide is of Galliard condensed on an electronic typesetting system, and I suppose it's meant to be a judgement on me for never having designed a proper condensed version. Sadists think this kind of distortion will make me miserable, but it doesn't really. Of course, I do notify the font police of all such violations. We have something called the Font DA, and there are plenty of deputy serifs, but they don't really enforce the law of the letter. My point in showing this slide is this: we have had 550 years of moveable type, now we have mutable type.

The fact is that type designers are only concerned with raw material; we are at rock bottom of the food chain, we are at the mercy of typographers, who are at the mercy of type directors, who are at the mercy of art directors, who nourish – eventually – the ultimate consumer, the reader. Anyway, down in the ooze, we type designers crave our feedback.

ITC Galliard (*Figures 1 and 2*) is a historical revival, based on a sixteenth-century French model. I like history. It has been called bunk. It has been called débris. I

Fig. 1. ITC Galliard

¶Hamburgefons†

EABCDEFGHIJLK,

BMNOOPQRSTUV.

XYZ-H&ŒWÆ §2 ‡

Fig. 2. ITC Galliard

think of it as manure: it fertilises the present. We are all agreed that typography is just a humble, utilitarian, workaday, sort of craft, with 'only accidentally aesthetic ends', as Morison put it. But you have to look to an art – and a fine art at that, like a painting, or music, or architecture – before you find a history more glorious than ours. I don't know what we did to deserve it, but since we have got it, we ought to act as good trustees of it.

I hear arguments about whether it is right to revive old types in a day and age when total originality is *à la mode*. For me, that is a boring debate – it has been

going on since the 1550s, for one thing, and, for another, I find it damn difficult to
draw the line between renovation and innovation in many typefaces, including
some of my own. I can more easily draw the line between tradition used as a fer-
tiliser, on the one hand, and nostalgia, on the other. The process of revival can
select what is good from the past and rejuvenate it; nostalgic pastiche does not dis-
criminate between good and bad so long as it is old.

The interesting debate about revivals concerns not the repeating of a remote history, but the repeating of one's own history (if you are old and lucky enough to have
one). Max Roach, the continuously innovative musician, in a newspaper interview
recently, put the challenge to the mature artist in this form: 'Don't write the same
book twice'. If you pick and choose from the past and allow for the fact that, as
Eliot said, 'the past should be altered by the present', it is remarkable how well our
typographic heritage adapts to the cutting-edge technologies. Here is the oldest
style of printing type reincarnated in the newest technology: Gutenberg's formal
blackletter decomposed into a mosaic of pixels on a computer screen (Figure 3).

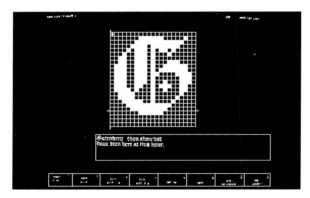

Fig. 3. Gutenberg decomposed.

Binary bit-mapped letterforms live on Cartesian co-ordinate planes whose axes are
vertical and horizontal. Blackletter, all straight lines and 45° angles, embraces the
raster grid sensuously. The only type better for bitmaps is also historical. The
cross-stitch from needlework samplers – the ultimate digital font (Figure 4).

I was facetious in showing these last two examples. It is not historical authentic-
ity, nor suitability to the prevailing production tool, that determine the viability of a
typeface. These examples are perfectly digital, but they are not perfectly legible.
They have not supplanted Roman and Italic in contemporary typography. And I
would have to confess that although this face is at least four years old by now, we
have not sold one single font of it.

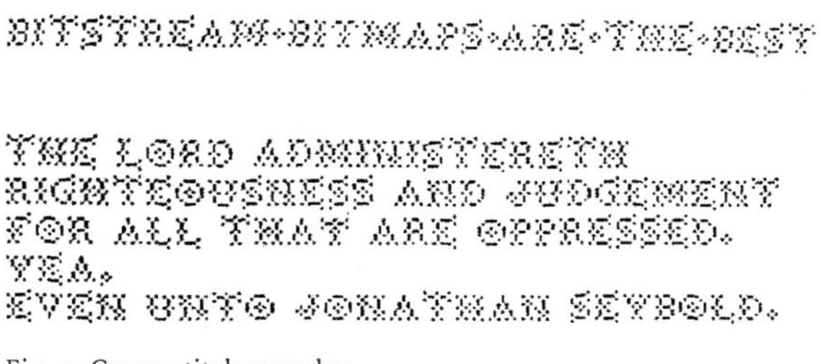

BITSTREAM·BITMAPS·ARE·THE·BEST

THE LORD ADMINISTERETH
RIGHTEOUSNESS AND JUDGEMENT
FOR ALL THAT ARE OPPRESSED.
YEA,
EVEN UNTO JONATHAN SEYBOLD.

Fig. 4. Cross-stitch sampler.

What the new technologies have to do, and what the previous technologies never had to do, is to render type in more than one form, simultaneously. The new imaging models, Apple Royal, Adobe Type Manager, Fontware and Speedo from Bitstream, Intellifont, Nimbus, make fonts at any output resolution. They convert outline fonts into bitmaps for screen fonts, for printer fonts and for typesetter fonts. These algorithmic fonts can do such versatile things thanks to inbuilt intelligence, known to its friends as hinting. Where does this leave the interrelationship between type and technology that I am concerned with? It leads in the end to this conclusion: in a world of multiple, coexisting, technologies we can no longer design type for a particular technology, even if we wanted to. Now, today, the life-expectancy of a decent typeface is longer than that of the technology that reproduces it. A type design dedicated to a particular technology is a self-obsoleting typeface.

The question of technically appropriate form came up in the design of Bitstream Charter, two-and-a-bit years old now, just a toddler in the springtime of the *new* new technologies of the digital desktop. If you buy a font of Charter, I cannot predict how you will use it – on a laser printer at 300, 400 or 600 dots per inch, typesetter at 1200 or 2000 dpi, on a screen display, film recorder, broadcast video system, architectural sign-making system. But I have to assume that sooner or later it will be used on all of those things, and probably more, as yet uninvented.

So the versatility of this omniverous digital technology, so reductive, increasingly independent of devices and their resolutions, requires a corollary in type design (*Figure* 5). Designing device-independent type, in practice, means avoiding certain pitfalls in the shaping of characters, a sort of damage-control by design. The difficulty for the designer in making a type that is all things to all devices is to give it some personality rather than a bland, committee-built, health-warning, Diet Coke, nondescriptness. And that is a new challenge for type designers. It is attempted in

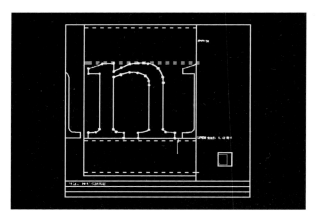

Fig. 5. Independent type.

Bitstream's Charter, and I think in Stone, designed by a good competitor and good friend at Adobe.

The central paradox of type design is that in an immediate sense we design letterforms, but letterforms are not our product. We are really word-shape designers; it is only in combination that letters become type. What readers read is word shapes, not individual component letters. Type designers have to look at letters set together in horizontal lines from the outset. It easy to think of type as black marks standing on a white background. Type designers think of type as white spaces separated by black marks.

Matthew Carter (1927–), from 'Communicating graphically', a talk given to the Royal Society of Arts in London and printed in the RSA Journal, June 1990.

AFTERWORD: THE BOOK AS OBJECT

The technicalities of type have occupied passionately (and I mean with fierce love) the lives of nearly all the men, and the one woman, whose contributions have made this book.

But, the technology of type production has been changing c.f. Matthew Carter. The first big change came before 1900, with the inventions in America of Monotype and Linotype composition. Yet for years books were still being set by hand. Even in 1936, when I went to work in Bernard Newdigate's Shakespeare Head Press in Oxford, I saw type being set by hand and proofed on a hand press which had once belonged to William Morris. They did use Monotype composition, for major books, but did not possess it. At the same time, I remember a lady historian, who had spent the day in the then great Oxford University Press, coming back in the evening delighted to have heard a compositor wandering along the cases saying 'Can anyone lend me a capital Q?'

Today (1995) even many professional typographers do not understand how type for books is produced. Yet books still look more or less the same as they have always looked. They are still printed on paper in what we choose to call roman type. The task facing book designers is the same as it has always been: to use existing materials and techniques, as they are offered, in the best way to help, not hinder, the flashpoint of communication between author/artist and reader. Not easy, but immensely interesting.

It is not just a question of plain communication: real reading takes in a bit more than the words on a page. Reading is a creative activity, going beyond the words to the ideas of the writer. The designer must not call attention to himself or herself (a point made by many of the authors in this book) but must stand aside, holding the door open. This doesn't always happen.

Real books – i.e. literature – are not less real than life: they actually are life, indeed they are life lived more abundantly than most people succeed in living it. They are not, as is sometimes alleged, a substitute for action, they are action, of a special kind.

That is the vital background to books: they are the life of men. Writing is an activity that only man has achieved. The old Scottish word for poet was 'maker'.

You can say that it does not matter how a book is printed, provided someone else can read it. We learned in 1940, with books in our gas-mask carriers, that a good book badly printed was more valuable than a bad book finely printed. But in the end, it does matter.

An elaborately decorated manuscript may, in fact, be difficult or virtually impossible to read, just as the Kelmscott Chaucer is not easily read: such objects are works of art in their own right, to be looked at and touched, like sculpture. Are they, then, books? Of course they are, because books, although they may contain words, are not for reading only, they are also for looking at. Whether a book, by definition, must contain words, is debatable. A picture-book, telling a story without words, may certainly be a book; but a collection of prints, like Audubon's Birds of America, the biggest book most of us have ever seen, is really not a book, although it was published in book form and sold as such.

The future of the book as object is uncertain. When I watch my own and other people's grandchildren glued to the TV, I wonder. A small children's book published in the United States some thirty years ago, called BOOKS!, ended with the sentence 'A book is full of surprises, feelings and learning and what growing up is like and loving and all the really big things there are'. And you can get all that out in a tent or a boat or up a tree where there is no electricity – if you have a book in your hand – remember?

R. McL.

words...

ideas...

thoughts...

books!

Some typefaces of the 1990's: FF Providence, Emigre Matrix, FF Kosmik, and Emigre Motion.